The Kogod Library of Judaic Studies
1

Also available in the Robert and Arlene Kogod Library of Judaic Studies

Ben: Sonship and Jewish Mysticism
By Moshe Idel

Judaism and the Challenges of Modern Life
Edited by Moshe Halbertal and Donniel Hartman

The Open Canon
By Avi Sagi

Transforming Identity
By Avi Sagi and Zvi Zohar

The Boundaries of Judaism

By

Donniel Hartman

continuum

Published by Continuum

The Tower Building, 11 York Road, London SE1 7NX

80 Maiden Lane, Suite 704, New York, NY 10038

www.continuumbooks.com

First published 2007

Reprinted 2008

British Library Cataloguing-in-Publication Data

A catalogue record for this book is available from the British Library

Typeset by Data Standards Ltd, Frome, Somerset, UK.

Printed on acid-free paper in Great Britain by Biddles Ltd, King's Lynn, Norfolk

ISBN-10: 0–8264-9663–6 (hardback)
       0–8264-9664–4 (paperback)

ISBN-13: 978–0-8264–9663-8 (hardback)
       978–0-8264–9664-5 (paperback)

He only says, 'Good fences make good neighbors'.
Spring is the mischief in me, and I wonder
If I could put a notion in his head:
'Why do they make good neighbors? Isn't it
Where there are cows?
But here there are no cows.
Before I built a wall I'd ask to know
What I was walling in or walling out,
And to whom I was like to give offence.
(Robert Frost, 'Mending Wall')

Contents

To my mother and father
    Who taught me to see myself and believe
    Who taught me to see others and care
    Who taught me to see Judaism and build there my home

Acknowledgements

This book has been the object of my research for many years and throughout this time, and indeed my whole adult life, I have been blessed with a wife, Adina, and then children, Michal, Yitzchak and Talya, who created an environment of love, joy, support and honesty, without which no growth, learning or creativity is possible. My debt to them is immeasurable and cannot be expressed in words.

The research on this book has been shaped by my community of friends and colleagues at the Shalom Hartman Institute. They have been the significant others with whom I have talked and from whom I have learned. Whether it is to learn together, share an idea, decipher a difficult text, or read a chapter of someone's manuscript, they always give of themselves and their time. In an ideal world, everyone will be able to live and grow in such a community. I have been blessed to live in such a world.

When creating and writing in the midst of an intellectual community, ideas are shared and at times the lines between one's thought and that of others is blurred. I have carefully attempted to give credit when I have referred to my colleagues' work in this book. If I have failed in any instance, I apologize and hope that these words of acknowledgement will serve as an expression of my indebtedness. There were a number of people in particular with whom I shared this work from the beginning and who played an invaluable role in shaping its outcome. I would particularly like to thank Avi Sagi, who more than anyone else gave of his time and his thought to me. He was also the one who first made me aware of the distinction between pluralism, tolerance and deviance, which became central to this work. I would also like to thank Zvi Zohar, who was always available to talk and who together with Avi Sagi and their joint work *Ma-agalei Shayahut*, and David Ellenson from HUC and his book *Tradition in Transition: Orthodoxy, Halakha, and the Boundaries of Modern Jewish Identity*, created the intellectual context within which this work was formed and grew. In addition, I would like to thank Moshe Halbertal, Menachem Lorberbaum, Shlomo Naeh and Adiel Schremer, who gave generously of their time and provided invaluable comments.

There would be no Shalom Hartman Institute were it not for our dedicated friends, supporters and board of directors. They not only sustain the institute, but also provided me with the financial support to write this book and the framework within which to pursue my life's work and dreams.

I owe as well a debt of gratitude to my doctoral advisors Izhak Englard and Paul Mendes Flohr for their patience, guidance and assistance; in particular to Paul Mendes Flohr, who at a difficult time in my graduate work responded with great kindness and provided me with a way to move forward. I would also like to thank the book's two editors, Charlie Buckholtz and Ilana Kurshan, who helped to tighten the arguments and make the language coherent, especially Ilana Kurshan, whose careful rereading and editing of the whole manuscript were invaluable and dramatically improved the quality and coherency of the book.

This book, *The Boundaries of Judaism*, grew out of my doctoral dissertation. It was inspired and shaped, however, by my work as a teacher in the Jewish community. I want to thank my friend, colleague and teacher, David Dubin *z"l*, who helped me to mediate and understand the living reality which is the Jewish people. I would also like to acknowledge my students, at the JCC on the Palisades, Aitz Hayim, and here at the Institute, who grounded me in a Jewish world in search of individual and collective meaning and who constantly guided and challenged both me and the arguments put forth in this book.

Last, but by no means least, I would like to thank my doctor and friend Perry Rosenthal and his wonderful institution, the Boston Foundation for Sight, without whom my writing and career would have been dramatically impaired. His kindness, gentleness and assistance to me during some of the more difficult times of my life, and to others on a daily basis, is an inspiration and model of *menschlikhkeit, tzedakah* and *tikkun olam*.

***

This book is dedicated to my mother and father, who have been the primary influence in my life. All that I have and am, I owe to them.

The Modern Problem of 'Who are the Jews?'

> The Lord spoke to Moses: 'Go down, for your people, whom you brought out of Egypt have acted corruptly.' (Exodus 32.7). What [did God] mean when [God said] 'Go down?' Rabbi Elazar said: The Holy One said to Moses: Moses, Go down from *your* greatness. I have only given you greatness for the sake of the people, and now that Israel have sinned – what need do I have for you? (BT, Tractate Berakhot 32a).

The sin of the Golden Calf did not simply result in the banishment of Moses from Mount Sinai, but more importantly, from his exclusive paradise. No matter how meritorious, the individual alone has no access to God in the Jewish tradition when standing apart from the Jewish people. God is interested in individuals only to the extent that the individual is grounded in, attached to and responsible for the Jewish people.

Judaism at its core is a collective enterprise, a religion invested in a people. However, it is precisely on this collective level that one finds one of the central paradoxes of contemporary Jewish life. On a national political level, in particular in times of crisis, the Jewish people are a paradigm of collective responsibility. However when it comes to issues relating to our collective religion, we cease to function as one people and allow sectarian and denominational forces to take over. We are a people who are willing to die for each other, but at the same time have great difficulty living with and respecting each other as Jews. In cities across North America, Jews from all denominational movements unite to march together at Israel Day Parades, but those same denominational rabbis will not share a public platform or sit on a shared rabbinic council, lest it be perceived that by doing so one is granting legitimacy to the other. Jews across the globe unite in times of crisis and raise unparalleled amounts of money for each other, but rarely share everyday ritual and holiday services together. A Russian new immigrant to Israel, the child of a Jewish father and a non-Jewish mother, is welcomed as a Jew into Israeli society and is able to serve in the most elite combat units in the Israeli army. However, if, God forbid, he is killed, he is not accepted for burial in a Jewish cemetery.

Who are the Jews? What do we mean when we refer to the Jewish people? What is it that all who are Jews share and hold in common, by virtue of which we are in fact one people? The problem is that Judaism, instead of serving as the uniting force around which our community is formed, has become itself the source of our divisiveness. One only has to look at the rancorous debate that arises any time the questions of 'Who is a Jew?' and Israel's Law of Return are put on the table. This law, which grants automatic citizenship in the State of Israel to anyone who is a Jew, obviously requires some common understanding of who is a Jew. Such an understanding, however, is sorely lacking. In one of the great paradoxes of contemporary Jewish life, it was decided that the definition of 'Jew' vis-à-vis the Law of Return is to be based on the Nazi definition as outlined in the Nuremberg Laws, i.e. a Jew is someone who is the child of a Jewish parent, or married to a Jew, or someone with one Jewish grandparent. Since we could not reach an agreement, we have adopted for ourselves the definitions of others.

In many ways the 'others' who surround us have always served as the ultimate protector of Jewish collective identity. We could always count on being a people segregated and persecuted by 'them', and the answer to the question of who is a Jew has often been those whom 'they' persecute for their Jewishness. In the context of an anti-Semitic world, Jewish collective life always had a measure of clarity to it. If Hitler did not distinguish between Orthodox, Conservative and Reform, or between the observant and non-observant, who are we to create boundaries on the basis of these considerations? However, as we enter the twenty-first century, a decline in anti-Semitism in many of the centres of Jewish life, in particular in Israel and North America, has created large communities of Jews for whom the hatred of others is neither existentially significant, nor a unifying force. Furthermore, even the classic 'safety net' of shared ethnicity is absent as we debate matrilineal vs. patrilineal descent, and as, at least outside of Israel, ever increasing numbers of Jews are born with only one Jewish parent.

If the Jewish people are to continue as a people – that is, as a community that is larger than any specific denomination and encompasses and indeed embraces diverse individuals who live in different locations and hold a multiplicity of ideas and commitments, we need our own answers to the question of what gives form and meaning to our collective enterprise.

This lack of collective clarity and cohesion is a strange condition for a people with a 3,000-year-old history. Its existence over such a long period of time is testimony to a commonality that must have been clear, self-evident and compelling to its members. Without this it would have been difficult to survive for so long even under normal conditions, not to mention the extraordinary conditions that have constantly challenged Israel's survival over the last 2,500 years.

The difficulties we face in understanding who are the Jews are in no small measure a modern phenomenon. Prior to the modern era, Jewish life was by and large shaped by a shared notion of tradition and clear boundaries distinguishing insider from outsider, 'us' from 'them'.[1] However, with emancipation and the encounter with modernity that began towards the end of the eighteenth century, there is a sense that the Jewish people have entered a new phase in their existence.[2] As the walls of the ghettos fell, and Jews, particularly those in Central and Western Europe, were granted the opportunity to participate fully in their surrounding cultures, the elements of Judaism and Jewish life that had informed these boundaries were challenged, reinterpreted, and often set aside. The traditional characteristics of Jewish life were exposed to the attacks of individuals and to strains of thought that preached change, integration, secularization, and a new interpretation of Jewish tradition appropriate to the spirit of modernity.[3] Debates and diverse policies regarding Jewish ideology and practice that in the past had been subjects of widespread consensus, such as belief in God, Shabbat and holiday observance, the centrality of mitzvah and ritual, to name but a few examples, now permeated communal life.

As a consequence of these sweeping changes, it became increasingly difficult to ascertain a shared ethos around which the Jewish community could remain unified. New and diverse notions of Jewish identity led to denominationalism and factionalism unprecedented in Jewish history. The advent and growth of the Reform movement, the formation of Orthodoxy as a distinct denomination, the rise of Zionist nationalist and secular approaches to Judaism and the subsequent development of the Conservative, Reconstructionist and Renewal movements – these are only the most prominent expressions of this pervasive trend. Within two centuries, the Jewish people were transformed from a more or less cohesive, traditional communal unit into 'A House Divided', as historian Jacob Katz famously put it.[4]

The attempt to construct or identify a community's shared ethos can take two different though not mutually excusive directions. The first reflects the premise that collective life in general assumes some notion of commonality shared by fellow members by virtue of which they belong to this particular group as opposed to another. This results in attempts to map out core principles or features which, one argues, are essential to the definition and identity of the group. But in the contemporary Jewish reality, all attempts to identify this commonality – be it practices and/or beliefs necessary for membership – will fail, as they are invariably founded on particular ideological premises that are simply no longer shared. More than serving to identify the core features of the Jewish people's common identity, most suggestions merely reflect the common identity of the particular denomination which espouses them, while leaving on the outside all those with different denominational affiliations.

Throughout social history, however, there is an additional tool that groups have incorporated – particularly in light of the reality of differences amongst their members – to demarcate their shared collective identity: the instrument of boundaries. As sociologist Kai Erickson explains, these boundaries may be understood as 'symbolic parentheses' delimiting a range of acceptable behaviours and norms. As a result of these boundaries, a community may be said to occupy a particular territory in the world, known as its 'shared cultural space'.[5] This cultural space sets the group apart and provides an important point of reference for its members.

Boundaries are particularly useful in the modern context, where people often carry multiple identities simultaneously. While in the past being Jewish may have been a more all-encompassing and exclusive identity, at present it is but one facet of a complex personality in which being, for example, a Jew and an Israeli; an American and a Jew; a Jew and a woman; a Jew and an upper-middle-class businessperson, coexist in the same person at the same time. Communities are thus made up of individuals who may share only one aspect of their identities, and in addition to their internal differences, bring to the collective table a whole array of alternate affiliations and values. In this context, while it may be difficult to positively identify that which is shared, it is still possible to locate that which all fellow members agree to reject, and it is through such an understanding that the process of constructing a shared cultural space can proceed.

In the bifurcated denominational reality that is the modern Jewish people, the process of demarcating a common identity through shared and agreed-upon boundaries is neither simple nor self-evident, and encounters challenges on both sides of the religious spectrum. Many members, in particular on the more liberal side of the community, feel ill at ease with any conversation about boundaries. Having built a conception of Judaism premised on the values of human autonomy and the right of individuals to construct a Jewish life in accordance with their individual consciences and religious sensibilities, they view any policy which aims to limit this autonomy as religiously and morally problematic. Their attitude towards individual religious expression is defined by the responses of pluralism and tolerance, rather than boundaries and the judgmental attitudes they are believed to engender.

In addition, large parts of the liberal Jewish community are, if not ideologically then functionally partially anarchic, operating with almost no central legal or institutional governing authority. The law and halakhic committees provide rulings for communities that, by and large, do not feel compelled or construed by these rulings. As evidence one can take the ever-decreasing levels of commitment by members to the guidelines of even the denomination to which they formally belong. Thus, for example, regular synagogue participation and ongoing involvement in the Jewish calendar life – although technically a part of all streams of Judaism – is statistically marginal in the liberal community. Almost fifty per cent of Jews outside of Orthodoxy intermarry with an individual outside of the Jewish faith, despite the fact that it is a practice that is officially denounced by all the Jewish streams. Conceptual conversations regarding standards and rules are by and large irrelevant, as they do not influence the actual life of the community.

The above attitude poses a challenge because it advocates for a community without boundaries, something that is a sociological anomaly. Social identity is, by definition, always exclusionary. At the foundation of every social structure, indeed in its conceptual definition, must lie some distinguishable characteristic or boundary by virtue of which its members can choose to belong to 'this' as distinct from 'that' social structure.[6] I am not arguing for the need to compel and limit the spiritual choices individuals may make, but rather to recognize that there is a need to distinguish between the right of an individual to choose, and the collective and political consequences of those choices. If the Jewish people are in fact to be one people, if there is to be an answer to the question 'Who are the Jews?', then we need to engage in the development of a shared boundary policy. Individuals are still free to make choices, but they must recognize that some of these choices might involve whether to remain or not remain a member of the Jewish people. As a collective identity, by definition Judaism cannot be determined solely by the actions or decisions of individuals, but must entail some shared common notion of boundaries which serves to demarcate the space which all who are Jews agree to share.

On the other side of the religious spectrum, individuals with a more traditional bent, in particular those often affiliated with Orthodoxy, have little difficulty with boundary language and formation. More than its fellow denominations, Orthodoxy views Reform, Conservative, Reconstructionist and secular approaches to Jewish life as having deviated from the central principles of Judaism, and from its perspective, as having breached the core boundaries which delineate the central and shared ethos of Jewish life.[7] The argument is made that Judaism must return to its roots and be in accord with its traditional laws and values, rather than reflect the new directions and directives of the Jewish people and modernity. To achieve this end, significant numbers of Orthodox Rabbinic figures regularly erect boundaries and utilize boundary claims and language to demarcate the core 'cultural space' of Judaism within the realm of their denominational affiliations.

While every social structure is built around boundaries, the difficulty with the boundaries often erected by Orthodoxy is that they do not serve to demarcate the Jewish people, but rather to bifurcate it further. Through the boundaries some Orthodox thinkers erect, ever-increasing numbers of Jews, if not the majority, find themselves ideologically outside the parameters of Jewish collective life. The sad state of contemporary Jewish boundary policies is that instead of serving to unite the Jewish people, they merely serve to separate Orthodoxy from the rest of the Jewish people – and at times to support a position that views Orthodoxy as the sole inheritor, the holy remnant of the collective mantle of Jewish peoplehood. What makes this situation even more troubling is that these boundary policies are represented as being *the* policies of the Jewish tradition, *the* necessary halakhic response to the challenges of modernity.

Contemporary Jewish life seems to be left in the predicament of having to choose between a policy that undermines the possibility of a coherent collective Jewish life by rejecting boundary policies altogether, and one that achieves the same end by advocating socially destructive boundaries. The aim of this book is to offer a third possibility.[8] This work is founded on the assumption that boundary policies are critical to Jewish social formation, and have always been critical, as I demonstrate through a survey of the boundaries of Jewishness throughout time. I argue, based on this analysis that precisely in the midst of our denominational disagreements, only boundary policies offer some hope of achieving a functional coherence regarding our collective identity. To achieve this end, however, Jewish political discourse is in need of a more sophisticated approach and understanding of boundaries: how and where to locate them, and identifying the tools used to maintain them. What is needed are boundary policies that serve to unite and not divide, which serve the ends of the Jewish people as a whole and not simply those of one denomination.

In exploring the boundaries of Jewishness, the chapter that follows will begin with an overview of the ways in which social structures deal with the reality of difference and distinguish between acceptable and unacceptable difference. In so doing I will analyse the three categories used to make this assessment – pluralism, tolerance, and deviance. Then, focusing on the treatment of deviance, I will characterize the various social arenas or spheres of membership in which the consequences of a Jewish boundary policy play out: the spheres of basic membership, loyalty, ritual and naming. The fact that a certain form of behaviour is classified as deviant and outside the shared boundaries of the community does not mean that the response to it is fixed and clear. At the heart of a constructive policy is a complex and varied array of responses influenced by the nature of the deviance and its social significance.

Next, in Chapters 2 and 3, I will trace and analyse the central Jewish legal precedents on the subject of boundaries and deviance as found in Rabbinic sources (approx. 50 BCE–500 CE) and the three major mediaeval halakhic codifications, Maimonides' (1135–1204) *Mishneh Torah*, R. Yaakov b. R. Asher's (1269–1343) *Tur*, and R. Joseph Karo's (1488–1575) *Shulhan Arukh*. It is in these sources that the language of boundaries and deviance was first discussed, developed and analysed. They therefore serve as the legal and intellectual basis for all contemporary halakhic discussion on the subject.

In developing its theories of boundaries over the centuries, Jewish law primarily utilized four categories of deviance. They are the *meshumad*, (which at the end of the Middle Ages was converted into the *mumar*), the *min*, the *apikorus* and the *kofer*. In re-constructing the legal precedents that shaped Jewish boundary theories, I will limit my analysis to the discussion that evolved around those forms of deviance that are classified under one of the above categories. In so doing, the primary tools for explicating the ideas contained in the various sources will not be the historical influences on the authors but rather the texts themselves, that is, the positions and rulings which can be gleaned from these halakhic sources.[9] As a result, much of the study in these chapters will entail close textual reading and analysis.

After presenting and analysing this historical legal precedent, I will turn in Chapters 4 and 5 to the modern (post-Enlightenment) period, where I will present and analyse a dominant and deeply problematic position of Orthodoxy vis-à-vis boundaries. This policy either calls for a complete physical segregation from the rest of the Jewish people, as is the case with ultra-Orthodoxy, or, as has become the case for the majority of modern or centrist Orthodoxies, involves a cultural, ideological and often social separation from those not living an Orthodox lifestyle. The two leading Orthodox halakhic authorities of this period have set the tone for these boundary policies: Rabbi Moses Sofer (Schreiber) (1762–1839), the Hatam Sofer, *(Hidushei Torat Moshe Sofer)*,[10] and Rabbi Moshe Feinstein (1895–1986).[11] The stature and significance of these two figures in shaping halakhic thinking and law in general, and on these issues in particular, is unparallelled.

The attitudes and rulings of the Hatam Sofer and Rabbi Moshe Feinstein on the boundaries of Jewishness represent two turning points in the history of the bifurcation in contemporary Jewish life. The first is at the beginning of the nineteenth century, when the internal divisions within the Jewish community first began to take root. The rise of assimilation and secularization, and the establishment of Reform Judaism redefined the rules for belonging to the Jewish community and necessitated a re-examination and restructuring of the collective Jewish boundaries. The one who took it upon himself to lead this re-examination within Orthodoxy was the Hatam Sofer.[12]

A second turning point took place when the actual boundaries of Jewish identity and communal life had been completely deconstructed and diversity of Jewish affiliations had become the norm. The Jewish community of North America in the middle and latter part of the twentieth century is perhaps *the* paradigm of this new reality.[13] The most significant Orthodox halakhic figure in America at this time was unquestionably Moshe Feinstein, who wrote extensively on this issue.

After completing this legal journey, the final chapter of this book will evaluate these legal precedents and attempt to offer, on the basis of Jewish tradition, an alternative theory of the boundaries that may demarcate the space inhabited by contemporary Jewry. In so doing I hope to show that the sectarian direction adopted by some boundary policies in the name of Jewish law and precedent in fact represents a significant legal innovation. I will argue that this innovation, while a response to the new challenges of modernity to Jewish collective identity, neither serves this identity nor strengthens it.

As stated, the focus of this work will be on the boundaries of Judaism, or, more precisely, on the way that Jewish law over the centuries has constructed a *theory* as to how and where to erect these boundaries, as well as how to govern and maintain them. In constructing a theory of boundaries I mean to distinguish this work from the project of historically mapping out what halakhic figures over the centuries deemed as 'beyond the Pale'. The answer to this question is relatively simple, ranging from idolatry and the public desecration of Shabbat to the intentional violation of law out of spite, to the Conservative and Reform and sometimes secular Jew in modern Orthodox halakhic discourse, to the universally rejected contemporary 'Jews for Jesus'. However, many of the particular details of past boundaries are by and large irrelevant in the context of the contemporary bifurcated Jewish community that has already breached almost every one of them. It is not the specific historical answers to the location of the boundaries, but rather the causes and reasons that lay at the foundation for their being so designated, which can serve as a guide in constructing a modern system of boundaries.

In developing a theory of boundaries, I will focus on three different sorts of questions:

1) What central factors influence the identification of certain positions and individuals as unacceptable? What categories of sin are deemed intolerable, and what factors are considered mitigating or aggravating when it comes to assessing this status? For example, does the deviance reflect a total flouting of the legal system, or is it limited to a localized offence? Does it fall within the parameters of heresy or delinquency? Is it carried out in public or private? Is it prompted by desire and appetite, or is its purpose to

anger and provoke? Are we speaking of a passive deviant, or only of one who actively denounces the social order? To what extent are the boundaries affected by the actual practices of the community?

2) What are the consequences of being designated as outside the boundary? Special attention will be paid to the diverse forms of marginalization assigned to different types of deviants, and to whether certain forms are associated specifically with certain sorts of deviance. Here too I will attempt to ascertain whether certain types of motivation and external circumstances are considered mitigating or aggravating when it comes to assessing sanctions.

3) What is the correlation between the individual's self-perception of his deviance and the social status given to that individual? I will explore whether a shift in status was descriptive (i.e. self-defined) or prescriptive (i.e. externally imposed). Is there a distinction between a deviant who sees himself as set apart from the community, and one who continues to see himself as a member in good standing?[14]

I first became sensitive to the importance of boundary policies twenty-something years ago, when I started my rabbinic career working as the Scholar-in-Residence of the Jewish Community Center on the Palisades in Tenafly, New Jersey. It was a teaching pulpit, and in that capacity, I instituted a weekly Torah study seminar for the board and leadership of the J.C.C., many of whom were prominent individuals who also served in Jewish leadership roles at a national level. One year into my work I received a call from the head of a national Orthodox movement, who upon hearing that an Orthodox Rabbi was working at the J.C.C., asked if I would come to meet him. At the meeting the head of the organization enquired about my willingness to jointly run a study weekend retreat for my leadership. I gladly agreed, but under one condition. Given the mandate of the J.C.C. as a community organization, we would need to respect the ideological diversity of the community, and as such, we could not run any program, especially on Shabbat, that was exclusively affiliated with one denomination alone. I explained that I would be happy to expose the leadership to his organization and ideology so long as the weekend was also open to rabbis of different denominations. Upon reflection, the rabbi also agreed, but again under one condition. He explained that as an Orthodox Jew, he had his *yehareg ve-al ya-avor*, aspects of Jewish law that he could not violate even upon pain of death. This phrase, which literally means, 'let him be killed and not violate (the law)', traditionally served to demarcate the main boundaries of Jewish life, boundaries that Jews cannot cross even if it meant forfeiting their lives.

As a young rabbi, I recognized the significance of the moment: a leading Orthodox rabbi was about to outline his position on the core of

Judaism, on the lines beyond which no compromise is possible. The rabbi then proceeded to say that he could participate in the retreat with other denominations so long as all prayer services included a *mehitzah*, the division between men and women during prayer services. I was astounded by his answer, for nowhere in Jewish law is *mehitzah* elevated to any level of exceptional significance, and certainly not to the level of *yehareg ve-al ya-avor*. He was also aware of many Orthodox synagogues that were members of his organization and who had been members for decades, despite not having a *mehitzah* in their sanctuaries. Furthermore, he could have raised far more important issues such as the observance of Shabbat law, *kashrut* and the like.

Reflecting later on his answer, I understood the rationale behind his peculiar choice. The significance of *mehitzah* as a boundary did not lie in its inherent importance, but rather in its role as a dividing mechanism between Orthodoxy and non-Orthodoxy. This rabbi knew that, just as Orthodox Jews will pray only in a synagogue with a *mehitzah*, non-Orthodox, although willing to compromise on many other matters, would not surrender the right to sit with men and women together in a synagogue. By demanding that all prayer be with a *mehitzah*, the rabbi was making it impossible for the weekend to happen unless people succumbed to his particular ideology.

The purpose of his boundary was not to define the core features of his beliefs, nor to challenge others to join him therein, but to serve to divide the community along denominational lines with Orthodoxy standing alone behind its new *yehareg ve-al ya-avor*. For this rabbi the *mehitzah* did not merely serve to divide men and women during prayer, but to divide the Jewish people. I understood that if Jewish collective life was to be possible, by which I mean a Jewish peoplehood that can transcend denominational lines and include all factions of Jewish life, we need to develop an approach to boundaries that allow for a common ground in which all can participate despite our differences. This is the aim of this work.

Notes

1 J. Katz, 'Jewry and Judaism in the Nineteenth Century', in *Jewish Emancipation and Self-Emancipation* (Philadelphia, 1986), p. 3.
2 For a more detailed analysis of the period, when it began, and the transformations which it engendered, see J. Katz, *Out of the Ghetto* (Cambridge, 1973); *ha-Halakhah be-Meitzar* (Jerusalem, 1992); *A House Divided: Orthodoxy and Schism in Nineteenth-Century Central European Jewry* (Hanover, 1988); *Tradition and Crisis* (New York, 1993), pp. 214–36; *Jewish Emancipation and Self Emancipation*, pp. 3–19; and 'Orthodoxy in Historical Perspectives', in P. Medding (ed.), *Studies in Contemporary Judaism* II (Bloomington, 1986), pp. 3–17; Y. Greenwald, *Sefer*

Mekorot ha-Torah ve-ha-Emunah be-Hungariah (Budapest, 1921), pp. 21–56; M. Samet, 'Halahkah ve-Reformah' (Doctoral Thesis, Hebrew University, 1967), and 'The Beginning of Orthodoxy', *Modern Judaism* 8, 3 (1988) 249–69; D. Ellenson, *Tradition in Transition: Orthodoxy, Halakha and the Boundaries of Modern Jewish Identity* (Lanham 1989) pp. 161–84; P. Mendes-Flohr and J. Reinharz, *The Jew in the Modern World* (New York, 1980), pp. 101–81; M. Meyer, *Response to Modernity* (New York, 1988), pp. 10–61; *Jewish Identity in the Modern World* (Seattle, 1990), pp. 3–32; *The Origins of the Modern Jew* (Detroit, 1967); M. Silber, 'Shorshei ha-Pilug be-Yahadut Hungariah' (Doctoral Thesis, Hebrew University, 1985); D. Philipson, *The Reform Movement in Judaism* (New York, 1907), pp. 3–56; J. Bleich, 'Rabbinic Responses to Nonobservance in the Modern Era' in J. Schachter (ed.), *Jewish Tradition and the Non-Traditional Jew* (Northvale, 1992), pp. 37–115. See also M. Meyer, 'Where Does the Modern Period of Jewish History Begin?', *Judaism* 24, 3 (1975), 329–38, who discusses the question of when to locate the turning point of modernity; as well as A. Shohet, *Im Hillufei Tekufot* (Jerusalem, 1960), who identifies the transformation as already occurring from the beginning to the middle of the eighteenth century.

3 See P. Berger, *The Heretical Imperative* (New York, 1980), pp. 25–6.

4 J. Katz, *A House Divided*.

5 K. T. Erikson, *The Wayward Puritans* (New York, John Wiley & Sons, 1966), p. 10.

6 Z. Eviatar, *The Fine Line* (New York, 1991), p. 41

7 See J. Katz, 'ha-Ortodoxia ke-teguvah le-Yitizia Min ha-Getto ve-la-Tenuat ha-Reformah' in *ha-Halakhah be-Meitzar*, pp. 9–20; M. Samet, 'Halakah ve-Reformah', p. 252; D. Ellenson, *Tradition in Transition*, pp. 162–3. On the other hand, Conservative, Reform, Reconstructionist and secular approaches to Judaism usually have less difficulty with the legitimacy of each other's policies and ideologies and with those of Orthodoxy. See C. Leibman, 'Orthodoxy in American Jewish Life', in *American Jewish Yearbook 66* (New York, 1965), pp. 38–9.

8 In so doing, I am indebted to the work of Gerald Bildstein in his article, 'Who is not a Jew?', *Israel Law Review* 11, 3 (1976), 369–90; David Ellenson in his book, *Tradition in Transition*; Avi Sagi and Zvi Zohar in their work *Ma-agalei Zehut Yehudit be-Sifrut ha-Hilkhatit* (Tel Aviv, 2000); and Adam Ferziger's *Exclusion and Hierarchy: Orthodoxy, Nonobservance and the Emergence of Modern Jewish Identity* (Philadelphia, 2005).

9 See A. Sagi and Z. Zohar, *Ma-agalei ha-Zehut ha-Yehudit*, p. 23.

10 For bibliographical and background information on the Hatam Sofer and his work, see J. Katz, 'Kavim le-Biographiah shel ha-Hatam Sofer', in *Halakhah ve-Kaballah* (Jerusalem, Magnes Press, 1984), pp. 353–86; and 'Conservatives in a Quandary', in *Out of the Ghetto*, pp. 157–60; M. Samet, 'Halakhah ve-Reformah' pp. 235–53, and 'Kavim Nosafim le-Biographiah Shel ha-Hatam Sofer', in M. Breuer (ed.), *Torah im Derekh Eretz* (Ramat Gan, 1987); M. Silber, 'Shorshei ha-Pilug be-Yahadut Hungariah', pp. 17–48; and A. Ferziger, *Exclusion and Hierarchy*, pp. 61–89.

11 For biographical and background information on Moshe Feinstein and his work,
see E. Rackman, 'Halakhic Progress: Rabbi Moshe Feinstein's Igrot Moshe on
Even ha-Ezer', *Judaism* 13, 3 (1964), 365–73; A. Kirshenbaum, 'Rabbi Moshe
Feinstein's Responsa: A Major Halakhic Event', *Judaism* 15, 3 (1966), 364–73; M.
Angel, 'A Study of the Halakhic Approaches of Two Modern Poskim', *Tradition*,
23, 3 (1988), 41–52; F. Rosner, 'Rabbi Moshe Feinstein's Influence on Medical
Ethics', in F. Rosner (ed.), *Medicine and Jewish Law* Vol II (Northdale, 1993), pp.
3–40; I. Robinson, 'Because of Our Many Sins: The Contemporary World as
Reflected in the Responsa of Moses Feinstein', *Judaism* 35, 1 (1988), 35–46; C.
Leibman, 'Orthodoxy in American Jewish Life', pp. 86–7; *Encyclopedia Judaica*,
'Feinstein, Moshe'; A. Rand, *Toldot Anshei Shem*, (New York, Hevrat Toldot
Anshei Shem, 1950); S. Finkelman, *Reb Moshe* (New York, 1986).

12 See M. Samet, 'Kavim Nosafim le-Biographiah Shel ha-Hatam Sofer'; and A.
Ferziger, *Exclusion and Hierarchy.*

13 See B. Lazerwitz, 'Denominations and Synagogue Membership: 1971 and 1990',
in D. Gordis and G. Dorit (eds), *American Jewry, Portrait and Prognosis* (West
Orange, 1997), pp. 199–220.

14 See Edwin Lemert's distinction between primary and secondary deviance in
'Secondary Deviance and Role Conceptions' in E. M. Lemert, *Social Pathology: A
Systematic Approach to the Theory of Sociopathic Behavior* (New York, 1951); and
Edwin Schur's notion of role engulfment in 'Role Engulfment', in E. M. Schur,
Labeling Deviant Behavior, (New York, 1971).

CHAPTER ONE

Pluralism, Tolerance and Deviance

A famous Jewish joke tells of a community which, after the death of its longstanding and revered rabbi, forgot its position on a certain central issue of Jewish law, leaving the community deeply divided between two factions. Not knowing what to do, the communal leaders went to the oldest member of the community, who was on his death bed. 'Reb Moshe', they pleaded, 'do you recall our tradition?' Immediately one faction began to press its point, arguing 'didn't we do it this way?' Not about to let their adversaries sway Reb Moshe, the second faction started to shout over the other, 'Reb Moshe, don't listen to those fools. In truth is this not our tradition?' The shouting continued unabated, with each side trying to drown out the other all throughout the day. When finally a moment of quiet descended on the room, Reb Moshe raised his frail hand and began to speak in a hushed voice. 'My memory is not what it used to be', he said, 'but this sounds very familiar. I remember that this same issue was raised in the community when I was a child. There were two factions each trying to shout over the other. The shouting, the debating – that is our tradition.'

The ability of individuals to live together in a common society and to construct their shared and agreed-upon boundaries is contingent on a delicate accommodation between two conflicting features of social life: commonality and difference. On the one hand, a community – as distinct from a crowd – is a collection of individuals who are bound together by virtue of their sharing some thing or things in common. Within the context of this community, the individual member or citizen is supposed to find like-minded individuals united by this commonality, which serves as both a foundation and a binding force for social life. What the group shares, on the basis of which it forges its union and boundaries, is dependent on the nature of the group as well as on how it understands and sees itself. Families, clubs, neighbourhoods, nations, religions, all define and perceive their common-ality differently. It may be, for example, a function of race, religion, values, culture, or national origin, or any combination of the above.[1] Regardless of what it is that is shared, the reality of something shared is the foundation and binding force for collective life.

At the same time, this need for a centralized ethos that circumscribes a community's cultural space often threatens the very collective existence it purports to serve. A community formed around a shared ethos, with all its members inhabiting some common cultural space and with clearly delineated boundaries distinguishing the 'insider' from the 'outsider', is challenged by the reality of complex social groups. Other than in very specific and narrowly defined social arrangements (e.g. cults), communal life built upon absolute uniformity is simply not possible. In every community, together with that which its members share, there is rarely only one monolithic set of rules, either in their form or in their meaning, accepted by all members or interpreted in the same way.[2] Furthermore, even if at one time there was a high measure of commonality and agreement about the community's boundaries, it is only temporary, as the boundaries themselves are rarely fixed; they shift constantly as the members of the group rethink the meaning and purpose of their collective identity in relation to those around them.[3]

Further adding to the complexity is the fact that rarely are communities constructed at some mythic founding moment, whereby those with a shared notion of a collective identity join together and form their social enterprise. These founding moments are generally 'imagined'. More often than not, we don't choose our fellow members – we inherit them, without a collective ethos shaping an admissions policy. We find ourselves bound to fellow members we did not choose and whom in reality we do not know. While collective life still requires that fellow members share something in common, the reality of difference and disparity among them pervades social life.

Those who participate in communal life must come to terms with the reality of difference and allow for disagreement between members on a wide range of issues, including those which are believed to be fundamental. This disagreement cannot be avoided. When a community cannot assimilate some degree of difference, its collective existence is threatened and its fate becomes one of constant factionalism, strife, and ultimately, bifurcation.

In trying to find the balance between the search for commonality and the reality of difference, social structures use three primary categories to assess, classify and ascertain which difference is allowed and which not. These three categories are pluralism, tolerance and deviance. When and why each is used is dependent on the nature of the differences, the communities, and the circumstances in question. The issue here is not to justify the use of one category over another in any given situation, but rather to point to the variety of responses that communities have at their disposal when attempting to strike the above-mentioned balance.

In this chapter, I will begin by exploring these three categories in terms of the role they play in maintaining social coherence and the way they comprise a spectrum and serve to police and protect communal boundaries. I will then consider the consequences of deviance and the range of responses available within Jewish law to differing forms of deviance. Finally, by way of illustration, I will conclude with the classical Talmudic debates between Bet Hillel and Bet Shammai, which involve an interplay between these categories.

Pluralism

Pluralism is that category which assigns equal value to certain differing positions. At the foundation of pluralism lies, as Isaiah Berlin states, the recognition that 'human goals are many, not all of them commensurable, and in perpetual rivalry with each other'.[4] Those in a pluralist community are cognizant of the differences among members, but are able to perceive equal value in a multiplicity of positions. While pluralism does not necessitate the acceptance of all positions, and is not to be equated with relativism, it does recognize the possibility of equally valuable though differing goals and values which 'cannot be graded on a scale, so that it is a matter of inspection to determine the highest'.[5]

Difference which falls under the category of pluralism is the easiest and least complicated for individuals and society to assimilate within one social structure. As they are viewed as having equal value, the diverse positions engender mutual respect amongst their respective advocates, and 'opposing' sides have little difficulty accommodating each other within the community's shared cultural space.

Tolerance

No community can be entirely pluralistic and all difference cannot be contained under the category of pluralism. In fact, if moral and principled judgments are not to be reduced to relativism, the application of pluralism is necessarily limited in its scope. In most instances, individuals neither can nor should assess all difference of opinion as being of equal value. It is natural and often logical that they view some other stances as in some way either wrong or inferior, even if recognizing the subjective nature of their perception; and it is precisely because of this valuation that they make their particular choices.

It is within this range of assessment of difference that tolerance comes into play. As distinct from pluralism, tolerance is reserved for difference which one believes to be wrong.[6] As the twentieth-century English moral philosopher, Bernard Williams, argues, 'Toleration, we may say, is required only for that which is in principle intolerable.'[7]

This negative appraisal of that which is tolerated, however, need not engender either defensive or punitive measures, but can in certain circumstances activate a response of tolerance which in essence involves 'allowing, leaving undisturbed, something which you think is wrong'.[8] The individual in question remains a member, an 'insider' in the full sense of the word, a person with whom one shares one's collective space, despite the disapproval that his or her behaviour may engender.

Once it is recognized that difference is not a passing episode but rather an inherent facet of all social structures, it is precisely tolerance which serves as the foundation for these structures' survival and viability. What is important about tolerance, as distinct from pluralism, is that it allows fellow members to live together despite not merely differing from each other, but also disagreeing. Disagreement is not something that needs to be feared, nor will it lead to sectarianism and social bifurcation – so long as fellow members can learn to accept the fact that monolithic uniform social groups are neither a plausible reality, nor a necessity, nor possibly even an ideal.

Deviance

Just as pluralism has its limits, so too does tolerance. Independent of the question of truth and the significance of debate and disagreement for human development, from a sociological perspective, boundaries must be erected, for 'each regime of toleration must be singular and unified to some degree, capable of engaging the loyalty of its members'.[9]

There is no viability for social life without some notion of boundaries and limits on the difference which it can accommodate. Without these boundaries it becomes impossible to locate that common core by virtue of which fellow members affiliate with one another and form a social entity.

That which serves to demarcate and govern these boundaries is the notion of deviance. As distinct from difference, which is assessed as tolerable and as such, left alone, deviance is that 'conduct which is generally thought to require the attention of social control agencies – that is, conduct about which "something must be done".'[10]

As the American sociologist Erich Goode defines it:

> By deviance, I mean one thing and one thing only: behaviour that some people in a society find offensive and that excites – or would excite if it were discovered – in these people disapproval, punishment, condemnation of or hostility toward the actor.[11]

Through the category of deviance, a community distinguishes between the forms of variability and diversity it conceives as threatening to its identity, and those it is able accommodate. Thus, in the societal balance, tolerance and deviance define one another: disagreement which is not deemed deviant is subject to tolerance, while that which is not tolerable is labelled as deviance.

Tolerable and Intolerable Deviance

The dividing line between deviance and tolerance, and the relationship between them, is, however, far from stable or clear. Further complicating matters is the fact that there is a line of tolerance that often passes through deviance itself, distinguishing between two types of deviance: that which is tolerated, and that which is not. Now, the notion of a 'tolerable deviance' seems an oxymoron. Deviance is by definition *that which is not tolerated*. In what sense, then, can we speak of deviance which is?

While many forms of deviance generate upon detection an immediate response, there are in reality many others that communities decide to leave alone. As anyone who has ever crossed the street at a red light in plain view of a police officer can attest, neither all rules nor all violators are treated equally.[12] While functionally tolerated, these un-enforced laws and boundaries serve at least to define what is understood by the community to be correct behaviour and representative of its values and norms. One of the more interesting and prevalent examples of tolerable deviance is adultery. While universally condemned in almost every moral system, it nevertheless remains generally unsanctioned both legally and even socially. One of the telling indicators for deviance which has become tolerable is the culture of jokes which can be associated with it. Intolerable deviance is never a laughing matter. Whether it is adultery or speeding, to name but two examples, humour represents the fact that the severity of the deviance is diminished in the eyes of society.

Why certain forms of deviance are treated as tolerable and some laws are left unenforced varies. It may reflect a sense that the deviance is only marginally unacceptable; or it may be the result of an abundance of violators of the law, making sanctions unfeasible. Regardless of the reason, the fact that no formal sanctions are directed against the individual warrants the deviance in question to be classified as tolerable.

As distinct from deviance which is tolerated, the intolerable deviant is one whose transgression is considered to so severely contravene communal standards that it constitutes a renouncement of core values and jeopardizes the integrity of shared cultural space. In this case, silence or the closing of the collective eye is neither possible nor desirable, and the community responds in a variety of ways. In its most extreme form, 'doing something' involves expulsion: stripping the deviant of his membership status and severing all personal and collective ties. It is this forsaking and forsaken figure that one can term the 'true outsider'.[13]

Though dramatically compelling, this lone, expelled stranger is in reality exceedingly rare. In the vast majority of instances, deviants, regardless of their crime, remain 'in' the community in the sense that they retain their basic status as members. Full expulsion is carried out sparingly, as a measure of last resort;[14] being branded an intolerable deviant in most instances entails relegation to the *margins* of membership and creates a status which may be termed an 'outsider within'. Through marginalization, basic membership status is retained, yet fundamentally altered. The anthropologist and sociologist Robert Scott describes this phenomenon in telling detail:

> When a deviant label has been applied to a person, he is often demarcated off from the rest of the group and moved to its margins. As a rule, he is excluded from participating fully in group activities, and he may even be denied the kind of freedoms that are accorded to others as a matter of right. He is sometimes physically confined and denied the sorts of privileges that are routinely granted to people who are considered to be 'in good standing'. Thus, when a person has been labelled a deviant, he becomes a second rate citizen, who is in a symbolic sense 'in' but not 'of' the social community in which he resides.[15]

The process of relocating the individual to the status of being not 'of' the community involves a 'something' which serves to change the deviant's status and marginalize the individual in question. Of course, it is important to remember that not every response serves to marginalize, and consequently does not reflect intolerable deviance status. A telling example is the legal and social response to different degrees of speeding violations. In an area where the speed limit is 65 mph, it is generally accepted that a 10 mph discrepancy is acceptable. Police do not enforce infractions of a lesser degree and such violations are generally not viewed as deviant at all; they are contained under the categories of pluralism or tolerance or in some cases, possibly, tolerable deviance. Speeding in excess of this 10 mph will generate a legal response in the form of a ticket. This response, however, while constituting 'doing something', nevertheless does not generate intolerable status, but still falls under the classification of tolerable deviance. The fine is not associated with, and does not carry with it, any social stigmatization or marginalization. The individual is still 'in' in the full sense of the word. As proof of this status, the guilty individual will openly tell others (as long as they are not his parents!) about the experience and often generate sympathy at 'being caught'. Furthermore, even from the perspective of the authorities, the status of the individual in question has not changed; once issued with the ticket, he is allowed to continue to drive, and merge back into traffic as if nothing had occurred. This is not the case, for example, with an individual who exceeds the speed limit by 30 mph or is caught driving under the influence of alcohol or drugs. Such an individual is taken off the road, an act which begins the process of status-change, and the penalty, whether suspension of licence or imprisonment, is intended to redefine the social status of and attitude towards the deviant in question.

This distinction between penalties which generate and reflect intolerable status and those which retain the status of tolerability is especially important when dealing with religious law in general and Jewish law in particular. Given that under Jewish law all violation (even inadvertent) of any negative precept engenders some sanction, the tolerable deviant who eludes penalty altogether will not be a common figure in Jewish legal sources. However, different sanctions – from the mildest fines to the strictest forms of corporal punishment – can be viewed in a strong (if not initially obvious) sense as reflecting tolerability. This formulation goes to the nature of sanctions. While initially seen as conveying intolerance, sanctions in fact simultaneously express a community's rejection of certain behaviours or ideas and its desire to retain all of its members – even those who may temporarily have strayed outside acceptable boundaries – and return them to good standing. Far from effecting a rejection of deviants, sanctions often serve as vehicles for their rehabilitation in society's eyes. A midrashic passage concisely illustrates the point:

> '*Then your brother should be dishonoured before your eyes*' (Deut. 25.3): Once he has been beaten, he is [again] your brother. Hence the Sages have said: As soon as those who are liable to the penalty of excision are beaten, they are immediately released from this liability. R. Hananiah ben Gamliel says: All along Scripture calls him wicked, as it is said, '*Then it shall be, if the wicked man deserve to be beaten*' (Deut. 25.2), but once he had been beaten, it calls him 'your brother' as it says, *then your brother should be dishonoured.*[16]

It is precisely through the processes of sanction that deviant behaviour can be expiated and the (former) deviant reintegrated into society. Indeed, it would not be inaccurate to refer to communities' standard repertoire of sanctions as mechanisms of toleration. It is only when sanctions entail an ongoing change in relationship or status and serve to marginalize the deviant in questions, such as, for example, incarceration or differing forms of shunning, that the sanctions represent the assessment of intolerable deviance.

Thus, what I will refer to in the following chapters as tolerable deviance includes cases in which the deviant is sanctioned, but not relegated to society's margins. He retains (or recovers) his standing as '*ahikha*', ('your brother') and despite deviant behaviour is still considered 'of' the community and not merely 'in' it. Conversely, when sanctioning involves exclusionary measures that amount not only to a rejection of deviant behaviour but the marginalization of the deviant himself, this deviance will be classified as intolerable.

The Relationship between the Categories

A community's ability to live with difference is enhanced in direct proportion to the rich variety of ways in which it is able to assess its diversity. Without some measure of pluralism, difference is always classified in terms of someone being right and someone wrong. It requires an act of significant self-restraint, humility and largesse of spirit to declare that one thinks the other opinion to be wrong, yet nevertheless, to fight for its right to not merely exist, but to grow and influence others. The notion of pluralism enhances our ability to accommodate difference by educating people in the prospect that difference may exist without there necessarily being a hierarchy of value. Without tolerance, however, individuals are taught that the only difference they can live with is that difference to which they are willing to ascribe equal value. Given the value conflicts which often lie at the core of our disagreements, especially in the context of religious life, such an assessment of the other is difficult and rare. More often than not, we see the other as wrong, and it is because of this assessment that we make our choices. Tolerance enables us to remain committed to our own truth while at the same time allowing others to decide for themselves, even if we believe their decisions to be wrong.

Finally, without the notion of tolerable deviance, the range of disagreement with which we can live would be too narrow. Tolerance is simply not broad enough a category to contain the spectrum of differences that modern multicultural and multi-religious societies must incorporate. In particular, in the contemporary context, when the sense is that even before the boundary is erected, there are some who have already crossed it, there is a need for a broader and more subtle array of responses towards difference if communal life is to be possible. Through tolerable deviance, one can make the distinction between that which is outside one's notion of socially sanctioned norms and the need always to respond to every breach of these norms. Through the notion of tolerable deviance one learns the virtue of sometimes ignoring that which one believes to be wrong. Modern multicultural collective life (not to speak of families with adolescent children) is well served by members who, while severely disagreeing, are still capable of not paying too close attention to everything that their fellow citizens say, do and believe.

The need for mutual accommodation notwithstanding, without intolerable deviance we would not be able to sustain communities of meaning, communities which have some measure of social cohesion. Some difference needs to be rejected, not just in theory, but in practice, if fellow members are to be able to identify the shared cultural space that they inhabit. Furthermore, while it seems counter-intuitive, it is precisely in the context of social realities where disagreement is most rampant that the category of intolerable deviance plays a central role in creating social cohesion. When it is most difficult to identify the positive content of a community's shared cultural space, instead of agreeing upon that which they hold in common, members can begin the process of creating their shared social identity by structuring an agreement with regard to that which they reject and place outside their cultural boundaries. This agreement with regard to that which every member rejects is strong enough to maintain social cohesion while undergoing the ongoing (and possibly never-ending) process of social identity building on a positive level.

While all the categories play an essential role in the formation of social identity and cohesion, it is important to be aware that their role is not identical. Shared collective life is possible even when fellow members do not agree whether a particular difference is to be assessed under the category of pluralism, tolerance or tolerable deviance. Regardless of the particular classification, in each instance the existence of the differing position does not necessitate a social or legal response. That is not the case when it comes to intolerable deviance. Here a high level of unanimity is necessary. Where there is debate as to what is beyond the boundaries, constant strife and sectarian tendencies will dominate, as one group attempts to marginalize some members with whom others live with in a condition of accommodation, if not tolerance or respect.

Second, in the social process of building and identifying a shared collective space, it is important to view pluralism, tolerance, tolerable and intolerable deviance as constituting a spectrum of social responses to difference, with pluralism and intolerable deviance serving as the extremes to be assessed more sparingly than tolerance and tolerable deviance. Where pluralism is used to encompass too broad a range of difference, a shared collective space becomes impossible to identify. Independent of the question of truth, social identity needs a specific identity, something that is unattainable if everything is of equal value and legitimacy. On the other hand, where intolerable deviance is assessed too expansively, this same identity becomes too narrow, leading to too many members finding themselves outside their society's boundaries. An unrestricted use of the category of intolerable deviance, while creating a clear and strong social identity, creates an identity which does not fit any real and complex social group. As a result, one of the more significant conditions for applying intolerable deviance is that it should not encompass too many members. Where that occurs, and the social structure is functioning well, that which is intolerable needs to be re-assessed as tolerable. If it is not, then the social group as it is presently known will disintegrate, and the social map will have to be redrawn.

Intolerable Deviance and its Spheres of Marginalization

Marginalization is not a mono-dimensional response, with all forms of deviance classified as intolerable being treated in a similar manner. The legal and social responses will vary in both their form and degree, often in accordance with the severity of the deviance in question and/or the danger that such deviance is perceived to pose to the community and to its common values. In fact, the mastery of the art of marginalization is as critical to social life as the boundaries it serves to protect. For our purposes we may consider four spheres of marginalization: basic membership, ritual, loyalty and naming.

1. Basic Membership

By definition, marginalization affects the various manifestations of membership. Being classified as an insider is accompanied by various consequences, rights and benefits, all of which may be called into question when one's basic status is being redefined. In its most radical form, as stated above, the process of marginalization affects the intolerable deviant's standing in the sphere of basic membership. The sphere of basic membership is that sphere which grants the first and most fundamental good distributed by society: membership itself. It serves to delineate and encompass all those who are members or insiders, distinguishing between citizen and non-citizen. Marginalization in this sphere leads to expulsion and to the intolerable deviant being designated as an outsider.

As stated above, marginalization within this sphere is rare, with societies preferring to keep the intolerable deviant within the community. One of the central reasons for this is not necessarily loyalty to the deviant in question, but rather, the social function that the deviant plays in helping to maintain social boundaries and norms. It is precisely by keeping the deviant within, in a status of 'in' but not 'of', that the deviant serves to remind others of what defines the shared cultural space of the community. Once they become outsiders, they cease to be able to serve this function, as they are outside the collective radar screen.

When it comes to the Jewish community and Jewish law, marginalization within this sphere was also rarely, and according to some, never used, for a different reason. True to its tribal roots, this community maintains an essentially familial structure inasmuch as the most basic way of acquiring membership is through birth. One of the central tenets of shared Jewish cultural space is common kinship and descent, an especially durable form of membership which in theory is immune to expulsion even in the face of the most extreme forms of deviance. No matter how badly a child behaves, and irrespective of the lengths to which a parent may go to distance themselves from their seed, the biological connection and the familial relationship it has engendered endure. Consequently, once defined biologically as a Jew – which is to say, once born[17] – according to most halakhic figures, one can never become a true outsider who has completely relinquished one's status as a Jew.

The classical formulation of the immutability principle of Jewish membership is found in the rabbinic pronouncement 'Even though they have sinned, they are still Israel.'[18] Based on this source, from the Middle Ages onward, it became axiomatic that, regardless of actions and beliefs, one's Jewishness could not be revoked. Even conversion to a different religion did not engender a complete loss of membership status.[19] Under Jewish law, one of the key expressions status of membership is the concept *kiddushav kiddushin*, i.e. that in the case of a Jewish male, his marriage act with a Jew is legally binding.

> When [the convert] comes up after his ablution he is deemed to be an Israelite in all respects. What is the practical consequence of this? In that if he retracted [his conversion and returned to his previous religious affiliation] he is regarded as an Israelite *meshumad* and his betrothal is valid (*kiddushav kiddushin*).[20]

As distinct from the non-Jew who is legally not capable of generating a binding marriage, being part of the 'Community of Israel' is attested by the right to marry within the community, a right that cannot be revoked given the immutable nature of one's membership.[21]

A powerful example of this notion at work is found in the responsa of Rabbi Eliezer Valdenberg, head of the Jerusalem Rabbinic court in the 1960s and 1970s, regarding the status of a woman who converted to Christianity and who petitioned the court to allow her to return to the fold of Judaism. Valdenberg ruled as follows:

> It is obvious and simple that according to Jewish law, a Jew is in no way capable of freeing him or herself from the bonds of the Torah and severing the ties and the roots of his connection to his people. A Jew's fundamental connection to the Jewish people is founded on the fact that he was born to Jewish parents, or more accurately to a Jewish mother ...

It is, therefore, a central principle of our religion and our holy Torah that no one of the offspring of Jacob can escape from it, whether voluntarily or non-voluntarily. Against his will, a Jew remains a Jew, connected to the religion of Moshe, with no recourse to free himself from it.

It is, therefore, simple and clear that the conversion to a different religion of this woman, who wants to return to Judaism, is something that never happened. She never left the framework of Judaism, either religiously or nationally, and her return to Judaism is like the return of a daughter to her mother.[22]

2. Ritual

The sphere of basic membership, however, does not exhaust the community's ability to marginalize and affect one's standing as a member *within* the community.[23] At issue is not merely the *fact* of membership, but the *nature and quality* of membership. Here, within the context of religious social structures in general, and Jewish law in particular, intolerable deviance status affects three primary spheres of membership rights. They are, as stated above, the spheres of ritual, loyalty and naming.

By the sphere of ritual, similar to Sagi and Zohar's notion of community of religion,[24] I mean the ability to participate fully in the ritual life of the community. Various sanctions within this sphere touch primarily the arenas of temple, synagogue or cemetery rituals, whereby the intolerable deviant is not given either the rights or honours allotted to members. Thus, for example, in the Talmud we find some deviants barred from the right to bring sacrifices: 'Of you' (Lev. 1.2) and not all of you, to exclude the *meshumad*,[25] who, as will be seen below is one of the intolerable deviants. In the modern context of the debate between Orthodox and liberal Jewish denominations, sanctions within the sphere of ritual often express themselves in the banning of those classified as intolerable deviants from fulfilling any leadership role in prayer services and public recitations of blessings.[26]

3. Loyalty

As for the sphere of loyalty,[27] it encompasses expressions of mutual care and assistance. As a result of loyalties, the members of a community treat each other as objects of concern. It is through loyalty that the community is transformed from being merely 'of' its members to being 'for' them.[28] Within this sphere, more than in others, one can find within Jewish legal sources a wide range of sanctions which serve to marginalize and separate the intolerable deviant. On one side of the spectrum one finds the Talmudic ruling that the intolerable deviant's spiritual well-being ceases to be of concern and, consequently, he is not allowed to offer the sin offering, so that he will not repent.[29] More extreme in nature, though not dissimilar, Moshe Feinstein encourages a teacher not to teach the children of intolerable deviants Torah.[30] And in one of its most extreme forms, the Hatam Sofer rules that all care and concern are removed, and the hope is expressed that the intolerable deviant will simply leave and be permanently separated from the community.[31]

4. Naming

On the surface the sphere of naming is simple. The member bears the name of the group while the outsider, or non-member, does not. Outsider-within status, however, creates complexities. On the one hand, by virtue of formally retaining one's status in the sphere of membership, one retains the group name as well. At the same time, in some instances, the name of Israel is reserved for members in good standing who participate more fully in the community's shared values and beliefs. Certain deviants, while legally incapable of being expelled from the Community of Israel, can, as a form of marginalization and shunning, be stripped of the name 'Israel' while still retaining basic membership status.[32] They remain formally a member, but lose the right to call themselves by the collective name. Thus, for example, the Hatam Sofer states:

> He is neither an Israelite nor a Christian nor a Muslim ... As a general rule it is as if his name has been erased from Israel.[33]

The varieties of forms of marginalization are not intended to simply increase the array of possible sanctions to which an intolerable deviant may be subjected. They are not only different in form but in degree as well, and as such carry different consequences for both the individual being so marginalized and the community that is doing the marginalizing. The art of marginalization is to use each sphere selectively while remaining cognizant of the differing costs and benefits which the use of each incurs. The difference between sanctions in the basic sphere of membership – whereby the deviant is reclassified as an outsider – and that of the other spheres – where the individual nevertheless remains a member – is relatively clear. There are also, however, significant differences between the sphere of ritual and loyalty and within the sphere of loyalty itself. Thus, it is one thing to declare that one cannot pray with a fellow Jew, for example, and quite another to declare that one cannot offer them or anyone associated with them any financial assistance in times of need. The sphere of ritual, while central to Jewish collective life, does not exhaust it. The proponents of differing opinions who view one another as deviant can still maintain social bonds of loyalty. Each will go to their own synagogue and never step into the other's, yet each will still care for others as fellow members and stand by them in times of need. Furthermore, within the sphere of loyalty itself, there is a critical difference between holding back assistance and a formal ban on all verbal, social and economic contact. While both generate significant measures of separation, the latter breaks all contact between the individual in question and the community in which he is formally a member.

Thus, just as it is critical to distinguish between tolerable and intolerable deviance, it is equally significant to distinguish between which intolerable deviance is marginalized in which way. Not all intolerability is of equal severity, and a society must use the various spheres of marginalization to express its varying assessments of differing forms of deviance. To treat, for example, financial and corporal crimes in a similar manner is to fail to give expression to the differing moral assessment that each has within one's social value system.

Furthermore, the truth is that a society can and is willing to live with certain forms of intolerable deviance as well. The fact that basic membership is not withdrawn implies a form of allowance for this deviance. The more complex a society's response to deviance, the more able it will be to weather the ongoing onslaught of difference to which it is subjected, and still maintain its collective framework. So long as the deviant is marginalized, the standards and shared cultural space of the society are maintained. The way in which one marginalizes is then dependent, for example, on the severity or the social prevalence of the deviance, to name but two possibilities. To severely marginalize in the sphere of loyalty all forms of deviance is to deny society its complexity of feelings towards differing forms and degrees of deviance, as well as its ability it continue despite the inevitability of some of its members adopting deviant positions.

It is precisely the result of a heightened sensitivity towards the different consequences of the various spheres, forms and degrees of marginalization that one becomes aware of one other status, beyond that of insider, outsider and outsider-within; that of 'functional-outsider'. It is true that the member in good standing and the outsider-within are indistinguishable vis-à-vis the sphere of basic membership. Nevertheless, their relationship to the community and their experience of communal life can differ so radically, especially when the outsider-within is sanctioned in the sphere of loyalty, that being 'within' becomes trivial. The rights and obligations conceded by *kiddushav kiddushin*, that is, that one's marriages are legally binding, hardly balances out forms of marginalization that can entail a cessation of all daily contact, cessation of all forms of social and economic assistance, a ban on marrying one's children, and in some cases being declared fair game for 'fellow' members to seek one's physical destruction. The persistence of, for example, ethnically maintained membership in these instances begins to seem at best a curiosity and at worst a kind of albatross, a shackle allowing the community to keep him close at hand for ongoing punishment and humiliation.

In actuality, the fact that formal membership is maintained within the sphere of basic membership often serves as a veil behind which the true reality of functional-outsider status is hidden. The fact that one accepts that an Israelite who has sinned is still an Israelite does not mean that one accepts the sinning Israelite into one's community, nor exhibits any degree of toleration. It is only by reviewing the whole spectrum of consequences that accompany intolerable status that one can assess the real implications of deviance within one's community.

In Conclusion: The Case of Bet Hillel and Bet Shammai

An example of the use and interplay between pluralism, tolerance, and tolerable and intolerable deviance within Jewish law can be found in the Talmudic account of the attempt to deal with the two consistently disagreeing schools of Bet Hillel and Bet Shammai. These two schools regularly offered conflicting interpretations of the law and engaged in a lengthy struggle for control, a struggle which went beyond the courts and study halls and involved at times, according to one account, bloodshed.[34] The Talmud in Tractate Eruvin tells that:

> For three years there was a dispute between Bet Shammai and Bet Hillel, the former asserting: The halakhah is in agreement with our views, and the latter contending: The halakhah is in agreement with our views. A *bat kol* [a voice from heaven] then came forth and declared: 'These and these are the words of the living God, but the halakhah is in agreement with the rulings of Bet Hillel.' Since, however, both are the words of the living God what was it that entitled Bet Hillel to have the halakhah fixed in agreement with their rulings? Because they were kindly and modest, they studied their own rulings and those of Bet Shammai, and were even so [humble] as to mention the actions of Bet Shammai before theirs.[35]

The section begins with the fact that the conflict between the two schools was being waged for years, as each argued for the exclusive legitimacy of their reading and wanted the shared rules of the community to reflect that fact. One of the more interesting and often overlooked facets of the above description of the debate is that it went on for so long, and each side claiming for itself the mantle of authoritative Jewish law, nevertheless did not stop arguing with the other. No side disqualified the other as a debating partner. No one left the room. In doing so, neither side classified the other as intolerable. The assumption of the text, however, is that a resolution to the debate had to be found. Since humans seemed to be at an impasse, God chose to intervene and resolve the conflict, but in a paradoxical manner. First God stated that 'these and these are the words of the living God'. In the eyes of God, neither is wrong; both fall within the range of opinions that represent different dimensions of the will of God. The infinite nature of the One God precludes a monistic approach to God's will. Pluralism is not in conflict with the notion of one God, but is rather its most logical conclusion. The positions of both Bet Hillel and Bet Shammai are deemed by God to be legitimate interpretations and expressions of the common ethos of the Jewish law that God promulgates. In essence, God is declaring that the proper way to assess the differences between the two schools is through the category of pluralism.

However, after this statement, God proceeds to grant the status of normative law (halakhah) to the opinions of Bet Hillel and not to those of Bet Shammai. What is important to recognize is that the Gemara is careful to remind the reader that the decision in favour of Bet Hillel is not the result of their being correct and Bet Shammai wrong. While both are the words of the living God, nevertheless, the position is taken that the law is to follow Bet Hillel, 'because they were kindly and modest, they studied their own rulings and those of Bet Shammai, and were even so [humble] as to mention the actions of Bet Shammai before theirs.'

The implication of being deemed the non-halakhic position is not explicated in the above source, but is subject to debate in BT Tractate Berakhot:

> Bet Shammai say: In the evening every man should recline and recite [the sh'ma], and in the morning he should stand, as it says, 'when you lie down and when you get up'.(Deut. 6.7). Bet Hillel, however, says that every man should recite it in his own way, as it says, 'and when you walk by the way.'(*Ibid.*) Why then does it say, 'and when you lie down and when you get up?' [The meaning of the verse is], at the time when people lie down and at the time when people rise up. R. Tarfon said: I was once walking by the way and I reclined to recite the *shema* in the manner prescribed by Bet Shammai, and I incurred danger from robbers. They said to him: You deserved to come to harm, because you acted against the opinion of Bet Hillel.[36]

The debate between Bet Hillel and Bet Shammai in this instance evolves around the manner in which one is to recite the *shema* prayer. What is important for our discussion is the final section of the Mishnah, where the opinion is expressed that deviance from the prescribed instructions of Bet Hillel makes one deserving of death. In the Gemara this opinion is repeated by R. Nahman b. Yitzchak who states that 'anyone who acts in accordance with (the ruling of) Bet Shammai, is deserving of death'.[37] Following Bet Shammai's rulings is defined as intolerable deviance, and one who does so must be removed.

This, however, is not the sole position. In the Gemara we find two other opinions.

> R. Ezekiel learnt: If one acts in accordance with the ruling of Bet Shammai one has done right, if one acts in accordance with the ruling of Bet Hillel one has done right. R. Joseph said: If one acts in accordance with the ruling of Bet Shammai it is as if one has done nothing.[38]

According to R. Eliezer, the rulings of Bet Shammai are classified as acceptable diversity and representative of the legitimate practices of the community. One who follows their instructions 'has done right'. 'These and these are the words of the living God' is not only a statement as to the legitimacy of the approaches in the eyes of God, but also in the eyes of the legal system. This opinion is stated with even greater clarity in Tosephta Yevamot:

> As a general principle, the halakhah follows Bet Hillel. On one who wants to be more stringent upon oneself and adopt the more stringent rulings of both Bet Shammai and Bet Hillel, may be applied the verse, 'A fool walks in darkness'. (Eccl. 2.14). One who adopts the more lenient rulings of both Bet Shammai and Bet Hillel is evil. Rather, if [one adopts the rulings of] Bet Shammai, [one must follow them both] where they are more severe and more lenient, or if [one adopts the rulings of] of Bet Hillel, [one must follow them both] where they are more severe and more lenient.[39]

While the law follows Bet Hillel, the law as understood and defined by Bet Shammai was accepted as legitimate behaviour and removed from the domain of deviance to that of acceptable difference. Members could choose, so long as they chose consistently and did not manipulate the diversity present in the system to support either a lenient or more stringent way of life.[40]

A third approach to the status of those who follow Bet Shammai's rulings is offered by R. Joseph. In the section from Tractate Berakhot just quoted he said, 'if one acts in accordance with the ruling of Bet Shammai it is as if one has done nothing'. Doing nothing is different both from an act which is deemed to be acceptable difference and thus of equal value, on the one hand, and intolerable deviance, on the other. There is a third category being played out here, whereby the rulings of Bet Shammai are rejected and placed outside the sphere of legitimate practice, while those who follow them are nevertheless not subjected to sanctions. They are acts which 'don't count'. This is a form of what I have referred to above as tolerable deviance

As a follow up to this discussion in the Talmud, it has become generally accepted that both the opinions of Bet Hillel and Bet Shammai fall under the category of acceptable diversity, and the tradition's ability to preserve both of them serves as an exemplar for the possibility of pluralism in Judaism. When any other approach argues for its legitimacy as an authentic reading of the tradition, and wants to be classified as acceptable diversity, it models itself and bases its argument on the pluralism implied by the precedent of Bet Hillel and Bet Shammai. Those who disagree, on the other hand, and who want to limit the range of pluralism, or classify the specific approach as deviant, present arguments which serve to show why the case in question is different and cannot be included under the Bet Hillel and Bet Shammai precedent.[41]

In summary, commonality and the various forms of accommodation of difference, in their own way, characterize and shape the nature and identity of our collective lives. Without commonality, we *would* not see each other as fellow members, but rather as strangers. Without accommodation for difference, we *could* not be fellow members, but merely individuals with no ability to form meaningful social ties with others. We attempt to find a balance between the two through the notions of pluralism, tolerance and deviance. Deviance, particularly intolerable deviance, sets the boundaries and creates the possibility of fellow members finding their commonality. Pluralism, tolerance and tolerable deviance, on the other hand, create the possibility of collective life despite our differences and disagreements. The building of a healthy and viable community requires that each have their place. Where one is removed, or when one becomes too dominant, the bond between members is weakened and the social fabric begins to unravel. Where pluralism is applied too broadly, it makes it difficult to identify a shared cultural space. While all members may get along, they may find themselves devoid of the commonality which makes getting along a virtue. At the same time, intolerable deviance, while a critical feature of every social group, has to be limited in nature. When it is too extensive, it begins to encompass too many members of the society, making sectarianism and social bifurcation inevitable.

What serves to limit both extreme forms of pluralism and radical expressions of intolerable deviance are the categories of tolerance and tolerable deviance. They are the dominant engines of social life. Without some measures of pluralism and intolerable deviance, however, they too are inadequate. If an individual cannot find any forms of difference to which one is willing to ascribe equal value and worth, the problem does not lie in the quality of the differing opinions, but in one's unbridled sense of self-aggrandizement and unwarranted self-certainty. Such a self-worshipper cannot live with others. At the same time, if one recognizes the existence of boundaries, but is never willing to do something about those who violate them, then one's real commitment to these boundaries and to the need of limits for one's community's common space is questionable. It is through a careful balancing between all four, together with a mastery of the art of marginalization, that social life becomes viable.

Notes

1 See O. Klineberg, 'The Multi-National Society: Some Research Problems', *Social Sciences Information* 6 (1967), 81–99.
2 See J. D. Douglas, 'The Experience of the Absurd and the Problem of Social Order' in R. A. Scott and J. D. Douglas (eds), *Theoretical Perspective on Deviance* (New York, 1972), pp. 189–214; and H. S. Becker, *Outsiders – Studies in the Sociology of Deviance* (New York, 1963), p. 15.
3 K. T. Erikson, *The Wayward Puritans* (New York, 1966), p. 12.
4 I. Berlin, 'Two Concepts of Liberty', in *Four Essays on Liberty*, (Oxford, 1969), p. 171.
5 *Ibid.*
6 See D. Heyd, *Toleration, an Illusive Virtue* (Princeton, 1996), p. 4; and A. Sagi, 'ha-Dat ha-Yehudit: Sovlanut ve-Efsharut ha-Pluralism', *Iyyun* 44 (April 1995), 175–200. M. Walzer, *On Toleration* (New Haven, 1997), pp. 10–12, on the other hand, argues for a continuum of attitudes within the category of tolerance itself, ranging from resigned acceptance to enthusiastic endorsement. He raises the question, 'But perhaps this last attitude (of enthusiastic endorsement) falls outside my subject: how can I be said to tolerate what I in fact endorse? If I want the others to be here, in this society, among us, then I don't tolerate otherness – I support it.' Nevertheless, he includes this under the definition of tolerance as well, 'for they coexist with an otherness that, however much they approve of its presence in the world, is still something different from what they know, something alien and strange'. The notion of tolerance as what Walzer calls 'resigned acceptance' is the central way the category will be understood in this work.
7 B. Williams, 'Toleration: an Impossible Virtue', in D. Heyd (ed.), *Toleration, an Illusive Virtue*, p. 18. See also M. Cranston, 'John Locke and the Case for Toleration', in S. Mendus and D. Edwards (eds), *On Toleration* (Oxford, 1987),

p. 10, who states, 'If there were not things we disapproved of, the concept of "toleration" need not be introduced at all. It would be enough to talk about "liberty" or "freedom". When we speak of people's liberty or freedom, no criticism is implied of the use to which they put their freedom ... we can say that only the undesirable – or at any rate, the undesired – is a candidate for toleration.'

8 D. D. Raphael, 'The Intolerable', in S. Mendus (ed.), *Justifying Toleration* (Cambridge, 1988), p. 139. See also J. Horton and P. Nicolson, *Toleration: Philosophy and Practice* (Aldershot, 1992), p. 2; and S. Mendus, *Justifying Toleration*, p. 6.

9 M. Walzer, *On Toleration* p. xii.

10 K. T. Erikson, 'Notes on the Sociology of Deviance', in H. S. Becker, *The Other Side – Perspectives on Deviance* (London, 1964), pp. 10–1.

11 E. Goode, *Deviant Behaviour*, (Englewood Cliffs, 1990), p. 24.

12 See J. R. Gusfield, 'Moral Passage – The Symbolic Process in Public Designation of Deviance', *Social Problems* 15 (1967), pp. 175–92, who distinguishes between the instrumental and the symbolic functions of law. The instrumental function lies in the enforcement of the law. Law also has a symbolic aspect, however, whose significance is independent of enforcement, shaping public consciousness and simply existing 'on the books' as an ideal expression of the community's shared ethos.

13 See H. S. Becker, *Outsiders*, p. 15.

14 R. A. Dentler and K. T. Erikson, 'The Function of Deviance in Groups', in R. A. Farrell and V. L. Swigert, *Social Deviance* (Philadelphia, 1975), p. 31.

15 R. A. Scott, 'Framework for Analyzing Deviance as a Property of Social Order', in R. A. Scott and J. D. Douglas (eds), *Theoretical Perspectives on Deviance* (New York, Basic Books, 1972), p. 15.

16 Sifre Deuteronomy, Piska 286. Translated by R. Hammer (New Haven, 1986).

17 Even the convert, it is proposed, undergoes a re-birthing process in becoming a Jew ('A convert who converted is as a baby who was born', BT Tractate Yevamot 62a), and thus all ties between him and his blood family are considered annulled. See for example BT Tractate Yevamot 22a, Kiddushin 17b. For a discussion of conversion as rebirth see A. Sagi and Z. Zohar, *Giyur ve-Zehut Yehudit* (Jerusalem, 1994), Ch. 14.

18 BT Tractate Sanhedrin 44a.

19 In addition, see Jacob Katz's article, 'Af Al Pi Shehata Yisrael Hu' in his *Halakhah and Kabbalah*, (Jerusalem, 1986). There he discusses the evolution of the concept through its transformation into a legal and binding principle by the mediaeval scholar Rashi. See Teshuvot Rashi 171, 173 and 175. See also G. Bildstein, 'Who is not a Jew?', *Israel Law Review* 11, 3 (1976), 369–90, who reviews the various Gaonic and mediaeval sources on the issue of the status of the *mumar*, including those who held the position that the *mumar* was an outsider. See also A. Sagi and Z. Zohar, 'Giyra ve-Zehut Yehudit', pp. 9–11.

20 BT Tractate Yevamot 47b. See also S. Leiberman, *Tosephta ki-Fshutah* (New York, 1962), D'mai, Chapter 2, p. 69, n. to line 11–12, who writes, 'However, a

convert who is suspected, even if he is suspected with regard to the whole Torah, is not expelled from his Jewishness, and has the status of an Israelite *meshumad* and *kiddushav kiddushin.*'

21 An example of this notion is found in Gen. 34.13–16, where Shimeon and Levi say to Shechem in the Dina story, 'We cannot do this thing, to give our sister to a man who is uncircumcised, for that is a disgrace among us. Only on this condition will we agree with you; that you will become *like us* in that every male among you is circumcised. Then we will give our daughters to you and take your daughters to ourselves; and we will dwell among you and become *as one kindred.*' (Emphasis mine.)

See also Ezra 9, where marriage is allowed only amongst those who share the 'holy seed'.

It is important to remember, however, that the primary emphasis with regard to maintaining the status of Jew is the persistent, immutable claim of one's legal *obligations*. For example, the main significance of *kiddushav kiddushin*, whose positive phrasing seems to connote the conferral of a right, is understood by Jewish law to lie in its halakhic corollary: that the marital bond can only be broken by an official writ of divorce, which the husband is obligated to provide in accordance with all rabbinic requirements and standards. For the intolerable deviant bound by blood to his community, this immutable membership, with all of its unwavering claims, can begin to seem more like an unrelenting burden than an inalienable right.

22 *Responsa* Tzitz Eliezer Part 13.93.

23 Rooted in an awareness of this nuance between rejection and marginalization, between the outsider and the outsider-within, Gerald Bildstein, 'Who is not a Jew?', p. 374, addresses the status of Judaism's classic intolerable deviant: the apostate. He argues for a reframing of the discussion away from the general question of membership to a more complex and pluralistic approach, which 'does not necessarily demand an answer of the either/or variety', but rather allows for the preservation of aspects of membership in certain areas and, simultaneously, exclusion from others. 'The Jewishness of the apostate is split', Bildstein argues, inasmuch as he may retain all the obligations of membership even as the rest of the community is relieved of significant obligations towards him. '"A Jew who sins remains a Jew nonetheless" – this refers [only] to marriage and divorce, where "brotherliness" (*ahva*) is no criterion' (i.e. there is nothing in the nature of these rituals that requires others to behave towards the deviant in a brotherly manner).

'"*Brotherliness*", the sharing of commitment and loyalty, is a criterion, however, in other areas such as interest-taking and the responsibility for [ensuring his basic physical] survival. Here the biological or purely national community is of no significance; the biological-national community confers status and assures continued obligation to the covenant – it does not sustain the bonds of fellowship and mutuality, nor does it compel the loyalty and responsibility of the community to its renegades' (p. 387).

Along similar lines, A. Sagi and Z. Zvi, in their work *Ma-agalei Zehut Yehudit* ba-Sifrut ha-Hilkhatit (Tel Aviv, 2000), addressing the membership status of the *mehallel Shabbat*, distinguish between two different spheres of membership. The first is membership in the ethnic community of Israel, a function of biological descent. The second is membership in the religious community, participation in the ritual life of Israel. As with Bildstein, the membership question here is not either/or, but *which*: which aspects of membership does the deviant relinquish and retain? In which spheres of communal life is he claimed by his fellows, and in which disavowed? Membership in the ethnic community, while a prerequisite for membership in the religious, is, however, in itself no guarantee: not every member of biological Israel is accepted as a participant in its ritual life.

24 A. Sagi and Z. Zohar, *Ma-agalei Zehut Yehudit be-Sifrut ha-Hilkhatit* (Tel Aviv, 2000).

25 BT Tractate Hullin 5a.

26 See Moshe Feinstein's *Igrot Moshe,* Oreh Haim 2.50.

27 This sphere is parallel to Bildstein's notion of 'brotherliness'. See G. Bildstein, 'Who is not a Jew?'.

28 G. Fletcher, *Loyalty* (New York, 1993), p. 20.

29 BT Tractate Hullin 5a.

30 *Igrot Moshe,* Yoreh Deah 2.107.

31 *Teshuvot Hatam Sofer,* Likutei She-eilot ve-Teshuvot 89.

32 One of the consequences of utilizing the sphere of naming as an independent sphere is that it allows for greater sensitivity in analysing various halakhic sources which prescribe that certain deviants are not to be included under the category of Israel, and are not a part of 'you' when it refers to Israel. Without the sphere of naming, these types of sources would be interpreted as entailing a call for expulsion, something which, while possible, is not necessarily what these sources are calling for.

33 *Teshuvot Hatam Sofer,* Hoshen Mishpat 195.

34 See JT Tractate Shabbat 1.4

35 BT Tractate Eruvin 13b.

36 Mishnah Berakhot 1.3.

37 BT Tractate Berakhot 11a.

38 *Ibid.*

39 Tosefta Yevamot 1.13

40 See Rashi, BT Tractate Rosh Hashanah 14b, *Mikulei Bet Shammai,* who argues that one can even alternate between the two schools, so long as one is guided by reason and not the desire for leniency or stringency.

41 See for example the following argument of A. Sagi in 'ha-Dat ha-Yehudit: Sovlanut ve-Efsharut ha-Pluralism', pp. 175–6: ' "These and these are the words of the living God", as a characteristic expression of the halakhic culture, is sometimes used as evidence for a philosophy of tolerance or even pluralism within the halakhic world. However, it is incorrect to deduce from the halakhic system's recognition of multiple opinions or even multiple religious practices that the halakhah sides with tolerant or pluaralistic positions. For the diversity which the Jewish religion recognizes is diversity within the system itself ...

However, all that which is not contained within the system is not considered a part of "the words of the living God". Rather, it is deviance towards which the halakhic system did not necessarily relate with tolerance, not to speak of with pluralism'.

CHAPTER TWO

Deviance, Boundaries and
Marginalization in Rabbinic
Literature

The aim of this chapter is to review the boundaries that the rabbis erected to
define the core shared cultural space of Judaism. What were the boundaries
that they believed could not be crossed? In exploring this question, the
analysis will follow the ways in which the four primary categories used to
denote deviants – *meshumad, min, apikoros* and *kofer* – were defined, used and
sanctioned during the rabbinic period. Through this study I hope to
reconstruct both a rabbinic theory of tolerable and intolerable deviance as
well as the rabbinic approach towards marginalization, i.e. which deviance
was marginalized in which way. As I hope to show, although the literature
does not provide a systematic statement regarding deviance, boundaries and
marginalization, it nonetheless presents several clear and consistent positions
on these issues.

Forms of Deviance

As stated, there are four primary categories of deviance used in rabbinic
literature. They are the *meshumad, min, apikoros* and *kofer*. Of the four, two
are used to denote intolerability: the *meshumad* and the *min*. Both terms are
used for a wide range of deviance, including some that were assessed as
tolerable – a fact that has lead to extensive scholarly debate as to the exact
nature of the intolerable deviance each designates.[1] In contrast, the *apikoros*
always represents a tolerable deviant, while the *kofer* does not appear as an
independent category as far as rabbinic literature is concerned.

Meshumad

The etymology of *meshumad* is based on the root meaning, 'to be
destroyed'.[2] When taking into account both Tannaic and Ammoraic
rabbinic sources, (the former referring to rabbis who flourished in Palestine
from approximately 70 CE to *c.* 220 CE, while the Ammoraim flourished in
Palestine and Babylon after the redaction of the Mishnah in 220 CE until the
final redaction of the Babylonian Talmud *c.* 500 CE) the category of
meshumad denotes a wide range of deviance, from complete rejection of the
covenant or apostasy to the impulsive violation of a particular law. Despite

this ambiguity, the *meshumad* of rabbinic literature demonstrates a set of consistent characteristics that add up to, if not a perfectly clear picture, then certainly a strong outline of intolerable deviance. Firstly, the *meshumad* is exclusively used as a category for delinquency, i.e. action-based deviance. However, in order to be classified as intolerable, this delinquency must also be expressive of a measure of heresy of differing forms and degrees. Non-heretical delinquency is always tolerable. Secondly, with the exception of the *meshumad ledavar ehad lehakhis*, the delinquent who violates one commandment out of spite, an exclusively Ammoraic and debated category, the intolerable *meshumad* is generally used to designate a radical, far-reaching deviant who has separated himself completely from either or both the Jewish people and Judaism. Any delinquency of a lesser measure, regardless of how severe the deviance, is either not a *meshumad* or is generally classified as tolerable.[3]

A paradigmatic source illustrative of the predominant nature of the *meshumad*'s deviance is found in BT Tractate Yevamot.

> When [the convert] comes up after his ablution, he is deemed to be an Israelite in all respects. What are the practical consequences of this? If he retracted [his conversion and returned to his previous religious affiliation], he is still regarded as an Israelite *meshumad* and his betrothals are legally valid (*kiddushav kiddushin*).[4]

By *meshumad*, the text is referring not to an individual who has simply deviated from one or some of the *mitzvot* or principles of Judaism, but rather an individual who has completely exited the social and religious framework of both Judaism and the Jewish people. While formally a Jew through conversion, he warrants *meshumad* classification by choosing to return to his non-Jewish status, with all its ideological and social commitments. The Tosefta in Tractate Succah speaks of the *meshumad* in similar terms. The reference speaks of the priestly family (course) of Bilgah, who were given an inferior status when it was their turn to officiate in the temple as a result of one of their daughters becoming a *meshumad*.

> Miriam the daughter of Bilgah ... became a *meshumad* and went and married an officer of the Greek king, and when the Greeks entered the temple she stamped upon the altar and declared: '*Lukos, Lukos*, you consumed Israel's money and yet did not stand by them in their time of oppression.'[5]

Miriam the *meshumad* is characterized as both a Hellenizer and a traitor.[6] Her offences (apostasy, intermarriage, treason, blasphemy) involve both delinquency and heresy. She is an all-inclusive type of deviant, rejecting both the community of Israel and the covenant with God upon which it is based.[7]

With the exception of the above two sources, the other Tannaic sources that refer to the *meshumad*, while following the same general understanding, do not offer as explicit an accounting of the nature of his deviance. They refer to terms such as one who rejects the covenant (*she-eino mekabel brit*),[8] and one who has separated himself from the community, (*poresh min hatzibur*);[9] however, there is no explicit reference to the nature of the deviance on the basis of which these terms are warranted. What the two terms have in common is that they refer to delinquency which both transcends any specific act and represents a radical transformation in the way the individual in question relates either to the Jewish legal enterprise as a whole or to the Jewish people.[10] This point is made more explicitly with reference to the deviance of the *meshumad* as *poresh min hatzibur* that appears in the Midrash *Seder Olam Rabbah*:

> The sentence of the wicked is [to be placed] in Gehenom for twelve months ... Upon concluding these twelve months, the wicked of Israel (*poshei yisrael*) who violated the commandments [are punished as follows:] their soul is destroyed and their body withers and is burnt; Gehenom discharges them and the wind spreads and disperses them and they become dust under the feet of the righteous ... But those who have separated themselves from the ways of the community (*parshu medarkhei tzibur*), such as the *minim*, the *meshumadim*, and the informers (*mosorot*), and the *khanifim*[11] and the *apikorsim* who deny the resurrection of the dead and who say the Torah is not from heaven – all these are locked in Gehenom and are sentenced therein for eternity.[12]

The *meshumad* is classified amongst a larger list of deviants who have separated themselves from the community. As such, they are distinguished from the mere wicked of Israel (*poshei yisrael*), defined as those who violate commandments. What is clear from the nature of the sanction, i.e. 'their soul is destroyed and their body withers and is burnt, Gehenom discharges them and the wind spreads and disperses them and they become dust under the feet of the righteous', is that the wicked of Israel are not the run-of-the-mill sinners, a category which in one way or another encompasses most people. They are a severe form of deviant who embody extensive and extreme delinquency. The one mitigating factor that saves them from eternal damnation is that, despite their delinquency, they nevertheless still view themselves as maintaining their overall connection and loyalty to the community. In contrast, the *meshumad* and the others are ones whose deviance is more than the 'mere' extensive violation of commandments. They are deviants of a more radical nature whose deviance is perceived to entail also the removal of oneself out of the confines of Israel's collective identity.[13]

The particularly Tannaic tendency not to clearly delineate the specific nature of the *meshumad*'s deviance, yet sanction him nonetheless, may be taken as further evidence of the all-encompassing and extreme form of deviance that it depicts. The *meshumad* in question is subjected to some extreme forms of marginalization, including a kind of extra-legal death penalty halakhically referred to as *moridin ve-lo ma-alin*.

> Non-Jewish idolaters and [Jewish] shepherds need not be raised up [from a pit into which they have fallen], though they may not be cast in [and left there to die] (*lo ma-alin ve-lo moridin*). The *minim*, *meshumadim* and informers, [on the other hand] may be cast in and need not be raised up (*moridin ve-lo ma-alin*).[14]

As distinct from non-member idolaters towards whom one need not offer assistance, a list of Jewish deviants, including the *meshumad*, may be actively placed in the direst of situations. This may involve such trickery as asking them to go down into a pit (*moridin*) in order to retrieve something and then removing the ladder (*ve-lo ma-alin*), thus causing them to die. What is particular about this extreme form of sanction is that it is not implemented by a court of law, which reviews evidence of guilt prior to issuing its judgment. Rather, *moridin ve-lo ma-alin* empowers regular citizens to take the law into their own hands in order to rid society of certain intolerable deviants. This fact alone further sets apart the deviance of the *meshumad* from regular sinners and identifies it as one that is extreme, transformative, clearly discernable and public in nature. Any broader a definition would lead to the possible endangering of innocents and to social chaos.

While much of the Ammoraic use of the category of *meshumad* follows its Tannaic sense as a total and comprehensive deviant, nevertheless in the Ammoraic period, there also emerges a significantly different use for the term. Rather than only encompassing the rejection of an entire system of behaviour and belief, the Ammoraic *meshumad* serves as a catch-all category for a broad and diverse range of deviances both tolerable and intolerable.[15] This change is most pointedly evinced by the appearance of the expression *meshumad le* ... (lit. '*meshumad* for ...'), which is indicative of a more partial and particular expression of deviance. Some instances of the classification of intolerability are equivalent to the prevalent sense of the term in the Tannaic period. Others, however, significantly expand the parameters of the boundary of intolerability.

One of the more central Ammoraic discussions of the nature of the *meshumad*'s deviance is found in BT Tractate Hullin 5a. After yet another Tannaic sanctioning of an unidentified *meshumad* appearing below in the first two paragraphs, the Ammoraic commentators offer the following analysis.

> 'Of you' (Lev. 1.2): and not all of you, to exclude the *meshumad*.
> 'Of you', with regards to you [i.e. Israel] I make distinctions [as to who can bring a sacrifice], but not with regards to the nations.
> 'Of cattle' (*ibid.*), to include people who are similar to animals. On the basis of this they say that sacrifices are accepted from Israelite criminals (*poshei yisrael*) so that they will repent, with the exception of the *meshumad*, one who brings wine libation [for idolatry] and one who desecrates the Shabbat in public.
> This is self-contradictory. It says, 'Of you and not all of you, to exclude the *meshumad*'; and then it says, 'Sacrifices are accepted from Israelite criminals (*poshei yisrael*)'. This is not self-contra-dictory. The former statement [prohibiting sacrifices] refers to one who is a *meshumad* to violate the whole Torah, while the latter statement [which permits *poshei yisrael* to bring sacrifices] refers to one who is a *meshumad* to violate one particular law.
> Consider now the last statement, 'with the exception of the *meshumad*, one who brings wine libation [for idolatry] and one who desecrates the Shabbat in public'. What is the definition of the *meshumad*? If it means one who is a *meshumad* to violate the whole Torah (*lekol hatorah*), then it is identical with the first part. If it means one who is a *meshumad* to violate one particular law then it is inconsistent with the middle section [which permits this class of *meshumad* to bring sacrifices]. Of necessity the reference [of the last class of *meshumad*] is, with the exception of the *meshumad* to bring wine libation [for idolatry] and to desecrate the Shabbat in public, proving that one who is a *meshumad* to worship idols is a *meshumad* to violate the whole Torah.[16]

The above Ammoraic analysis creates three different types of *meshumad*: 1) the *meshumad lekol hatorah kullah* (lit. '*meshumad* for the entire Torah'); 2) the *meshumad ledavar ehad* who is either an idol worshipper or a public desecrator of the Shabbat; and 3) the more limited *meshumad ledavar ehad* (lit. '*meshumad* for one thing') defined as one whose particular violations entail any individual commandment with the exception of either idolatry or the public desecration of the Shabbat. Intolerability is limited to deviance of the first two kinds, while the general *meshumad ledavar ehad* is classified as tolerable.

The first, the *meshumad lekol hatorah kullah*, is a metaphorical expression, not a literal description of a sinner who violates every single commandment, for this is technically impossible. Rather, it is meant to represent this *meshumad*'s *attitude* towards the system in *total*, which entails a complete rejection of the authority of Jewish law, and is thus parallel to the Tannaic use of the term as found, for example, in the Sifra's *meshumad she-einan mekablei brit*, or with regards to the deviance of Miriam the daughter of Bilgah. Conversely, the third category, the general *meshumad ledavar ehad* could, in actuality, violate any number of commandments and maintain his tolerable appellation, as long as these individual sins do not reflect a rejection of the system as a whole. The distinction between the *meshumad lekol hatorah kullah* and the *meshumad ledavar ehad* does not reflect a quantitative measure of sin, but a difference in perspective and disposition. It is not the mere delinquent who is marginalized, but the delinquent who willfully renounces and exits the system.

The second category, which is also intolerable, is the *meshumad* who either worships idols or desecrates the Sabbath in public.[17] What is important about this category is that it entails individual sins that nonetheless have the power, *on their own*, to generate intolerability. What the Talmud does not explain, however, is why these forms of deviance bear this unique power.

Regarding idolatry, it is not difficult to formulate a rationale. The *meshumad* who worship idols is not simply violating one aspect of Jewish law; he is effectively becoming an apostate. Idolatry and idolatry alone provokes the rabbinic dictum: 'One who accepts idolatry rejects the whole Torah and one who rejects idolatry accepts the whole Torah.'[18] In this sense the idolater is not merely a *meshumad ledavar ehad* of an especially severe nature, but a form and extension of *meshumad lekol hatorah kullah*.[19] What is unique about idolatry is that even though it is a particular act, it is nevertheless indicative of a comprehensive rejection of all of Torah.[20]

The inclusion of Shabbat desecration as a form of intolerable deviance on a par with idolatry is far less self-evident, and, indeed, it is subject to debate within the Talmud itself.[21] The Hebrew term used for this category of deviance is *mehallel Shabbat befarhesia*, which literally means 'one who desecrates the Sabbath in public'. Rashi offers an explanation for the equivalency with idolatry, based on the heretical qualities associated with each. Just as the idolater rejects belief in God as defined by Jewish tradition, 'so too the *mehallel Shabbat* rejects the belief in God's deeds and bears false witness that God did not rest in the act of creation'.[22] In other words, Shabbat desecration and idolatry distinguish themselves by being singular deviancies that are uniquely indicative of a larger, specific heretical position. It is this particular combination that makes the deviant behaviour intolerable.

This justification, however, has an obvious flaw. The deviance that is compared to idolatry is not the desecration of the Shabbat in general, but is limited to the *mehallel Shabbat befarhesia* ('in public').[23] Were merely the heresy of the *mehallel Shabbat* at issue, there would be no distinction between private and public, a distinction which, significantly, is absent with regard to idolatry. For heresy, location is irrelevant.[24] Limiting the intolerable deviance of the *mehallel Shabbat* to that which occurs in the public realm argues against heresy as a defining factor for his deviance status.

The public desecrator of the Shabbat is deemed intolerable, I would argue, not because of the heresy implied in his behaviour, but rather because of the statement about his association with the community implied by his public flaunting of the law. Designating him an intolerable deviant stresses the centrality of public fidelity to the Shabbat as a defining characteristic of the Rabbinic Jewish people's shared cultural space, to use Erikson's language. As a rule, no specific act of deviance, even one performed publicly, has the power, on its own, to define and serve as an indication of an individual's overall affiliation with the community of Israel. That is, a *meshumad* is not generally considered a *poresh min hatzibur* unless he is a *meshumad lekol hatorah kullah*. Shabbat is the exception to this rule, and endowing it with this extra measure of consequence reinforces its integral role. The deviant who publicly desecrates Shabbat thus renounces his communal affiliation, and is a form of *poresh min hatzibur*. The desecration of the Shabbat is thus unique in that, despite its apparent limited scope, it nevertheless serves as an indication for a larger shift in an individual's loyalty and collective identification.

In their defining of the idolater and the public desecrator of the Shabbat as intolerable, the Ammoraim here are thus not altering the core Tannaic criterion for intolerability. Through the notion of *meshumad ledavar ehad*, however, they are expanding the use of the term *meshumad* to include deviance of a tolerable nature. In BT Tractate Gittin, we see the Ammoraim both expand the use of the category and the criteria for intolerability:

> A certain [Jewish] man sold himself to the [non-Jewish] Lydian tribe and then appealed to R. Ami saying: Redeem me. So he [R. Ami] said: We have learned, 'If a man sells himself and his children to a heathen he is not to be redeemed, but his children are to be redeemed after the death of their father, to prevent their going astray.' All the more so here, where there is a danger of their being killed. The rabbis said to R. Ami: This man is an Israelite *meshumad* who has been seen eating non-kosher meat (*neveilot* and *treifot*). He [R. Ami] said to them: Possibly he did so because he was motivated by desire (*teiavon*)? They said: There have been times when he had the choice of permitted and forbidden meat and he left the former and took the latter [thus indicating that the motivation was spite and not desire]. He

thereupon said to the man: Be off, they will not let me ransom
you.[25]

While the community is legally obligated to redeem its members who fall
into captivity, this particular case involves an individual who sold himself
into captivity, an act which generally absolves the community of its
responsibility. R. Ami nonetheless argues for intervention on the grounds
that the captors are Lydians, whom some commentators identify as
cannibals, [26] and whom others say ran gladiator events with their slaves. [27]
In doing so, he invokes a special clause, a kind of loyalty failsafe: in a case
with clear life-or-death ramifications, the exemption from redeeming one
who sells himself is overridden.

The rabbis, who appear to generally accept this premise, nonetheless
dismiss R. Ami's claim in this particular case. This is due to the fact that the
individual in question is a deviant out of spite and not out of desire. They
argue that he is an intolerable deviant towards whom there are no bonds of
loyalty. [28] In doing so this text radically extends the range of intolerable
delinquency to include seemingly any *meshumad ledavar ehad* so long as the
motivation for the deviance is spite. The new condition for intolerability is
thus heresy even if the heresy is not all-inclusive and comprehensive. An
individual sin, when not triggered by weakness or appetite, constitutes some
measure of rebellion against the halakhic system as a whole and a rejection of
the binding nature of the covenant. Conversely, when a sin can be
explained as motivated by *teiavon,* the deviant is essentially given the benefit
of the doubt, construed as a victim of human fallibility and deemed devoid
of any broader ideological malice. [29]

In the final analysis, however, the *meshumad* in the above source has
only violated one law, and one with no inherent or obvious resonance vis-à-
vis the covenant or community as a whole. Thus, he can be compared
neither to the *meshumad she-eino mekabel brit* nor to the *meshumad lekol hatorah
kullah* or even to the *mehallel Shabbat befarhesia.* He thus constitutes a
significant deviation from and expansion of Tannaic definitions of the
intolerable *meshumad.* Perhaps in opposition to this expansion, R. Ami
dismisses the *meshumad* with 'Be off, they will not let me ransom you.' This
closing remark indicates a clear sense of discomfort with the decision of his
colleagues. Though he does not dispute their designation of the Jewish
captive as a *meshumad lehakhis,* he clearly is not comfortable with the
marginalization prescribed by his colleagues in this case.

Min

The second category used to designate intolerable deviance is the *min*. The category itself, as distinct from the *meshumad*, is primarily used to denote deviance of a heretical nature;[30] however, in no case do the rabbis explicitly direct sanctions against the *min* as heretic alone. In fact the vast majority of the references to the *min* are devoid of any mention of marginalization. It is only when the heresy of the *min* is accompanied by delinquency that the issue of marginalization is broached.[31] There are two types of delinquency that may characterize this *min*: either he is an idolater, or else he is a Jewish Christian – a term used to refer to individuals of Jewish descent who are believers in the redemptive significance of Jesus.

In accordance with its heretical underpinning, one finds in rabbinic sources numerous references to people identified as *minim* ideologically challenging the rabbis around doctrines of faith.

> 'And God said: Let us make man.' (Gen. 1.26). The *minim* asked R. Simlai: How many deities created the world?[32]

> *Minim* asked Rabban Gamliel: How do we know that God will resurrect the dead? He responded [with proof] from the Torah, the Prophets and the Writings, and they did not accept it. [33]

> A certain *min* said to R. Hanina: Now you [Israelites] are certainly impure, as it states: 'Her uncleanness clings to her skirts.' (Lam. 1.9). He replied: Are you aware what is said about them: 'Which abides with them in the midst of their uncleanness.' (Lev. 16.16). Even when they are unclean, the Divinity resides amongst them. [34]

The *minim* in the above sources question monotheism, the resurrection of the dead, and the election of Israel, all of which are fundamental tenets of Jewish tradition. The *meshumad*, as distinct from the *min*, is never depicted as engaging the rabbis in such doctrinal debates. Although his deviance involves heresy, it is primarily characterized by delinquency; the *min*, on the other hand, is one whose deviance consists of a rejection of Judaism's doctrines of faith.

Despite the wide range of heresies denoted by the *min*, there is one central defining feature of his deviance: he is primarily an enemy deviant. He is not merely a heretic, but an individual who actively challenges rabbinic articles of faith; he is constantly on the attack. The expressions, 'The *minim* asked ...'[35]; 'Because of the claim of the *minim*, so that they wouldn't be able to say ...'[36]; 'So that the *minim* won't say ...'[37]; 'After the *minim* ruined and said ...' [38] and the like, which attend almost every mention of the *min*, attest to his contentious stance. In fact, the rabbis invoke the term *min* as a way of referring to general attacks on rabbinic Judaism, as the following midrashic passage demonstrates:

> Once I was walking along the road and I happened upon a man who came to me in the manner of a *min (derekh minut)*. He knew the Bible but not Mishnah. He said to me: The Bible was given to Moses at Sinai but not the Mishnah.[39]

The aggressive posture of the *min* led to a whole genre of sources aimed at helping individuals defend themselves against their doctrinal attacks. Jewish law itself was even viewed as being altered in order to avoid the *min*'s manipulation and influence:

> Rav Matnah and Shmuel bar Nahman both said: By law the Ten Commandments should be read every day. They are not read, however, so that the *minim* would not be able to say that they alone were given to Moses at Sinai.[40]

Indeed, their antagonism was considered so significant that attempts to pre-empt it were read polemically into the Bible itself. Thus according to the rabbis, any time the Bible refers to God in the plural, it also takes pain to add a reference to God in the singular to avoid heretical *minim* manipulating it to claim God's plurality.

> For all the passages which the *minim* use as a basis for their heresy, another passage which refutes their interpretation is always close at hand. 'Let us make man in our image', (Gen. 1.26), and 'God created man in His own image'. (Gen. 1.27). 'Come let us go down and there confound their language', (Gen. 11.7), and 'And the Lord came down to see the city and the tower'. (Gen. 11.5)[41]

Furthermore, as an enemy, the *min* goes further than merely questioning Jewish beliefs; he frames these questions using the texts and practices of the tradition itself. Even the non-Jewish *min* knows Scripture and uses it to attack Israel.[42] He engages Jewish tradition in a battle on its own turf in order to prove that it is based on lies. It is this particularly insidious brand of antagonism that brought R. Meir to pray for the death of the *min*:

> There was once a certain *min* who lived in the neighbourhood of R. Meir who caused him trouble with Bible verses. R. Meir accordingly prayed that he should die.[43]

Consistently, then, the *min* – whether as sectarian, heretic, or non-Jew – is not simply an ideological deviant who rejects some aspect of Jewish law, nor only an apostate who rejects Judaism in its entirety. He is rather a subversive figure who works actively to *undermine* the community, its faith and way of life. He does not merely adopt attitudes and practices considered threatening or dangerous, but functions consciously and proactively to convince others to adopt them as well. Not content to be alone in his deviance, he works to undermine the beliefs and practices of rabbinic Jews, and ultimately rabbinic Judaism, as a whole.[44]

To summarize, the categories of *meshumad* and *min* represent three primary criteria for intolerability, all of which combine delinquency and heresy of varying degrees. The *meshumad* depicts the individual who has either completely rejected all of Torah (*meshumad lekol hatorah kullah, meshumad she-eino mekabel brit* or the idolater) or who has completely separated himself from the community (*poresh min hatzibur* or *mehallel Shabbat befarhesia*). The marginalized *min* adds to the classification of intolerability the deviance of the Jewish Christian who in rabbinic eyes combines heresy and delinquency with the condition of enemy deviance. In addition to the above three criteria, some Ammoraim add the *meshumad ledavar ehad lehakhis*, who, while not rejecting all of Torah, nevertheless includes a strong heretical and ideological foundation to his delinquency. This addition, however, is not present in Tannaic sources, and as will be seen below, is also not uniformly accepted amongst the Ammoraim.

Apikorus

As distinct from the *meshumad* and the *min*, categories that depict both tolerable and intolerable deviants, the *apikorus* is always tolerable in the sense that it is never subjected to legal or this-worldly sanctions. Like the *meshumad* and *min*, it too is a complex category evoking a spectrum of meanings and uses.[45] The term is primarily used as a category for heresy alone – deviance unaccompanied by delinquency. It thus constitutes a distinct classification from both *meshumad* and *min*.[46] Similar to these other categories, it too is often used without specification as to the nature of the offence.[47] A classic Mishnaic reference to the *apikorus* neatly illustrates this trend:

> The following have no share in the world to come: one who says there is no resurrection after death, and [one who says] the Torah is not from heaven and the *apikorus*.[48]

Unlike its counterparts in the above Mishnah, the deviance of the *apikorus* is not explicitly detailed. However, what is made explicit from the fact that the *apikorus* is placed within in a list of fellow heretics is that it, too, is a form of heresy. As for sanctions, the only consequence in the Mishnah for his heresy involves an exclusion from the world to come, with no sanctions in this world resulting from his deviance.

This lack of sanctions is particularly interesting in light of the identification of the *apikorus* in rabbinic sources, like the *min*, as an enemy deviant:

> Rabbi Eliezer states: Be alert to study in order to know what answer to give an *apikorus*. Know before whom you are striving, and who is your employer who will pay you the reward for your labour.[49]

The warning '... know what answer to give an *apikorus*' identifies him as not merely a passive holder of opinions, but as one who challenges the beliefs and ideas of others. Like the *min*, the *apikorus* is not merely a heretic, but an enemy subversive, and thus, as with the *min*, one finds in rabbinic literature debates between rabbis and *apikorsim*, as well as statements about how the tradition as a whole defended itself against his heretical claims.[50] Nevertheless, the classification of the *apikorus* as tolerable serves as a significant testimony to the rabbinic position that intolerability is conditional on the presence of both delinquency and heresy.

With regards to the *apikorus* there is, as well, a usage that is hyperbolic, a way of expressing the distastefulness and potential dangers of behaviour that would more aptly be characterized as inappropriate rather than as delinquent.

> 1. *Apikorus*: Rav and R. Hanina both taught that this means one who insults a rabbinic scholar.
> 2. R. Yohanan and R. Joshua b. Levi maintain that it is one who insults one's neighbour in the presence of a rabbinic scholar ...
> 3. R. Joseph said: One who says: Of what use are the rabbis to us? It is for their own benefit that they read and for their own benefit that they study ...
> 4. R. Nahman b. Isaac said: One who was sitting before one's teacher when the discussion turned to some other subject, and the disciple remarked: We said so and so on that matter, instead of: Thus did the master say ...
> Raba said: One who is like the family of Benjamin the doctor who says: Of what use are the rabbis to us? They have never permitted us to eat (the biblically forbidden) raven and have never forbidden (the biblically permitted) dove.[51]
> ... R. Nahman said: One who calls one's teacher by name.[52]

Instead of heretical opinions, *apikorus* is used here to characterize, to varying degrees, a lack of reverence, respect, and/or recognition of the authority of the rabbis.[53] There are, in fact, four levels of *apikorus* depicted here. The one that is least severe involves a rabbinic student who lacks or forgets to use the proper etiquette with his rabbinic teachers, revealing implicitly some measure of arrogance and disrespect. The second consists of individuals who, by insulting their neighbour in the presence of a Rabbi, exhibit an acute form of callousness. The third entails individuals who insult the rabbis themselves, probably in the context of some argument, while the fourth derides the entire institution of rabbinic scholars. Only the fourth of these represents a heresy in line with the more classic use of the *apikorus* category. The other three lack ideological content, describing rather individuals who are inappropriate, careless, or at worst, disrespectful.

This hyperbolic usage is the only instance in rabbinic literature in which a category of deviance is used in this manner. In general, the rabbis were very careful and precise in their use of the categories. It would be too dangerous to use categories hyperbolically that can generate marginalization; however, the *apikorus*, because there are no sanctions associated with him, can be used in this manner.

Kofer

Even though it does not appear in rabbinic sources as an independent category, the *kofer* is worthy of mention as it will recur in later sources. In rabbinic sources the category of *kofer* is used as an adverb describing the rejection of a wide spectrum of Jewish practices and beliefs. One can be amongst other things, a *kofer* in the covenant of Abraham;[54] the *mitzvot*;[55] the Ten Commandments;[56] the commandment to lend without interest;[57] the Exodus from Egypt;[58] the commandment of tzitzit;[59] and in the essence of Judaism – *kofer ba-ikar*.[60] Possibly the most well-known use of the term is found in the context of idolatry: 'All who accept idolatry reject (*kofer*) the whole Torah in its entirety and all who reject (*kofer*) idolatry accept the whole Torah in its entirety.'[61]

Forms of Marginalization

A boundary policy is more than the demarcation of the line between tolerance and deviance and between tolerable and intolerable deviance. One of its most significant features involves the varying ways that it treats whatever or whoever it classifies as intolerable. Now, as stated in the previous chapter, in Jewish boundary policy discussions one can identify four distinct spheres of marginalization: basic membership; ritual; loyalty; and naming. Nowhere in rabbinic sources does one find the *meshumad* or the *min* explicitly subjected to sanctions either within the sphere of basic membership or naming.[62] Quite the contrary: the apostate *meshumad* who seeks to revoke his conversion is explicitly referred to as an *Israelite meshumad*.[63] Furthermore, even when marginalizing the *meshumad* and *min*, the Talmud clearly distinguishes between the sanctions directed towards them and the treatment or status of a non-Jew, as seen above both with regard to the offering of sacrifices and the punishment of *moridin ve-lo ma-alin*.[64] The fact that in both instances being classified as members engenders more severe sanctions is not the point. The deviance of the *min* and *meshumad* does not affect their status within the sphere of basic membership.

Marginalization of intolerable deviants is expressed within the spheres of ritual and loyalty. The *meshumad*'s ability to function as a full-fledged member in the religious life of Israel is curtailed, and his sacrifices are deemed unwanted. This applies not only to voluntary sacrifices (*korban nedavah*),[65] but penitent sacrifices (*korban hatat*) as well.

> Sacrifices are accepted from Israelite criminals (*poshei yisrael*) *so that they will repent*, with the exception of the *meshumad*. [66]

What is not clear is whether this exclusion also pertains to other obligatory sacrifices, essentially removing the intolerable *meshumad* from temple worship in general. The verse in Leviticus 1.2 quoted as the basis for the sanction, 'Speak unto the children of Israel, and say unto them, when any man of you bringeth an offering', specifically refers to voluntary sacrifices. As seen, however, the Baraita includes also penitent sacrifices, showing that the context of the verse is not seen as binding.

A parallel type of more general exclusion within the sphere of ritual is evidenced by the addition of *Birkat ha-Minim*[67] to the daily prayer of the *Amidah*. In its original forms as used in rabbinic times, it states as follows:

> For the *meshumadim* let there be no hope. And let the arrogant government be speedily uprooted in our days. Let the *nosrim* (Jewish Christians) and the *minim* be destroyed in a moment. And let them be blotted out of the Book of Life and not be inscribed together with the righteous. Blessed art thou, O Lord, who humblest the arrogant.[68]

While the above prayer does not formally banish the *meshumad* and *min* from the synagogue, it does clearly indicate that they would not be welcome. Those who are in the synagogue have no desire to be in their presence. Given that a person would not want to pray for one's own demise, nor participate with others who do so, the inclusion of the blessing within the everyday ritual will cause the *de facto* exodus of both deviant types from the ritual life of the synagogue.

As to marginalization within the sphere of loyalty, the above-mentioned exclusion from *korban hatat* transcends the sphere of ritual to impact as well on the sphere of loyalty. While as a rule, community members who sin (*poshei yisrael*) are encouraged to repent, the exclusion from *korban hatat,* a primary vehicle for repentance, effectively blocks the *meshumad*'s path towards rehabilitation. The member to whom it is applied is implicitly, but decisively, removed from the sphere of communal concern. The community no longer feels compelled to look after his spiritual well-being, much less facilitate it through ritual means.

One of the more significant expressions of marginalization within the sphere of loyalty, shared by both the *meshumad* and the *min*, is found in the sanction of *moridin ve-lo ma-alin* briefly discussed above.[69] In the normal course of communal life, members understand as fundamental the responsibility to protect one another from physical danger and imminent harm. Towards the intolerable *meshumad* and *min*, however, not only is this basic form of care suspended, but overt acts of aggression are actually encouraged. It is important to remember that the sanction of *moridin ve-lo ma-alin* is not meant as a form of expiation or rehabilitation similar to the court-sanctioned death penalty;[70] on the contrary, its only goal is to mark, marginalize, and ultimately banish the *meshumad* and *min* through intimidation and/or death. Similarly, the relinquishing of the responsibility to redeem the *meshumad* from captivity, even when the consequences will be the loss of his life, is further evidence of his marginal standing within this sphere.

It is interesting to note that this extreme marginalization in the sphere of loyalty did not lead, at least on the Tannaic level, to the abolishment of the requirement to return the *meshumad*'s lost property.[71] Despite the forfeiture of responsibility to his life implied by the sanction of *moridin ve-lo ma-alin,* no such parallel forfeiture was made regarding his property. While there is a measure of incongruity here, it is possible that the overall responsibility to return lost property is based on the biblical injunction to return the lost property of one's brother, *ahikha.*[72] As a result, any exclusion of the *meshumad* from this law would have been perceived as an exclusion from the category of *ahikha,* an act which implies sanctioning within the sphere of basic membership, a step that the rabbis were unwilling to take.[73] In any event, it is precisely a sense of this inconsistency that motivated the Ammora, R. Yohanan, to argue for the removal of the sanction of *moridin ve-lo ma-alin* from the *meshumad.*

> Whereupon R. Yohanan remarked: I have been learning that the
> words: '*And so shall you do with every lost thing of your brother (you
> may not hide yourself)*', (Deut. 22.3), are also applicable to the
> *meshumad*, and you state he may be thrown down; leave out
> *meshumad* [from the list of those cast in]![74]

In its attempt to respond to R. Yohanan's reservation, the Talmud returns
to the Ammoraic distinction between *meshumad leteiavon* and *meshumad
lehakhis*, arguing that the *meshumad* against whom one applies the law of
moridin ve-lo ma-alin is the *meshumad lehakhis* while the *meshumad* included
under the obligation of returning his lost property is the *meshumad leteiavon*.
The implication of this explanation is the expansion of sanctions towards the
meshumad within the sphere of loyalty through the removal of the
responsibility towards the *meshumad lehakhis'* lost property. This expansion,
however, is nowhere present within Tannaic sources or in Ammoraic
sources that discuss the laws of lost property, raising questions as to its legal
weight in the rabbinic period. In any event, an interesting feature of the
above two instances of marginalization of the *meshumad* in the sphere of
loyalty is that they are both contested. As seen above, with regards to the
cancelling of the obligation to redeem the *meshumad* who sells himself to
captivity, R. Ami states: 'Be off, they will not let me ransom you',[75]
thus clearly distancing himself from the ruling. Similarly, as stated, R. Yohanan
argues against the sanction of *moridin ve-lo ma-alin*. It is possible that this
represents a reservation regarding the application of sanctioning within the
sphere of loyalty towards non-enemy deviants.

Similar reservations, however, are nowhere expressed vis-à-vis the *min*.
On the contrary, it is precisely within the sphere of loyalty that the most
extensive forms of marginalization of the *min* are found. These sanctions,
directed exclusively against the *min*, are of the most severe and radical found
in rabbinic writing, and involve total shunning and the breaking off of any
and all social and business contacts. It is important to note that not only are
these forms of sanctions never applied to the *meshumad*; even within the
category of *min*, sanctions of this type are limited to the *min* as Jewish-
Christian. The most prominent example of this is found in Tosephta Hullin.

> If meat is found in the hands of a Gentile, its use is permitted; but
> if found in the hands of a *min*, its use is forbidden. That which
> comes out of a house of idolatry is considered to be the meat of
> dead offerings, for they have said that the meat which is
> slaughtered by the *min* (is regarded as) intended for idolatry. Their
> bread is the bread of Cutheans; their wine is considered as wine
> used for idolatrous libation; their fruit is *tevel*; their scrolls of the
> Law are considered to be books of soothsayers; and their children

are bastards. It is forbidden to sell anything to them or buy from them, to negotiate or engage in any transactions with them, to teach their children a trade and to be healed by them, whether healing your property or your body.[76] It happened that R. Elazar ben Damah was bitten by a snake and Yaakov Ish Kfar Sama[77] came to heal him in the name of Yashua b. Pantera (Jesus),[78] and R. Yishmael did not let him. [R. Yishmael] said to him: Ben Damah, you are not allowed. [Ben Damah] replied: I will bring evidence that will allow him to heal me, but he died before he was able to bring the proof. R. Yishmael said: How lucky are you ben Damah, that you exited [the world] in peace and did not violate the decree of the rabbis. For anyone who breaches a fence of the rabbis, in the end disaster befalls him, as it says: 'He who breaches a stone fence will be bitten by a snake.' (Eccl. 10.8). It happened that R. Eliezer was arrested on the charge of *minut*; they brought him up to the tribunal to be judged.[79] Said the governor to him: How can a sage such as yourself occupy himself with such things? He replied: I acknowledge the judge to be right. The governor thought he was referring to him but in reality he was referring to his Father who is in heaven ... When he was exonerated he was upset at being accused of *minut*. His students came to console him but he would not listen. R. Akiva said to him: Master, may I say something which may relieve your sorrow? He replied: Say it. He said: Perchance one of the *minim* said to you something pertaining to *minut*? He replied: From the heavens I am reminded. Once I was walking in the upper market of Sepphoris and I came across Yaacov of Kfar Sakhnin who said some words of *minut* in the name of Yashua b. Pantera and he caused me joy. It is for this reason that I was arrested on the charge of *minut*, for I transgressed the words of the Torah: 'Keep yourself far away from her. Do not come near the doorway of her house.' (Prov. 5.8). [80]

The deviant with whom all contact must be severed is the Jewish Christian, as indicated by the reference to Yaakov ish bar Sama who came to heal R. Eliezer in the name of Yashua ben Pantera (Jesus). The general rule governing the treatment of this *min* is summarized by a verse from Proverbs at the end of the above quotation that came to exemplify the status of the *min*: 'Keep yourself far away from her'. In other words, all contact with the *min* is forbidden.[81] He is not to be spoken to, all business transactions are forbidden, and assistance may be neither offered to his children nor received from him. To enforce and reinforce this ban, all food he produces is forbidden,[82] his books may not be read, and his children are banned from marrying other Jews. This ban is so severe that it is to be upheld even if one's life is in danger: it is preferable to die than to be healed by a *min*. To use R. Yishmael's language, it is preferable to die from the bite of a real snake than to suffer from the bite of the allegorical 'snake' which attacks those who would be as presumptuous as to breach this rabbinic decree.[83]

This total ban on contact that is unique to the *min*[84] does not stem from an assessment of the inherent severity of his deviance. The *meshumad lekol hatorah kullah*, whose deviance is by definition as severe as is possible, is never subjected to this degree of shunning. The directing of this level of marginalization is the result, I believe, of the perception of the *min* as not merely a deviant, but an *enemy* – a danger to anyone with whom he might interact. The *min*, as distinct from the *meshumad* – even a *meshumad* as apostate – is feared. As BT Tractate Avodah Zarah, quoting and commenting on this Tosephta, notes: 'It is different with the teachings of the *minim*, for it is alluring, and one may be lured into it.'[85] This fear is so profound as to make death a preferable alternative even to the most limited association.

There may be an additional element to this fear, beyond the fact of the *min*'s proactive antagonism. The *meshumad*, at least in most rabbinic sources, is a deviant who has left the system; in his rejection of normative Judaism, he does not offer an alternative reading of what Judaism 'really' is or what the sources 'really' mean. The *min* as Jewish Christian, even if he is part of a group which has parted ways with Judaism before the end of first century, still uses traditional Jewish sources and claims to belong to the real children of Israel. Consequently, he poses a far greater danger than the idolater or Hellenist who, by his own admission, has stepped outside of Jewish textual and ideological discourse. Furthermore, if, as the Talmud scholar Daniel Boyarin argues, there was no such clear early break, and the two religious traditions ('*rabbinic* Judaism and *orthodox* Christianity') grew together within Judaism and continued to interact for centuries,[86] the threat posed by the *min* in rabbinic eyes is that much more comprehensible. As to competing ideologies within Judaism, there was ongoing contact and battle, to which the sources marginalizing the *min* bear witness. It is the 'insider' who is to be feared more than one who has already chosen to leave.[87]

A similar consideration may be at play with regards to the Ammoraic expansion of intolerability to the *meshumad ledavar ehad lehakhis*. It may be that the Ammoraim view precisely this individual's lack of total apostasy as his most dangerous feature. The *meshumad lekol hatorah kullah* has, after all, separated himself or herself both from Judaism and the community. Whatever damage he or she has caused to communal morale has been done;

this *meshumad* poses no further danger. On the other hand, the threat of principled deviants who remain full members, left to travel and speak freely within the community's midst, is far more dangerous.

Returning to the *min*, a further expression of the rabbinic ire and dread which the *min* as Jewish Christian aroused can be found in the following source pertaining to the *min*, which scholars too have identified as referring to the Jewish Christian:

> The *Gillyonim* [in all probability the Gospels] and the books of *minim* are not to be saved from the fire [on Shabbat]. Rather they are to be allowed to burn, they and the Divine names mentioned therein. R. Yossi the Galilean said: On weekdays one must cut out the Divine names which they contain, store them and then burn the rest. R. Tarfon said: May I bury my son if I would not burn them together with their Divine Names if they came to my hand. For even if one was pursuing me to slay me, I would enter a Temple of idolatry [for refuge], but not one of their houses, for the idolaters do not know of God and therefore deny Him, while they know of God yet still deny Him.[88]

Striking a note consistent with the previous source, the exclusion of the *min* is expressed again in the preference of death over any form of contact. What is added here is the requirement to burn the books of the *minim*, a particularly powerful expression of the fear associated with this deviant.[89] Burning books does not merely reflect a desire to establish boundaries precluding contact. Rather, it seeks actively to protect members from exposure to a message which it is understood (and has possibly been demonstrated) as having the power to influence and attract.

The passage quoted above also provides a window into what the rabbis understood to be the source of this unique attractive power, and thus why the shunning of the *min* is more severe and urgent than that of the non-Jewish idolater. According to R. Tarfon, the beliefs of the idolatrous non-Jew are not founded on a rejection of God but on ignorance; they never knew otherwise.[90] The *min*, on the other hand, is a former believer who wilfully rejected one set of beliefs and embraced another. The individual who was once an insider, a believer 'like us', who discards one system for another, implies an ideological critique of the system in ways that the individual who was always an 'outsider' does not. He or she is an ideologue who has principled reasons for rejecting Judaism, and is thus far more threatening. These reasons can be influential on others, and it is for this reason that their books are not simply viewed as representative of an alternative faith system, but as potentially entailing an internal critique of Rabbinic Judaism.

An important question to raise here, one which will be relevant throughout the remainder of this study, is whether intensive marginalization, particularly in the sphere of loyalty, generates a status that is *de facto* akin to that of 'outsider'. While it is true that one who is marginalized is a member by definition – that only a community member can be placed at the community's margins – it may also be possible for this marginalization to impose a status which, while *formally* upholding membership ('*kiddushav kiddushin*'), effectively constitutes reclassification of certain deviants outside the margins of the community.

This question takes on pointed resonance when it comes to assessing the actual status of the *min*. In addition to the application of *moridin ve-lo ma-alin*, all contact and interaction with the *min* is forbidden; anything he writes or produces is ruled taboo; and his children are deemed off-limits for marriage by members in good standing. One begins to see these measures as part of a larger, concerted effort to erect a boundary demarcating two distinct social frameworks. Are not the *min*, and to a lesser degree the *meshumad*, transformed into *de facto* outsiders? It is possible that objecting to this reality is what motivated the objections of R. Ami to the exclusion of the *meshumad* from the requirement to redeem captives and R. Jonathan to including him in the sanction of *moridin ve-lo ma-alin*. Marginalization in the sphere of ritual is one thing. Casting a member outside of the sphere of loyalty and banning any and all contact is something else altogether.

Prescriptive vs. Descriptive Marginalization

Vis-à-vis the question of prescriptive versus descriptive application of intolerable deviant status, there is a possible difference between the category of *meshumad* and that of *min*. When it comes to the *meshumad*, application of intolerability is generally descriptive, i.e. imposed upon those who have committed acts which, according to cultural consensus with which they are familiar, place them outside of tolerable communal norms. The one significant exception may be in the Ammoraic and debated sanctioning of the *meshumad lehakhis*, who possibly still sees himself as partially committed to the halakhic system and the community.

With respect to the *min* as enemy deviant, there are two possibilities. The first, which derives from the status of the *min* as enemy deviant, would also render any process of marginalization descriptive as well: the essence of being an enemy deviant entails a hostility and degree of separation from those whom one is attacking. On the other hand, in their capacity as Jewish Christians, while clearly distinguishing themselves from rabbinic Judaism, they do not necessarily perceive or define themselves as being outside the community or religion of Israel. While this is indeed an open question and subject to significant debate, the severity of exclusionary measures directed exclusively towards Jewish Christians may point to a use which is prescriptive. One who has already removed themselves from the community does not have to be marginalized with such severity; the separation has already been effected. It is the insider who offers an ideological alternative and who promotes a different way of life who must be feared and marginalized. The fact that he does not see himself as separate is not a cause for leniency, but rather an impetus for a harsher response.

To summarize, the main points regarding the rabbinic theory of boundaries are as follows. Regarding the definition of the intolerable, firstly, it is applied only to the extent that the deviance incorporates both delinquent and heretical features. Neither the heretic nor the delinquent alone are classified as intolerable. Secondly, within the confines of the above conditions, there are two primary and universally accepted forms of intolerability, i.e. being either a *meshumad lekol hatorah kullah* or an enemy deviant. Being a *meshumad lekol hatorah kullah* involves either the complete rejection of all of Torah (apostasy or idolatry) or a complete separation from the community (*mehallel Shabbat be-farhesiah* or a *poresh min hatzibur*). Among the Ammoraim, there are some who expand the category of intolerability to the *meshumad ledavar ehad lehakhis*, a move that, as will be seen below, became common place in halakhah, but which was nevertheless contested within the rabbinic period. When it comes to the application of intolerable status, it is almost exclusively done in a prescriptive manner. The one significant possible exception is the *min* as enemy deviant, which might indicate a willingness to prescriptively marginalize enemy deviants depending on one's assessment of the connection of Jewish Christians with the Jewish community.

For all these categories, marginalization is limited to the spheres of ritual and loyalty. No consideration of sanctions in the sphere of basic membership is contemplated. Nevertheless, the scope of sanctions within the sphere of loyalty applied in particular towards the *min* as enemy deviant are so extreme as to create the status of a functional outsider. Beyond the particulars of marginalization within the spheres of ritual and loyalty, what is most significant about the rabbinic discourse regarding marginalization is the care that is used in its application. While there are very few mitigating factors staying the application of intolerable status, the rabbis, as distinct from the mediaeval halakhists of the next chapter, limited the application of particular sanctions to particular forms of deviance. Thus, while the *meshumad* and the *min* both receive the sanction of *moridin ve-lo ma-alin*, their paths basically part, with the *min* being subjected to an array of sanctions in the sphere of loyalty that never apply towards the *meshumad*. Overall one may characterize the general trend within rabbinic sources regarding deviance as follows:

1. Intolerable deviance is generally limited to deviance of the most severe and radical form and reflects the self-perceived status of the deviant in question.
2. Great care and precision is exercised in the application of forms of marginalization, with the latter contingent on the nature of the deviance.
3. The status of the *min* as enemy deviant is radically different from that of the *meshumad lekol hatorah kullah*.
4. As a result, it is of paramount significance under which category of deviance one is classified.

Notes

1 Regarding the category of *meshumad*, Saul Lieberman argues that the Talmudic meaning was one who was coerced to worship idols or violate the law, and that its meaning was later expanded to include intentional sinners. See S. Lieberman, *Tosephta Ki-Fshutah* (New York, 1962), 3 Eruvin Chapter 5, p. 402, n. 45. Louis Finkelstein claims the term had multiple meanings and referred to different levels of sinners, including both a) heretics who, despite being Hellenizers, still maintained some of the elements of the faith of Israel; and b) delinquents who, while violating some elements of halakhah, continued faithfully to observe many others. See L. Finkelstein in *Sifra on Leviticus* (New York, 1989), p. 195. In a general sense, he says, the *mumar/meshumad* refers in the Talmud to those who, in their overall behaviour, deviated from the traditions and practices of Israel. Lawrence Schiffman similarly argues that the term encompasses a broad range of sins, generally denoting an individual 'who ignores the commands of the Torah and the demands of the Jewish law'. See L. H. Schiffman in *Who was a Jew?* (Hoboken, 1985), p. 47. Jakob Petuchowski agrees the term is only anachronistically translated as apostate. While bearing multiple meanings, its primary sense is not of one who has exited the system, but one who has become alienated from the system within which he continues to live: 'a type of sinner living completely within the structure of Jewish community life, and on the whole, abiding by the provisions of the Torah'. See J. J. Petuchowski, 'The *Mumar*: A Study in Rabbinic Psychology', in *Hebrew Union College Annual* XXX (1959) (New York, 1968), p. 189. Milikovsky and Flusser agree that the original meaning of *meshumad* refers not to the convert, but rather to the Jew who rejects the authority of Judaism. See H. Milikovsky, 'Gehenom ve-Poshei Yisrael al pi Seder Olam', *Tarbitz* 55, 3 (1986), pp. 332–3, and D. Flusser, 'Miktzat Ma-asei ha-Torah u-Birkat ha-Minim', *Tarbitz* 61 (1992), p. 340. As to the meaning and usage of the category of *min*, see Y. Sussman's extensive footnote in 'Heker Toldot Ha-Halakha U-Megliot Midbar Yehudah', *Tarbitz* 59 (1989–90), 53–4, n. 176; L. H. Schiffman, *Who was a Jew?*, p. 41 n. 55; and S. S. Miller, 'The *Minim* of Sepphoris Reconsidered', *Harvard Theological Review* 86, 4 (1993), 377–8. Reuven

Kimelman, 'Birkat Ha-Minim and the Lack of Evidence for an Anti-Christian Jewish Prayer in Late Antiquity', in E. P. Sanders, A. I. Baumgarten and A. Mendelson (eds), *Jewish and Christian Self-Definition, Vol. Two: Aspects of Judaism in the Graeco-Roman Period*, (Philadelphia, 1981), pp. 226–44, also points to the multiplicity in uses, but ascribes this diversity to the fact that *min* was used by numerous individuals, in different sources, over a period of 500 years. For Kimelman, the significant issue was whether *min* referred to non-Jewish Christians. He concludes that in Tannaic and Palestinian Amoraic texts there is consistency in that the *min* referred only to Jewish sectarians and deviants, including Jewish Christians. In Babylonian texts, on the other hand, owing to the lack of *minim* as sects, the term was used more loosely, which for Kimelman meant that it referred to non-Jews as well. On the other hand, Saul Leiberman, in *Greek and Hellenism in Jewish Palestine* (Jerusalem, 1962), p. 109. n. 196; E. E. Urbach, in *The Sages* (Jerusalem, 1982), pp. 482–3; A. Buchler, in *Studies in Jewish History* (London, 1956), pp. 245–74; and S. S. Miller, 'The *Minim* of Sepphoris Reconsidered', p. 378, disagree with the position taken by Kimelman, pointing to the usage of the term to denote Gentiles as well. R. T. Herford, in 'The Problem of the "Minim" Further Considered' in S. Baron and A. Marx (eds), *Jewish Studies in Memory of George A. Kohut* (New York, 1935), and A. F. Segal, in *Two Powers in Heaven* (Leiden, 1997), pp. 262–7, argue that the original identity of those who hold the belief in 'two powers' often referred to as *minim*, were Jewish Christians. G. G. Scholem in *Major Trends in Jewish Mysticism* (New York, 1971), p. 359 n. 24, and S. Leiberman, in 'How Much Greek in Jewish Palestine', in A. Altmann, *Biblical and Other Studies* (Cambridge, Harvard University Press, 1963), p. 135, point to the common use of *min* to refer to the Gnostics. H. Milikovsky, 'Gehenom ve-Poshei Yisrael al pi Seder Olam', p. 332 and n. 92, and G. Alon, in *Toldot ha-Yehudim be-Eretz Yisrael be-Tekufat ha-Mishnah ve-Hatalmud* (Israel, 1977), p. 180, point to the uniqueness of the *min* as distinct, for example, from the *mumar*, in that it is a category which refers to deviant *sects* and not individuals. Milikovsky identifies him in particular with the sect of Jewish Christians.

2 See L. Finkelstein, *Mabo le-Massektot Abot ve-Abot d'Rabbi Natan* (New York, 1950), p. xxxix; and L. H. Schiffman, *Who was a Jew?*, p. 47. In rabbinic sources, the designation is always *meshumad* – see R. Rabbinovics, *Sefer Dikdukei Sofrim* (Jerusalem, 1948), 'Introduction to Berakhot' p. 22; S. Leiberman, 'Some Aspects of After Life in Rabbinic Literature', in S. Leiberman (ed.), *Harry Austryn Wolfson Jubilee Volume, English Section Volume II* (Jerusalem, AAJR, 1965), pp. 531–2; and D. Weis Halivini, *Mekorot Umesorot* (Jerusalem, 1982), Eruvin 69a, p. 180. Later censors changed it to the softer *mumar*, from the root 'to be changed' – see S. Leiberman, *Tosephta Ki-Fshutah* 3, Order Moed, Eruvin Chapter 5, p. 402 n. 45. While in some mediaeval and most modern halakhic sources the term used is *mumar*, as this chapter is an analysis of rabbinic sources, I will also use the nomenclature of *meshumad*.

3 There are two instances within the Tannaic sources, both within the Tosefta, where the *meshumad* is used to depict a deviant of either tolerable or a more

limited nature. In Tosefta Hullin 1.1 it states, 'All are legitimate to ritually slaughter animals, even the *Kuti*, even the uncircumcised and even the Israelite *meshumad*. The ritual slaughter of the *min* is considered idolatry. The [ritual slaughter of] the non-Jew and that of the monkey are illegitimate, for it states, "and you shall offer and you shall eat" (Deut. 12.21), ["you"] and not the offering of a non-Jew'. The *meshumad* in the above source is of a completely different character, for example, from the *meshumad she-eino mekabel brit* of the Sifra, who rejects the covenantal requirements in their entirety. The fact that his ritual slaughter is trusted assumes some loyalty to the tradition as a whole. Furthermore, as distinct from both the Sifra Diburah D'nedavah 2.3 and BT Tractate Hullin 5a, to be discussed below, where the inclusive category of 'you' (referring to Israel) is understood to exclude the *meshumad*, the tolerable *meshumad* in Tosefta Hullin is considered a part of 'you' – emphasizing his acceptance, despite his sins, as one of 'us'.

An instance where the deviance of the *meshumad* is explicitly of a more limited nature is found in Tosefta Horayot 1.5: 'One who eats loathsome creatures is a *meshumad*. If he ate *neveilot* and *treifot*, loathsome creatures and reptiles, if he eats the meat of swine, drinks *yein nesekh*, and the desecrator of the Shabbat, and the *mashukh*. R. Jose son of R. Judah said: also one who wears *killaim*. R. Shimeon son of Elazar said: even one who does that towards which one has not desire'.

According to this source, *meshumad* status is earned through a wide range of individual and specific types of deviance and does not necessarily involve the categorical rejection of either Jewish law and/or the Jewish people's collective identity. This position is an anomaly amongst Tannaic sources and is more representative of one of the moves we will see in the Amoraic period. In any event, the specific list is remarkably eclectic, and is in fact inscrutable. There seems no discernable internal logic, either in terms of what is included or what is omitted and as such it is a problematic text on which to base any larger theory. In any event, as no sanctions are mentioned it is not clear whether the *meshumad* mentioned is to be classified as intolerable.

4 BT Tractate Yevamot 47b.

5 Tosefta Succah 4.28.

6 S. Leiberman, *Tosefta Ki-Fshutah*, Succah Chapter 4, p. 278.

7 A further example of the *meshumad* as a deviant of an all-encompassing nature is found in BT Hullin 5a: 'On the basis of this they say that sacrifices are accepted from Israelite criminals (*poshei yisrael*) so that they will repent, with the exception of the *meshumad*, one who brings wine libation [for idolatry] and one who desecrates the Shabbat in public.' In the above Baraita, the *meshumad* depicts a deviant who is distinct from both the idolater and the *mehallel Shabbat be-farhesiah*, deviants who are also marginalized. They are, however, not included under the category of *meshumad*. The *meshumad* is not a category for one who violates a particular individual commandment, no matter how severe. It is a category for the Hellenist or apostate who rejects the whole system in total. Other deviants, even the individual who 'only' worships idols, are not denoted by the category.

8 Sifra, Diburah D'nedavah 2.3. The reference is as follows: ' "Speak unto the

children of Israel and say unto them, when any man of you bringeth an offering"
(Lev. 1.2): The expression "any man" embraces the proselyte. The expression
"of you" excludes the *meshumad*. Why do you accept this view? Let us rather say
the expression "any man" embraces the *meshumad* and that the expression "of
you" excludes the proselytes. [The reply is that] after Scripture was inclusive [in
reading "any man"], it was exclusive [in reading "of you"]. [The quandary thus
created is resolved by] the passage, "Children of Israel". This is to be interpreted,
"Just as the children of Israel have accepted the covenant, so also the proselytes
who have accepted the covenant [may bring an offering]": this excludes the
meshumadim, who do not accept the covenant (*she-einan mekablei brit*). Or shall we
say, "Just as the children of Israel are descendants of those who accepted the
covenant (*binei mekablei brit*), so also the *meshumadim* who are descended from
those who accepted the covenant [may bring an offering]"? This excludes the
proselytes who are not descended from those who accepted the covenant.
Therefore Scripture says "of you" [indicating that only a portion of those
addressed may bring an offering]. Hence it follows that we can say only that just
as Israel means those who have accepted the covenant, so [we should include] the
proselytes who have accepted the covenant, to the exclusion of the *meshumadim*,
who have not accepted the covenant as it states: "The sacrifice of the wicked
man is an abomination" (Prov. 21.27).'

9   Seder Olam Rabbah, Chapter 3.

10 See L. Finkelstein, *Sifra on Leviticus* Vol. II, *Diburah D'nedavah* 2.3, p. 21, note on
    line 25. See also A. Shemesh, 'King Manasseh and the *Halakhah* of the
    Sadducees', *Journal of Jewish Studies* LII, 1 (2001), p. 28, on the category of *meifer
    brit*. Shemesh explains that in that context *brit* can refer either to the covenant of
    circumcision or to Torah in general. There is, however, some ambiguity
    exhibited within the text. Finkelstein remarks on the fact that the *meshumad*
    mentioned here still wants to offer a sacrifice in the Temple, a desire which
    makes it difficult to classify him as one who has rejected his religion altogether.
    See L. Finkelstein, *Sifra on Leviticus*, p. 195.

11 Meaning unclear, possibly people who do not believe. See H. Milikovsky,
    'Gehenom ve-Poshei Yisrael al pi Seder Olam', p. 334.

12 Seder Olam Rabbah, Chapter 3. For a general exposition of the source, see H.
    Milkovsky, 'Gehenom ve-Poshei Yisrael al pi Seder Olam', pp. 311–43, and D.
    Flusser, 'Miktzat Ma-asei ha-Torah u-Birkat ha-Minim', pp. 333–46. For a
    parallel source to Seder Olam Rabbah, see Tosefta Sanhedrin 13.4–5. There, the
    poresh medarkhei tzibur is not a general category, the other deviants its sub-
    categories, but rather an independent category alongside the others.

13 See S. Lieberman, *Tosefta Ki-Fshutah*, Berakhot Chapter 3, p. 54 n. 96. See also
    H. Milikovsky, 'Gehenom ve-Poshei Yisrael al pi Seder Olam', pp. 328–9, who
    explains the distinction between the tolerable *poshei yisrael* and the *poresh
    medarkhei tzibur* as lining up on the axis of behaviour vs. belief. The former
    exhibit delinquency alone, while the latter rebel ideologically against God,
    provoking a harsher sanction which in turn reflects and expresses a prioritization
    of faith over observance (p. 337). See also D. Flusser, 'Miktzat Ma-asei ha-Torah

u-Birkat ha-Minim', pp. 338–9, who similarly argues that *poresh medarkhei tzibur* refers to 'sinners who rebelled against God in that, ideologically and in practice, they deviated from the people and their beliefs, and so cause harm to the community of Israel, its Torah and its existence' (pp. 338–9). These two explanations would identify the *meshumad* in Seder Olam with the *meshumad* in the Sifra, highlighting the shared element of heresy to explain his or her harsh sanction as contrasted with the more 'standard' delinquency of *poshei yisrael* who yet maintain their basic fidelity to God and Torah.

14 Tosefta Baba Metzia 2.33.

15 See, for example, BT Tractate Horayot 11a, which sees *meshumad* status as indicative of one who violates commandments which are well known (*mefarsem isura*). Such a violation is expressive of a measure of *poresh min hatzibur*, though it is not comprehensive. Whether the *meshumad* in question is tolerable or intolerable is not stated.

16 BT Tractate Hullin 5a.

17 This use seems explicitly at odds with the Tannaic position taken in the Baraita, which defines these two as separate from the *meshumad*.

18 Sifra Deuteronomy 54.

19 See also Rashi, BT Tractate Eruvin 69b *Ad Dehavei*. The same logic of Tractate Hullin 5a, which transforms the idolater into a *mumar lekol hatorah kullah* also applies to the *mehallel Shabbat be-farhesiah*. This is the argument of R. Ashi in BT Tractate Eruvin 69b.

20 The only dissenting opinion is held by R. Anan, who presents the position that an Israelite idolater is still tolerable. This position is summarily rejected. See BT Tractate Hullin p. 4b–5a. See also Rashi (Hullin 5a), who offers a different gloss on the unique status of idolatry. Rashi explains that the deviance of the idolater is intolerable due to the inherent heresy involved in denying the unity of God. It would follow, then, that the standard (i.e. non-idolatrous) *meshumad ledavar ehad* is tolerable because he or she is not necessarily a heretic, thus placing heresy as a necessary (though insufficient) criterion for intolerability.

21 See the opinion of Rav Ashi in BT Tractate Eruvin 69b, and Rashi, *ibid*. See also Rashi BT Tractate Hullin 5a, *Alma Mumar*, who states that it is one individual's opinion. See also Teshuvot Rashi, 169.

22 Rashi, BT Tractate Hullin, 5a. See also Maimonides, Hilkhot Shabbat, 30.15, Hilkhot Eruvin 2.16, Sheggaggot 3.7, Shehitabh 4.14 and Ma-aseh Korbanot 3.4, who offers a similar argument.

23 See too BT Tractate Eruvin 69b and the Tosefta Eruvin 5.18.

24 Furthermore, if location were viewed as determinative, one could argue that the result should be reversed. Such is the case with the distinction between *gezeliah* and *geneivah*, where sin performed *be-tzinah* is viewed as more heretical that that done *be-farhesiah*. See BT Tractate Baba Kama 79b.

25 BT Tractate Gittin 46b–47a.

26 See Rashi, *ibid.*, 46b.

27 See Maurice Simon, *Commentary on the Talmud* (London, Soncino Press, 1990), Tractate Gittin 46b, n. c4.

28 For further use of the *leteivon/lehakhis* distinction see Tosefta Horayot 1.5 (Zuckermandel) in which R. Shimon b. Elazar associates the category of *meshumad* with one 'who sins (lit. 'does something') when one's inclinations do not yearn for it'. This would leave the deviant motivated by inclination outside the category of *meshumad*.

   In Amoraic sources, the category of *meshumad okehl neveilot leteiavon* is common and is always classified as tolerable. See, for example, BT Tractates Hullin 3a and 4a, and Sanhedrin 27a. See also BT Tractates Aovdah Zarah 26 and Horayot 11a, where the opinion is presented that it is precisely the motivation of *teiavon* that makes the deviant a *meshumad*, while the more severe deviance which is motivated by *lehakhis* is classified under the more stringent category of *min*.

29 Evidence to the perception of the *meshumad leteiavon* as maintaining fidelity to the system as a whole can be found in BT Hullin 4a. See also BT Horayot 11a where, quoting Raba, it is universally accepted that one who is a *meshumad* to eat suet is not thereby considered a *meshumad* to eat blood.

30 See, for example, Mishnah Sanhedrin 4.5; Tosefta Berhakhot 7.21; Tosefta Sanhedrin 8.7; JT Berakhot p. 3.3; BT Tractate Berakhot 12b; BT Tractate Sanhedrin 38b and 90b; Genesis Rabbah 8.8–9; Deuteronomy Rabbah 2.13; Midrash Tanhumah, Bereishit, 7, Kedoshim 4 and Naso 30.

31 One possible exception is found in Tosefta Baba Metzia 2.33, quoted above, which marginalizes both the *meshumad* and the *min* with the sanction of *moridin ve-lo ma-alin*. The particular features of the *min* in question are not explicated. However, the extra-legal nature of the sanction, as argued above, points to a form of deviance which is extremely public and easily recognizable. Heresy devoid of delinquency would not meet this criterion.

32 Genesis Rabbah 8.9. Parallels to this source appear throughout midrashic sources. See for example Midrash Tanhumah Bereshit 7 and Kedoshim 4; Deuteronomy Rabah 2.13. See also Tosefta Sanhedrin 8.7, BT Tractate Sanhedrin 38b and JT Tractate Berakhot 1.4.

33 BT Tractate Sanhedrin 90b.

34 BT Tractate Yoma 56b–57a.

35 Bereshit Rabbah 8.9, p. 62.

36 JT Berakhot 81.4 p. 3.3.

37 BT Mishnah Sanhedrin, 4.5.

38 Mishnah Berakhot 9.5.

39 Midrash Eliyahu Zuta, Parshah 2. See also Sifri Bamidbar, Piska 16, 'Basefer Emkha', which gives further testimony to the contentious character of the *min*, referring to their books as ones which 'cause contempt, hatred and envy'.

40 JT Berakhot p. 3.3. For other similar references see Berakhot 9.5; see also Tosefta Berakhot 7.21, p. 17.

41 BT Sanhedrin 38b.

42 It is possible that only when they enter into a conflict with rabbinic Judaism do non-Jews become categorized as *minim*. See R. Travers Herford, 'The Problem of the "Minim" Further Considered', p. 120, for a similar argument about the non-Jew as *apikorus*.

43 Midrash Psalms 104.27. See the parallel account in BT Berakhot 10a, where instead of *min* the term *biryoni* is used. The correct rendition for Midrash Psalms is *min*, for, according to the Midrash, the trouble caused by the individual in question is with *kra-ei*, which does not fit the difficulties posed by *biryoni*. In fact, in the Talmud where the term *biryoni* is used, the trouble it refers to is of a more general type.

44 This point takes on a paramount importance in the context of Feinstein's classification of the Conservative and Reform Jew as a *min*.

45 S. Lieberman, in 'How Much Greek in Jewish Palestine', p. 130, claims that the term functioned as a figure for heresy in general. He argues that there is no evidence that the rabbis were familiar in any way with any Greek philosophies or philosophers. All they knew of Epicureans were some general phrases about the world moving automatically and being uncared for. Given the particular danger that they perceived in the doctrine, and not because of its prevalence or popularity, they chose the name *apikorus* as a figure for all heresy. E. E. Urbach, in *The Sages*, pp. 23–4, and Y. Geiger, in 'Letoldot ha-Munakh Apikorus, *Tarbitz* 42 (1973), pp. 499–500, agree, but add that the term was already commonly understood to connote one who did not believe that the gods are involved or active in the affairs of this world. On the other hand, L. Finkelstein, in *Mabo le-Massektot Abot ve-Abot d'Rabbi Natan*, p. 229, n. 6, disagrees and dates the first use of the term to the Hasmonean period, where it did refer to a follower of the Greek philosopher Epicures, whose ideologies were popular at that time. H. Fischel, in *Rabbinic Literature and Graeco-Roman Philosophy* (Leiden, 1973), pp. 14, 23–4, 114–5 n. 113, 133 n. 52, similarly argues for the familiarity with Epicurean beliefs and the presence of anti-Epicurean polemic in rabbinic sources. He claims that in the early Tannaic period, *apikorus* clearly denotes an Epicurean, who denies providence, while already in later Tannaic sources the term was reinterpreted as antinomian or synonymous with *min* in the general sense of heretic. H. Milikovsky, 'Gehenom ve-Poshei Yisrael al pi Seder Olam', pp. 334–5, argues that the term had the dual meaning of denying the resurrection of the dead and the divine origin of the Torah, two expressions of God's providence. L. H. Schiffman, *Who Was a Jew?*, p. 44, claims, with Urbach, Geiger and Milikovsky, that Epicureanism was understood to refer to an individual who rejected divine providence. He adds that, given the debate between the rabbis and the Sadducees on the specifics of God's rewards, in particular doctrines of the resurrection and the world to come, the term *apikorus* was used to refer to these Saducees. See also M. Hengel, *Judaism and Hellenism* (Philadelphia, 1974), Vol. II, p. 115 n. 447. R. T. Herford, in *Christianity in the Talmud and the Midrash* (Eugene OR, Wipf and Stock, 2003), pp. 119–20, argues that the term is plainly borrowed from the Greek Epicures, but that its main sense is based on a play on the Hebrew word *pakar*, which means to be free from restraint. Consequently, he claims that the term does not imply the holding or rejecting of specific doctrines, but rather the assertion of liberty of thought and the rejection of external authority in all subjects. In this capacity, the term denoted Jews and non-Jews who were in conflict with rabbinic figures.

Continuing this line of thought, A. Buchler, in *Studies in the Period of the Mishnah and the Talmud* (Jerusalem, 1967), Ch. 4, particularly p. 63; and Albek, Hanokh, Mishnah Sanhedrin 10.1, claim that the *apikorus* was used to refer to an individual who had no respect for, and even derided, the rabbis.

46 One exception to this rule can be found in Sifre Numbers 112, where the *apikorus* is used to depict act-based deviancy: 'Because he has spurned the word of the Lord – this is the *min* – and violated his commandment – this is the *apikorus*.'

47 One source which may provide some insight into the explicit definition of the heresy of the *apikorus* is found in *Seder Olam Rabbah* Chapter 3, discussed above at length, in the section on *meshumad*. It provides one of the few possible explicit definitions of the heresy of the *apikorus*.

But those who have separated themselves from the community (Heb. *parshu medarkhei tzibur*), such as the *minim*, the *meshumadim* and the informers (Heb. *mosorot*) and the *khanifim* and the *apikorsim* and those who deny the resurrection of the dead and who say the Torah is not from heaven, they are locked in *Gehenom* and sentenced in it for eternity.

There are two versions of this source, one which includes the word 'and' (*ve-*) after *apikorsim* and one which does not. Without the *ve-*, the text appears to explain the heresy of the *apikorus* as a denial of the resurrection of the dead and the divine origin of the Torah ('... and the *apikorsim* who deny the resurrection of the dead and who say the Torah is not from heaven...'), which would support a strong linkage of *apikorus* to the tenets of Epicureanism. If, on the other hand, the prefix is left in place, then each heresy, including *apikorus*, is a category unto itself, and the window on a possible explication of the term is once again closed. See H. Milikovsky, 'Gehenom ve-Poshei Yisrael al pi Seder Olam' *Tarbitz* 55, 3 (1986), p. 335 n. 104. Even with the addition of *ve* the meaning may not be 'and' but rather as a '*ve*' which serves to explicate. See A. Schremer in Ktav Yad Umesorot Nusah Shel Moed Katan, *Sidra* 6 (1990), p. 132 n. 51. With regard to sanctions, here too, as in the Mishnah quoted above, the sanctioning of the *apikorus* appears to be metaphysical and not connected to the legal processes of this world.

48 Mishnah Sanhedrin 11.1. By being distinguished from one who denies life after death or the divine origin of the Torah, it would seem that *apikorus* is a heretic of a different type, or a heretic in general, as argued for by Leiberman and not as argued by many of the other scholars mentioned above.

49 Mishnah Avot 2.19 (Kaufman manuscript). Note that here, too, the nature of the *apikorus*' deviance is not spelled out. Basing himself on the concluding words of the Mishnah, which speak to the doctrine of divine providence, Urbach argues that this points to the *apikorus* as an individual who denies, in particular, this principle of faith.

50 See for example Yalkut Shimoni, Bereishit 39, Mishpatim 359, Balak 766 and Pinhas 781.

51 In other words, they are limited by what is written in the Bible, and are thus of no use.

52 BT Sanhedrin 99b-100a.

53 For a similar use of the category, see JT Sanhedrin 10.1 p. 27d.

54 BT Tractate Shabbat 41a.

55 Sifra Behukotai 2.2.

56 Sifre Numbers 111.

57 Sifra Bahar 5.5.

58 Sifra Shmini 10.12.

59 Sifri Zutah 15.

60 BT Tractate Sanhedrin 38b.

61 Sifre Deuteronomy 54

62 One possible exception is Sifra, Diburah D'nedavah 2.3 quoted above in Note 8. According to Finkelstein, the exclusion of *meshumad* from the category of 'you' is so definitive as to suggest banishment from the sphere of basic membership. See L. Finkelstein, *Mabo le-Massektot Abot ve-Abot d'Rabbi Natan*, pp. xxviii–xl.

63 BT Tractate Yevamot 47b.

64 See for example BT Tractate Hullin 5a, and Tosefta Baba Metzia 2.33.

65 See Sifra, Diburah D'nedavah 2.3. See also Rashi, BT Tractate Hullin 5a, *Mikem*.

66 BT Hullin 5a. Emphasis mine.

67 Beyond its name, mentioned in Tosefta Berakhot 3.25 and BT Berakhot 28b–29a, the specific wording of the prayer is not cited in rabbinic sources. There are numerous versions of the blessing and, as scholars have found, it is difficult to identify the original with certainty. As to the specific identity of the *min* mentioned in the prayer, his identity has been the subject of much scholarly debate. Possibly composed by Shmuel ha-Katan in the time of R. Gamliel II, some argue that its aim is directed specifically and exclusively at Jewish Christians. See Y. M. Elbogen, *Hatfillah be-Yisrael be-hitpat-hutah ha-Historit* (Tel Aviv 1972), pp. 27–9, 31–2, 40; L. Finkelstein, 'The Development of the Amidah' in L. Finkelstein (ed.), *Pharasaism in the Making* (Hoboken, 1972], p. 263; G. Alon, *Toldot ha-Yehudin be Eretz Yisrael be-Tekufat ha-Mishnah re-Hotalmud*, pp. 172–92; L. H. Schiffman, *Who Was a Jew?*, pp. 53–61. Others posit that it was a revision of a previous, broad-based condemnatory blessing that referred to *minim* in the general sense, as well as *meshumadim* and others who had broken away from the community, and later adapted by Shmuel ha-Katan to specifically target Jewish Christians. See S. Leiberman, *Tosephta Ki-Fshutah*, Berakhot pp. 53–4 n. 96; D. Flusser, 'Miktzat Ma-asei ha-Torah u-Birkat ha-Minim', pp. 333–74. All these positions share a consensus that by the end of the first century, the *min* of the blessing had become consolidated into this particular, highly recognizable deviant, thus fitting the condition demanded above – that if you want to sanction someone the particular nature of his or her intolerable deviance has to be clear and distinct.

68 This rendition of the blessing is based on the Genizah version as translated by Kimelman, 'Birkat Ha-Minim and the Lack of Evidence for an Anti-Christian Jewish Prayer in Late Antiquity', pp. 226–44.

69 Tosefta Baba Metziah 2.33.

70 As explained in the previous chapter, legal sanctions and even the death penalty are not necessarily indications of marginalization. Formal sanctions can actually

be an expression of loyalty, as the vehicle through which the punished party achieves atonement. See Tosefta Yoma 4.8 and Sifri, Davarim, Piska 286.

71 See Mekhilta, Mesekhta de-Kaspa, Mishpatim 20, *Shor Oivekha*.

72 See Deut. 22.1–3.

73 Maimonides, on the other hand, as will be seen in the next chapter, who considers marginalization within this sphere, does sanction intolerable deviants in the area of lost property as well.

74 BT Tractate Avodah Zarah 26b.

75 BT Tractate Gittin 47a.

76 See parallel in BT Hullin 13a–b. The words 'whether healing your property or your body' appear in the Hebrew as *ripui mamon* and *ripui nefashot*, here translated as interpreted in BT Avodah Zarah 27a.

77 See parallel in BT Avodah Zarah 26b, which refers to Yaakov Ish Kfar Sakhnin specifically as a *min*.

78 A common name for Jesus. See S. Leiberman, 'Notes on Chapter 1 of *Koheleth Rabbah*', in E. E. Urbach, R. J. Zwi Werblowsky and C. Wirszubski (eds), *Studies in Mysticism and Religion Presented to G. G. Scholem*, (Jerusalem, 1968), pp. 172–3; and D. Rokeah, 'Ben Sitra Ben Pantira Hu', *Tarbitz* 39 (1970), 13–14. See also D. Boyarin, *Dying for God*, (Stanford, 1999), p. 32.

79 Christianity was then illegal under Roman law. See S. Leiberman, 'Roman Legal Institutions in Early Rabbinics and in the Acta Martyrum' *JQR* 35 (1944–5), 20–1.

80 Tosefta Hullin 2.20–24 (Zuckermandel). See parallel in BT Avodah Zarah 16b–17a.

81 The forbidding of all contact with the *min* is a common sanction. See also Avot d'Rabbi Natan version 2 Chapter 3, which states, ' "Keep yourself far away from her" (Prov. 5.8). R. Joshua b. Korhah said: This refers to the ways of *minut*. A person is told to not go to *minim* nor listen to their words so as not to fail and fall into their deeds. If the person retorts: I am confident in myself for even though I will go, I will not listen to their words nor will I fail and fall into their deeds, reply to him, Despite your confidence, do not go. For this reason it states: "Keep yourself far away from her", and it states: "For many are those she has struck dead" (Prov. 7.26).' In the above, the identity of the *min* is not explicated. See also Mekhilta de-Rabbi Yishmael, Tractate Kaspa, Mishpatim, Parshah 20.

82 See also Tosefta Hullin 1.1.

83 See BT Tractate Avodah Zarah 27b, which explains that the bite of the snake of one who breaches a rabbinic decree is never healed, implying a continued punishment in the world to come.

84 A partial exception to this rule may be the prohibition on allowing the *mehallel Shabbat meshumad* who does so openly and brazenly (*be-gilui panim*), to cancel his share in a public courtyard, thus allowing the other partners to erect there an *eruv*. Now, the laws of the Shabbat prohibit the transporting of items from one domain to another, i.e. a public to private or vice versa. A common housing arrangement in the Talmudic era was the shared courtyard formed by the homes surrounding it and held in common by the owners of those homes. The legal issue under

discussion is the permissibility of carrying something on the Shabbat from one's home (private domain) into the courtyard, or the opposite. Because the courtyard has no sole owner, it was ruled to constitute a domain unto itself, requiring the establishment of an *eruv*, a ritual wire barrier which serves to unite the private property with the shared property and transform the area into one contiguous domain. The Mishnah in Tractate Eruvin states: 'One who lives in a courtyard with a heathen or with one who does not acknowledge the principle of *eruv* causes one's usage of the courtyard to be forbidden.' (Mishnah Eruvin 6.1.)

Shared use of the courtyard requires that all the partners, together, erect an *eruv*. Partnership is defined, it seems, by equal ideological investment in the *eruv*'s creation. Since a non-Jew does not require an *eruv*, and a Jew who does not acknowledge the laws of *eruv* does not care if one is erected or not, neither of these figures can join with the other homeowners to form the necessary partnership. In order to circumnavigate these impasses, and allow the erection of the *eruv* to benefit the Shabbat-observing Jewish tenants, the rabbis generated two solutions. From the non-Jew, the Jewish partners must rent his share in the common courtyard, and only thus are they able to include his property while excluding his person. For the non-*eruv*-believing Jew, a more lenient ruling was offered in that it is sufficient that this Jew renounce his share in the common courtyard without the requirement that the remaining tenants rent it from him. The Baraita in BT Tractate Eruvin 69a states that 'a *meshumad gilui panim* is not entitled to renounce his share', so that with respect to this issue, a *meshumad gilui panim* has the same status as a non-Jew. He cannot relinquish his share, but must rent it out before the others can erect their *eruv*.

Now, on the surface, this ruling seems to sanction the upstanding partners in the courtyard far more than the deviant himself. It is they who are penalized financially simply for wanting to remain in accordance with Jewish law. Actually, though, it is the consequences of this prospective penalization for the deviant that is this Baraita's primary concern. As explained by Maimonides, the purpose of legislation obligating the rental of the non-Jew's share is to make it less attractive to live in a common courtyard with non-Jews. (See Maimonides, Hilkhot Eruvin 2.9.) Including the *meshumad gilui panim*, while not prohibiting contact as in the case with the *min*, nevertheless aims to create barriers to social intercourse and to maximize, where possible, the separation between the community and the *meshumad mehallel Shabbat*.

85 BT Tractate Avodah Zarah p. 27b.
86 D. Boyarin, *Dying for God*, pp. 1–41.
87 A similar consideration may be at play with regard to the Amoraic expansion of intolerability to include the *meshumad ledavar ehad lehakhis. Meshumadim* who incorporate more severe forms of deviance have, after all, left the community – either literally through apostasy or conversion, or effectively through descriptive marginalization as 'outsiders within'. Whatever damage they have caused to communal morale is finite, and, most importantly, it is finished; they pose no further damage. On the other hand, the threat of principled deviants who remain full members, left to travel and speak freely within the community's midst, is

what they fear most. It is possibly this ominous scenario, the implicit threat of corruption by insider deviants, which motivated the Amoraim to cast him out despite the less than obvious legal or conceptual justification for doing so. They are not 'misreading' the Tannaic use of *meshumad* but co-opting it, employing it as a model for addressing what they perceive as a similar but even more severe threat.

88 Tosefta Shabbat 13.5. S. Leiberman in Tosefta Shabbat 13.5, p. 58, and *Tosefta Ki-Fshutah*, Shabbat p. 206, explains that *Gillyonim* refers to the Gospels and, following the uncensored edition of BT Shabbat (see *Didukei Sofrim*, Shabbat 116b, p. 260 n. 60), interprets 'books of *minim*' as writings of Christians interwoven with biblical verse. The incorporation of scripture gives further credence to the internal nature of the Jewish–Christian debate.

Rashi interprets 'books of *minim*' as referring to Bibles written by idolaters for idolatrous purposes. See Rashi, BT Shabbat 116b, *Sifrei Minim*. Given the extensive parallels between this source and the Tosefta above, this interpretation is unlikely. In addition, *sifrei torah* written by *minim* in the Talmud are called precisely that, and not *sifrei minim*. See BT Gittin 45b.

89 See also BT Tractate Gittin 54b which similarly states:

'R. Nahman said: We have it on tradition that a scroll of the Law which has been written by a *min* should be burnt, and one written by a heathen should be stored away.'

90 In a certain sense, then, they can be compared to the *tinok shenishbah*. See BT Shabbat, 68a–b. See also BT Hullin 13b, where the Talmud states, 'R. Yohanan said: The Gentiles who live outside the land [of Israel] are not idolaters, but rather they hold to the customs of their fathers.' As distinct from the non-Jewish idolaters, the *min*, portrayed as an ideologue, is defined here as a Jewish idolater. See also Rashi, BT Tractate Hullin 13b, 'Min'. This may be the source for Rashi's interpretation of the *min* in BT Tractates Shabbat 116b and Gittin 45b as a Jewish idolater.

CHAPTER THREE

Intolerable Deviance and its Forms
of Marginalization in Mediaeval
Halakhic Writing

From the rabbinic period until the Middle Ages, several significant shifts in
the understanding of boundaries can be noted, both in the definition of
intolerable deviance and the forms of marginalization that intolerability
engendered. These shifts played a major role in the formation of modern
halakhic responses to the breakdown in boundaries within the Jewish
people. In the mediaeval period the Jewish tradition witnessed, for the first
time, a systematic cataloguing of Jewish law, and this analysis of mediaeval
sources will focus on the three most significant codifiers of the period:
Maimonides (1135–1204), R. Yaakov b. R. Asher (*Tur*, 1269–1343), and R.
Joseph Karo (*Shulhan Arukh*; 1488–1575).

The primary focus of the chapter will be on the rulings of Maimonides,
who, in post-rabbinic legal discourse, was the most significant figure on the
issue of deviance and boundaries. In his halakhic writing, the phenomenon
of deviance – its definition and the ways in which it impacts one's
communal standing – gives rise to a nuanced and multi-layered discussion
with distinctly modern resonances. In addition, his rulings are the most
widely quoted and debated, and are often viewed as even more precedent-
setting than those found in rabbinic sources. By contrast, the treatments of
deviance in the *Tur* and *Shulhan Arukh* were less broad-based and far-
reaching than that of Maimonides, whose precedents in most cases were also
incorporated into their rulings. As a result, the primary focus for their
analysis will be on the handful of instances in which they diverge from his
precedents.

Intolerable Deviance

The most comprehensive statement regarding the nature of intolerable
deviance in medieval halakhic codifications is found in Maimonides'
Mishneh Torah, Hilkhot Teshuvah. In the context of his discussion of sin,
repentance and atonement, Maimonides offers a wide-ranging exposition of
the more severe forms of deviance that, as distinct from regular sin, exclude
one from redemption in the world to come. This list, generally structured
along the lines of the thirteen principles of faith outlined in his *Commentary*

on the Mishnah, Tractate Sanhedrin, Introduction to Perek Helek,[1] presents those forms of deviance which he classifies as intolerable.[2]

Utilizing as his framework the categories of *min, apikorus, kofer* and *meshumad,*[3] amongst others, and, in a striking departure from Talmudic style, Maimonides details with great specificity and nuance both the sins that are intolerable and the distinct deviance category within which each falls. An interesting feature of Maimonides' writing is that while what constitutes intolerable deviance in Hilkhot Teshuvah is by and large consistent with his other writings, the category to which each particular deviance is associated changes all the time.[4] For Maimonides the important issue is what constitutes intolerability and not the category under which it is classified. While such confusion would be unacceptable in rabbinic sources given the particular forms of marginalization that were specifically applied to each category, Maimonides makes no such distinctions. As will be discussed further below, intolerable deviance in all its forms and expressions, with the exception of idolatry and the public desecration of the Shabbat, are treated in the same manner. For Maimonides, once one is classified as intolerable, the whole battery of sanctions automatically applies, regardless of the nature of the deviance in question. Furthermore, given the explicit nature of the way he uses the categories, even where there are exceptions, the marginalization is clearly directed against a particular form of deviance and not against one of the categories.

Turning to Hilkhot Teshuvah, Maimonides utilizes the various deviance categorizes in the following manner. The *meshumad,* following its use in rabbinic sources, denotes the delinquent, i.e. one whose deviance is expressed primarily in behaviour. In doing so he too distinguishes between the *meshumad ledavar ehad* and the *meshumad lekol hatorah kullah.* The former is defined by Maimonides as a person whose deviance is motivated by spite, who 'commits the transgression habitually and has become notorious for it',[5] and for whom 'the precept is regarded by him as no longer binding'.[6] As to the *meshumad lekol hatorah kullah,* Maimonides defines him in new terms as one 'who at a time of religious persecution converts to a non-Jewish religion, clings to them, saying: "What advantage is it to me to adhere to the people of Israel, who are of low estate and persecuted. It is better for me to join these nations who are powerful." '[7]

The *min, apikorus* and *kofer,* on the other hand, are used to denote deviants of a primarily purely heretical nature. Thus the *min* is used for the heretic with mistaken notions about the existence, identity and essence of God:

> Five classes are termed *minim:* one who says there is no God and
> the world has no ruler; one who says that there is a ruling power

but that it is vested in two or more persons; one who says there is one ruler, but he is a body and has form; one who denies that God alone is the First Cause and Rock of the Universe; likewise, one who worships any one besides God, to serve as a mediator between the human being and the Lord of the Universe. Whoever belongs to any of these five classes is termed a *min*.[8]

The *apikorus* is one who holds heretical beliefs as to God's relationship with the world:

> Three classes are called *apikorsim*: one who denies the reality of prophecy and maintains that there is no knowledge which emanates from the Creator and directly reaches the human mind; one who denies the prophecy of Moses, our teacher; and one who asserts that the Creator has no cognizance of the deeds of the human beings. Each of these is an *apikorus*.[9]

Finally, the *kofer batorah* status, a new and non-rabbinic category, is assigned to the heretic who, while accepting what Maimonides advances as Jewish tradition's understandings of the identity of God and God's relationship with the world, rejects its claims about the divine origin and eternality of the Written Torah, as well as the authority of the Oral Torah and its authors. The term *kofer* is also used for those who believe that they have superseded the Torah and rendered it obsolete, similar to the claims of Christians and Muslims. These heresies, as distinct from most of the heresies of the *min* and *apikorus*, will also ultimately have a direct effect on behaviour as well.[10]

Independent of the particulars, what is most striking in the above discourse and the subsequent discussion of deviance in his halakhic writing is the prominence of heresy in Maimonides' framework of intolerable deviance. Maimonides elevates heresy to a degree of significance found nowhere in rabbinic literature.[11] There, intolerability was conditional on the presence of both heresy and delinquency. For Maimonides, on the other hand, heresy alone is sufficient to activate intolerability status. Thus he states, with regard to belief in his thirteen articles of faith (*ikarim*) in his *Introduction to Perek Helek*:

> But if a man doubts any of these [thirteen theological] foundations, he leaves the community [of Israel], denies that which is fundamental, and is called a sectarian (*min*) *apikorus*, and one who 'cuts among the plantings'. One is required to hate him and destroy him.[12]

The mere doubting of or failing to believe in one of the articles of faith designates an individual as one whom the community is required to hate and destroy. Similarly, Maimonides rules in Hilkhot Mamrim:

> Whoever repudiates the Oral Torah is not the rebellious elder mentioned in the Torah, but rather is one of the *minim*, who any person has a right to put to death. Once it is made clear that he indeed repudiates the Oral Torah, he is cast into [a pit] and not rescued from it (*moridin ve-lo ma-alin*), similar to the other *minim*, *apikorsim*, those who say that the Torah is not from heaven, informers and *meshumadim*. All of the above are not a part of Israel, and do not require witnesses, prior warning, or judges [before being put to death]. Rather anyone who kills one of them has fulfilled a great *mitzvah* and removed a stumbling block.[13]

The central role Maimonides accords to heresy in determining intolerability parallels the central role he accords to knowledge of God within his overall understanding of Judaism. For Maimonides, the essential feature of the identity of Israel, the core of its 'shared cultural space', is as a nation that 'knows God'.[14] Furthermore, the central religious value is this knowledge, and it is exclusively through one's knowledge of God that closeness to God is attained.

> He who knows God is the one who finds favour in His eyes, not one who only fasts and prays, but each who knows Him is the favoured and the close (*mekorav*), and one with foolish ideas [about God] is hated and spurned [by God]; in accordance with knowledge or foolishness will be favour or contempt, closeness or scorn.[15]

A more careful analysis of the forms of deviance included in Hilkhot Teshuvah under the various categories, in particular that of the *meshumad* and *min*, points to a number of other significant Maimonidean innovations with regards to the definition of the intolerable.

When it comes to the *meshumad*, the delinquent, Maimonides makes two important additions to the rabbinic discussion. The first is that, similar to the Ammoraic position, the *meshumad ledavar ehad*, under certain conditions, may be classified as intolerable. However unlike these Ammoraim, the presence of the motivation of *lehakhis* alone is not sufficient to activate intolerable status. In addition to deviating out of spite, the *meshumad ledavar ehad* has to also 'commit the transgression habitually and has become notorious for it' in order to be classified as intolerable. He cannot merely be an episodic sinner, but rather one who consistently violates a particular law, and furthermore, is known for this fact. The aggregate of these conditions reveals that he is adopting a public and consistent ideological position vis-à-vis this law in particular and the authority of the legal system in general. Meeting these conditions paints the intolerable *meshumad ledavar ehad* as more of an outsider from the perspective of the norms of the community. In so doing, Maimonides is adopting a position somewhere between the Tannaic and Ammoraic positions outlined above. On the one hand, like the Ammoraim, he expands the scope of intolerable *meshumad* beyond the *meshumad lekol hatorah kullah*, idolater and *mehallel Shabbat befarhesia*; but on the other hand, like the Tannaim he demands more evidence of heresy than *lehakhis* alone.[16]

Maimonides' second addition to the discussion of intolerability pertains to the category of *meshumad lekol hatorah kullah*, who is now granted an explicit and particular identity. For Maimonides, this individual denotes one who is a *poresh min hatzibur*.[17] What is interesting about this classification is that Maimonides considers him intolerable even if he does so for reasons of *teiavon*, in this case, the desire to survive.[18] Unlike the *min*, who is a believing idolater, the *meshumad lekol hatorah kullah* is not a heretic. He joins a different religion, whether monotheistic or idolatrous, not out of ideology, but rather, solely out of the desire to be separated from the *fate* of the Jewish people during a time of religious persecution (*shemad*). As characterized by Maimonides in Hilkhot Teshuvah, this *meshumad* states 'What advantage is it to me to adhere to the people of Israel, who are of low estate and persecuted? It is better for me to join these nations who are powerful.' For Maimonides, this reasoning does not serve to ameliorate the severity of the deviance; the act of separation from the community, regardless of the motivation, is sufficient to warrant intolerable status.

When it comes to Maimonides' definition of the *min*, what is particularly important is his inclusion of belief in the corporeality of God within the category of intolerability. The question of divine corporeality was the subject of much debate in mediaeval Judaism. Evidence of this debate can be found in the barbed response of the Rabad (Rabbi Abraham Ben David of Posquieres, *c.* 1125–1198), one of Maimonides' most famous and formidable critics, to his identification of this belief not only with being a *min*, but with heresy of any sort:

> ['He who says there is one ruler, but he is a body and has form']: Why did he (Maimonides) call such a person a *min*? There are many people greater and superior to him who adhere to such a belief on the basis of what they have seen in verses of Scripture and even more in the words of those midrashic passages which corrupt right opinion about religious matters.[19]

Clearly, the validity of this belief had been neither unequivocally or definitively resolved and no normative consensus had been reached. What Maimonides is doing is imposing the status of intolerable deviant on individuals who clearly and justifiably view themselves as operating squarely within the parameters of traditional and communal norms; yet Maimonides labels them as intolerable deviants, ascribing to them a social status radically at odds with their own self-perception. In doing so, Maimonides is deviating from the central mode of classification in rabbinic sources, particularly Tannaic, which was primarily descriptive, i.e. reserved for individuals who left Judaism and the Jewish community. In addition, even if it is argued that Jewish Christians saw themselves as Jews, rendering their marginalization prescriptive, they were clearly aware of the universal rejection of their position on the part of rabbinic leadership. Marginalization was therefore hardly a surprise. In the case of corporeality, however, it is clear that the issue is under significant debate. Nevertheless, Maimonides is willing to impose intolerable status even in this case, a fact that expands the use of the classification of intolerability and which consequently unleashed the Rabad's anger.

Under the category of *min*, Maimonides also includes the individual who 'worships any one besides God, to serve as a mediator between the human being and the Lord of the Universe'.[20] In general, Maimonides limits the deviance of the *min* to the heretic. The inclusion of the delinquent idolater is thus a puzzling exception. Furthermore, the nature of this idolater is very particular. The individual in question is not a 'regular' idolater, but rather one who may be termed a delinquent monotheist and, in the language of Maimonides in Hilkhot Avodah Zarah, holds a position which is the precursor to idolatry.[21] He still believes in one God, but he mistakenly believes that there are intermediaries who can and must be worshipped; an error that Maimonides warns will ultimately lead to the adoption of idolatrous beliefs. Now, in defining the *min*, Maimonides already includes the polytheist. By including the delinquent monotheist as well, he seems to be engaging in the classical rabbinic practice of building a fence around serious transgressions. Along with sanctioning the pure heresy of believing in many gods, he slates for marginalization also that which at present is ideologically benign, but which might, in the end, also lead to heresy.

This move by Maimonides introduces an additional feature into the way intolerability can be assessed. Marginalization is permitted not only on the merits of the inherent deviance in question, but also on the basis of its potential consequences. In a certain sense, a very broad measure of deviance that hitherto was deemed tolerable, can, under these conditions, be classified as intolerable. The significant criterion ceases to be the nature of the actual deviance and its correlation to the core features of a community's shared cultural space, but rather the society's degree of comfort or fear regarding the stability of this space. When this comfort is eroded, a society may tend to include under the category of intolerability marginal forms of deviance under the argument that 'A' may lead to 'B' which may lead to 'C', etc. Furthermore, this latter argument is often devoid of governing rules, and is dependent on the associative thought process of the individual making the argument. Which 'A' may lead to 'C' is often dependent on who is deciding. By opening the classification of intolerability to these types of considerations, Maimonides is dramatically expanding the categories of deviance that may be subjected to this classification. As distinct from rabbinic sources, which by and large limited intolerability to deviance of an extreme and radical nature, this move by Maimonides thus allows for far more moderate expressions of deviance to be deemed intolerable. One limiting factor is that this move, which appears in a number of other instances in his halakhic writing,[22] is only used with regard to idolatry. According to Maimonides, the Jewish people, whose identity is that of being the people who know God, and whose Torah's core purpose is to promulgate the rejection of idolatry, must not only render all exhibitions of idolatry intolerable, but must also erect as wide a net as possible around this deviance to ensure that it does not penetrate the society through some back door.

Finally, Maimonides disassociates from the *min* any element of subversiveness or enemy deviance. In general, the notion of enemy deviant, that is, one whose deviance is also associated with attacks and attempts to alter the religious life of the community, is by and large absent from Maimonides' discussion of intolerability. The major exception is the category he entitles *makhtiei harabim*, i.e. those who cause others to stray. In this case, however, it is a category exclusively for *leaders* of deviant ideologies who cause others to follow them and sin, such as Jeroboam, Menashe (in the Bible) and Jesus, and does not apply to regular deviants.[23]

In the *Tur*, written approximately a century later, the discussion of intolerable deviance is far more limited with intolerability generally confined to four forms: the idolater,[24] the apostate,[25] the *mehallel Shabbat befarhesia*[26] and the *meshumad lehakhis*.[27] All of the above are contained under the categories of the *min* and *meshumad*,[28] with the two basically treated as synonymous.[29] Most importantly, as distinct from Maimonides, and returning to the rabbinic position, the *Tur* refrains from sanctioning heresy alone, requiring instead that some measure of delinquency must also be present for intolerability to be assessed. At the same time, as with Maimonides' *meshumad*, delinquency alone is similarly viewed as insufficient to warrant intolerable classification, but must be accompanied by or be indicative of larger heretical beliefs.

The case is not similar to that of one who eats non-kosher meat *lehakhis*, for he [who eats non-kosher meat *lehakhis*] is able to eat that which is permitted and instead sets it aside in his rebelliousness, and eats that which is forbidden. In doing so *he intends to rebel and is, therefore,* called a *min*.[30]

It is the intent to rebel that generates the status, not the delinquency per se, that is problematic. Conversely, delinquency motivated by *teiavon* is always tolerable.[31]

In the *Shulhan Arukh*, the definitions of intolerable deviance basically follow the precedents set by Maimonides and the *Tur*. This work, too, focuses primarily on the idolater,[32] the apostate,[33] the *mumar lekol hatorah kullah*,[34] the *mehallel Shabbat befarhesia*,[35] and individuals who violate individual commandment *lehakhis*.[36] The deviance categories are limited to *mumar*, as in 'one who has been changed' (henceforth in Jewish legal sources the term is *mumar* and not *meshumad*, i.e. 'one who has been destroyed') and *apikorus* exclusively, the former being the most predominantly used, while the latter serves as a substitute for *min*. *Mumar* always signifies action-based deviance, and again, what makes it intolerable is the presence of heresy accompanying the delinquency.[37] The category of *apikorus* is also used in a number of cases to refer to heresy devoid of delinquency, and in a few instances is also classified as intolerable.[38] However, this position is nowhere as prominent as it was in Maimonides, as there is no comprehensive statement regarding the place of heresy in intolerability in the *Shulhan Arukh* similar to that found in Maimonides' Hilkhot Teshuvah or his *Introduction to Perek Helek*.

Forms of Marginalization

As was the case with the definition of intolerability, when it comes to marginalization, the *Tur* and the *Shulhan Arukh* generally follow the precedent set by Maimonides and thus the discussion here will focus on Maimonides' writings. The one major exception pertains to the spheres of basic membership where, as will be seen below, the *Tur* adopts a different position from that of Maimonides, with the *Tur*'s position ultimately coming to dominate traditional Jewish law.

With regard to the sphere of ritual, Maimonides basically sticks to rabbinic precedent. Thus the *meshumad* who worships idols or who desecrates the Shabbat in public is denied the right to offer sacrifices. Maimonides emphasizes that this pertains to 'sacrifices of any kind',[39] including those 'sinners' sacrifices' which were established for the very purpose of restoring the sinner's relationship with God. As stated in the previous chapter, such sanctions affect not only the sphere of ritual but loyalty as well, as the community ceases to care about the spiritual well-being of the individual in question. The above two categories of deviants, together with the heretic who denies the Torah and the authority of Moses,[40] are not trusted to participate in the ritual slaughter of animals[41] – the stock criterion used as an indication of an individual's trustworthiness to faithfully perform any part of the law.

There is one form of marginalization of the *min* in the sphere of ritual to which Maimonides gives a particular explanation, which consequently had broad-ranging implications for the contemporary halakhic discussion of marginalizing deviance. At issue is who can write a sacred scroll, i.e. a document that can bear holiness and be used as a Torah, *tefillin* or *mezuzah*. Once written, such a document is considered sacred writ, and may therefore not be destroyed. When rendered unusable, it must be stored in a special depository known as a *genizah*. Despite this fact, rabbinic precedent states that a Torah scroll written specifically by a *min* (as distinct from a regular idolater) must be destroyed.[42] In explaining the reasons for this ruling, Maimonides states as follows:

> It is forbidden to burn or otherwise by one's act destroy any of the sacred Scriptures, their commentaries or expositions. Whoever by his act does so destroy them, is punished with lashes of rebelliousness (*makat mardut*). This rule applies only to Scriptures written by an Israelite who is conscious of their sacred character. But if an Israelite *min* wrote a scroll of the Torah, it is to be burnt with all the Names of God contained therein. The reason is that he does not believe in the sanctity of the Divine Name and did not write it for God's sake, but regarded it like any other writing. This being his view, the Divine Name that he wrote never became sanctified. It is a religious duty to burn it, so as to leave no record of *minim* or their works. But if an [idolatrous] non-Jew wrote the Divine Name, it is put away in a place of concealment (*genizah*).[43]

The burning of sacred scrolls, especially of a *Sefer Torah*, is clearly serious business. Various interpretations of the rabbinic source text[44] attempt to associate this ruling with the fear that the scrolls were written for the sake of idolatry. Maimonides explains the issue differently. Rather than asserting that the sacred scrolls become invalidated by bad intent, he questions whether they ever become sanctified in the first place. Sanctification of a written text only occurs, he argues, when a text including God's name is written by one who believes in the sanctity of God's name. The *min*, who is defined here as one who does not accept this sanctity and views God's name as equivalent to any other word, thus cannot create a sacred text. Consequently, the text he writes need not be preserved.

However, once the ban is lifted, Maimonides activates another consideration, which is mentioned in this instance alone and is specified as being unique to the *min*: one is required to leave no record of *minim* or their works. This requirement is based primarily on the rabbinic sources that mandate the burning of the books of the *min*, there referring to the *min* as Jewish Christian.

It is important to emphasize that the above ruling regarding sacred scrolls is limited in nature and does not apply to the *min* per se, but to a particular type of heretic who does not recognize the sanctity of God's name. It is only because of this particular belief that the scroll he writes is not sacred, and consequently may be burnt. It follows that according to Maimonides, other types of *minim* and heretics, who do uphold the sanctity of the divine name (e.g. a Sadducee), can generate sacred writing upon which the prohibition against burning or otherwise destroying would fully apply.

As to the sphere of loyalty, its more severe forms, i.e. shunning and the cessation of all contact, are for the most part not discussed by Maimonides. With the absence of the category of enemy deviant, Maimonides loses as well the unique sanction associated with it. Nevertheless, in other forms, the sphere plays a central role in Maimonidean marginalization. A concise and powerful statement as to its application and parameters appears in Maimonides' *Commentary on the Mishnah, Introduction to Perek Helek*, partially quoted above.

> When all these foundations are perfectly understood and believed in by a person he enters the community of Israel and one is obligated to love and pity him and to act towards him in all ways in which the Creator has commanded that one should act towards his brother, with love and fraternity. Even were he to commit every possible transgression, because of lust (*teiavon*) and because of being overpowered by evil inclination, he will be punished according to his rebelliousness, but he has a portion [of the world to come]; he is one of the sinners of Israel. But if a man doubts any if these foundations, he leaves the community [of Israel], denies the fundamental, and is called a sectarian (*min*)[45], *apikorus*, and one who 'cuts among the plantings'. One is required to hate him and destroy him.[46]

The responsibilities generated by the sphere of loyalty require that we treat fellow members as brothers with love and fraternity. This applies to members in good standing as well as other tolerable deviants (who do not deny one of the articles of faith). On the other hand, when one is an intolerable deviant, marginalization within this sphere entails the require-ment 'to hate him and destroy him'.

An expression of this requirement is the sanction of *moridin ve-lo ma-alin*, found in rabbinic sources, whereby individuals are actively encouraged to find ways to take the deviant's lives.

> The *minim*, by this are meant Israelites who worship idols, and the sinner *lehakhis* . . . and the *apikorus* from amongst Israel who denies the validity of the Torah and prophecy, it is a commandment to kill them. If one had the power to slay them publicly by the sword, he should do so. If not, one should plot against them in such a way as to bring about their death. Thus, if one saw that one of the above [deviants] had fallen into a well containing a ladder, he should remove the ladder, giving the excuse that he wanted it to get his son down from the roof, and would bring it back afterward, and do similar acts. However, [when it comes to] the heathen against whom we are not at war or the Israelite raisers of small cattle, one is not to bring about their death. It is, however, forbidden to save them from dying.[47]

Maimonides explicitly includes in this sanction not only the idolater, but the heretic, and following Ammoraic precedent,[48] also the *meshumad ledavar ehad lehakhis*. Both moves significantly extend the parameters of intolerability beyond the Tannaic precedent.

The exclusion of the intolerable deviant from the love and care one is obligated to direct towards one's brother in his *Introduction to Perek Helek* is followed up by Maimonides in his cancelling the obligation to return their lost property. Now, in the Torah, the obligation of returning lost property in its Deuteronomy reference specifically refers to the lost property of one's 'brother', '*ahikha*'.

> If you see *ahikha*'s ox or sheep going astray, do not ignore it: you must take it back to *ahikha* . . . You shall do the same to his ass; you shall do the same with his garment; and so to shall you do with anything that *ahikha* loses and you find; you must not remain indifferent. (Deut. 22.1–3)

The significant question is who is included under the category of *ahikha*. Now, as seen in the previous chapter, on the Tannaic level, the Jewish deviant is always included. On the Ammoraic level the issue is debated, with R. Yohanan arguing that the tradition includes the *meshumad* within the category of *ahikha* for the issue of lost property (and for that matter the laws of *moridin velo ma-alin*), while the unnamed voice of Gemara posits that only the *meshumad leteiavon* is to be included in the laws of returning lost property. Ignoring the Tannaic precedent and the position of R. Yohanan, Maimonides rules as follows:

> The return of lost property to an Israelite is a positive commandment, for Scripture says 'you must surely take it back to your brother.' (Deut. 22.1) ... if one takes lost property and does not return it, he disregards a positive commandment and transgresses two negative ones ... Even if the owner of the lost property is wicked and would eat improperly slaughtered meat *leteiavon*, or do anything similar, to return his lost property to him is still a commandment. But if one eats improperly slaughtered meat *lehakhis*, he is deemed a *min*, and it is forbidden to return lost property to *minim* from amongst Israel and the *apikorsim*, and idol-worshipping Israelites and the desecrators of the Shabbat in public, just like it is (forbidden to return lost property) to a heathen. The lost property of a heathen may be kept, for Scripture says: '[return] the lost property of your brother'. (Deut. 22.3) Furthermore if one returns it, he commits a transgression, for he is supporting the wicked of the world.[49]

Similar to his ruling in the *Introduction to Helek*, the intolerable deviant ceases to be considered and treated as a brother. The care and loyalty expressed to those whose lost property one has found only extend to those who are brothers. The intolerable deviant's property may thus be kept by those who find it.

Some of Maimonides' more innovative and complex positions on marginalization appear in his discussion of the spheres of basic membership and naming. As stated above, the first involves the stripping of the right of basic membership in the community, and the designation of the deviant in question as an outsider. The latter resists going so far and rather entails a form of linguistic shunning whereby certain deviants cease to be allowed to carry the name of Israel. As seen above, neither sphere is incorporated within the rabbinic arsenal of sanctions.

When it comes to the sphere of basic membership, Maimonides' position is inconsistent. On the one hand, he often follows the rabbinic precedent maintaining the intolerable deviant's status in this sphere. Thus, in Hilkhot Teshuvah, after enumerating the various classes of intolerable deviants, he explicitly states: 'All these twenty-four classes which we have enumerated, *even though they are Israelites*, nevertheless have no place in the world to come.'[50] In addition, again following rabbinic precedent, he rules that the convert who reverts back to his previous religious affiliation nevertheless still maintains his status as a member of Israel with the consequence that his marriage acts are still legally binding (*kiddushav kiddushin*). This individual also retains his status in the sphere of naming and is referred to by Maimonides as an *Israelite meshumad*.[51] Similarly, the intolerable deviant is considered an Israelite from the perspective of the laws of Levirite marriages, forcing his deceased brother's childless widow to receive from him either *yibum* (Levirite marriage) or *halitzah* (Levirite divorce).[52] Furthermore, in numerous instances, Maimonides explicitly distinguishes between the legal status of the Israelite deviant and that of the non-Jew. It is the Israelite intolerable deviant who cannot bring an offering, while every non-Jew, regardless of his or her behaviour and beliefs, can.[53] It is only the Israelite intolerable deviant whose life is forfeited through the laws of *moridin ve-lo ma-alin*, while the non-Jew receives the more lenient sanction of *lo ma-alin ve-lo moridin*, wherein there is no obligation to save him but it is forbidden to actively cause his demise.[54]

Together with the above, however, Maimonides also takes the reverse position. In his *Introduction to Perek Helek*, quoted above, beyond sanctions within the sphere of loyalty, Maimonides also clearly excludes the intolerable deviant from the sphere of basic membership.

> When all these foundations are perfectly understood and believed
> in by a person he enters the community of Israel... But if a man
> doubts any if these foundations, *he leaves the community [of Israel]*.[55]

According to the above, one becomes a member of Israel not by birth but by adhering to certain dogma; it is one's fellow believer rather than one's biological kin who is called 'brother'. In the same way that one becomes a member through the adoption of correct beliefs, Maimonides seems to be arguing that one loses one's membership through the rejection of these beliefs. While tolerable deviants maintain their status as insiders in the sphere of basic membership and are referred to by Maimonides as 'one of the sinners of Israel', the heretic, on the other hand, is defined as one who 'leaves the community of Israel'.

However, it remains unclear to what extent we are meant to take the above statement of Maimonides literally. Given the fact that it is not located in his halakhic codification, some have argued that it was not intended to have legal consequences.[56] In numerous instances throughout his *Mishneh Torah*, Maimonides compares certain intolerable deviants, in particular the idolater and the *mehallel Shabbat*, with the non-Jew. Thus for example, he states:

> An Israelite who worshipped idols is like a non-Jew in every
> respect (*ke-goy lekol devarav*) and not like an Israelite who

committed a transgression the punishment of which is death by stoning. [57]

> Observance of the Shabbat and abstention from idolatry are each equivalent to the sum total of all other commandments of the Law. Furthermore, the Shabbat is an eternal sign between the Holy One, blessed be He and ourselves. Accordingly, if one transgresses any of the other commandments he is merely a wicked Israelite (*rishei yisrael*), but if he publicly desecrates the Shabbat he is the same as an idol worshipper, and both of these are regarded as non-Jews in every respect (*ke-goyim lekol divreihem*).[58]

However, what Maimonides means by the statement *ke-goy lekol devarav* is not clear, as no sanctions are mentioned. The simile '*ke*' [like] may be seen as countervailing the language of '*kol*' and limiting the inclusiveness of the comparison. They are not heathens, only 'like' heathens, and thus they remain members. At the same time, the all-inclusive nature of the statement, being like a non-Jew 'in every respect', makes it at least plausible to argue that Maimonides means that the intolerable deviant and the non-Jew share a similar status within the sphere of basic membership.

Given the uncontestable fact that in certain instances he clearly does maintain the status of the intolerable deviant in the sphere of basic membership, it is possible that in some of the cases the sanction implied is not in the sphere of basic membership, but in the sphere of naming. Certain forms of deviance, in particular, but not exclusively, the idolater and *mehallel Shabbat*, have crossed a line by deviating from such foundational features of Jewish shared cultural space. As a result, they lose their right to be called Israel, even though their status in the sphere of basic membership remains the same. Thus Maimonides rules:

> Whoever repudiates the Oral Torah is not the rebellious elder mentioned in the Torah, but rather is one of the *minim*, whom any person has a right to put to death. Once it is made clear that he indeed repudiates the Oral Torah, he is cast into (a pit) and not rescued from it (*moridin ve-lo ma-alin*), similar to the other *minim*, *apikorsim*, those who say that the Torah is not from heaven, informers and *meshumadim*. All of the above *are not a part of Israel*, and do not require witnesses, prior warning, or judges (before being put to death). Rather anyone who kills one of them has fulfilled a great *mitzvah* and removed a stumbling block.[59]

Maimonides explicitly states, 'All of the above are not a part of Israel'. The consequence is that they may be put to death without witnesses or judicial proceedings under the rule of *moridin ve-lo ma-alin*. However, as seen above, this rule applies exclusively to Israelites, while those who are 'not a part of Israel' are subjected to the more lenient *lo moridin ve-lo ma-alin*.[60] While effort need not be expended to save them, no overt actions of harming them are sanctioned either. 'All of the above are not a part of Israel', in this instance is clearly not a sanction in the sphere of basic membership, but an appellation they are given, i.e. a sanction in the sphere of naming.

It seems unlikely, however, that all the instances of comparison with the non-Jew can be subsumed under the sphere of naming; they are probably evidence of Maimonides' willingness to marginalize in the sphere of basic membership as well. Maimonides' statement in his *Introduction to Perek Helek* is thus not an exaggeration, but one, albeit inconsistent, feature of his marginalization policy. One instance where this becomes apparent pertains to the case of returning lost property discussed above with regards to the sphere of loyalty. The responsibility to return an individual's lost property is contingent on the owner of the lost property being classified as one's 'brother'. On this basis, Maimonides excludes the intolerable deviant, comparing his status to that of the non-Jew. While this seems to pertain only to the sphere of loyalty, in another instance he explicitly expands the implications of such a sanction. There, arguing for the full status of the intolerable deviant in the sphere of basic membership he states:

> Even if he reverts to his previous state and worships idols, he is considered merely an *Israelite meshumad*, whose acts of marriage are valid (*kiddushav kiddushin*). It is a *mitzvah* to return his lost property, for once he immerses himself, he attains the status of an Israelite.[61]

Two factors serve as evidence for the maintaining of one's status in the sphere of basic membership. The first is that one's marriages are valid, and the second is that others are obligated to return one's lost property. Yet in Hilkhot Aveidah, as seen, he argues the opposite,[62] and specifically excludes intolerable deviants from the category of 'brother' and the subsequent right to have their lost property returned. While inconsistent, the consequence of Maimonides' sanction in Hilkhot Aveidah is the marginalization of the intolerable deviant in the sphere of basic membership as well.

One of the more important cases which provide evidence for Maimonides' willingness to institute sanctions in the sphere of basic membership is found in Hilkhot Eruvin, which deals with the laws of *eruv*, a ritual barrier that serves to unite a private and public property into one domain, thus permitting the transportation of items therein on Shabbat. The laws of Shabbat prohibit the transporting of items from one domain to another, i.e. public to private or vice versa. A common housing arrangement, whose status is discussed in Jewish legal treaties over the centuries, pertains to a shared courtyard formed by the homes surrounding it and held in common by the owners of those homes. At stake is the permissibility of carrying something on the Shabbat from one's home (private domain) into the courtyard, or the opposite. Because the common courtyard has no single owner, it was ruled to constitute a domain unto itself, requiring the establishment of an *eruv* around the whole complex – thus uniting the various private properties and the courtyard. The legal debate to be discussed below involves various attempts to regulate the consequences of different types of deviant neighbours on the building of this *eruv*. The Mishnah in Tractate Eruvin, which serves as the basis for the discussion, states as follows:

> One who lives in a courtyard with a heathen or with one who
> does not acknowledge the principle of *eruv*, causes one's usage of
> the courtyard to be forbidden.[63]

Shared use of the courtyard requires that all the partners together erect an *eruv*. The Mishnah teaches that this partnership in the *eruv*'s creation requires equal ideological investment in the process. Since a non-Jew does not require an *eruv*, and a Jew who does not acknowledge the laws of *eruv* does not care if one is erected or not, neither of these figures can join with the other homeowners to form the necessary partnership. In order to overcome these impasses, and allow the erection of the *eruv* to benefit the Shabbat-observing Jewish tenants, the rabbis generated two solutions. If a non-Jew is part of the housing arrangement, the Jewish partners must rent his share in the common courtyard, and only thus are they able to include his property while excluding his person. For the non-*eruv*-believing Jew, a more lenient ruling was offered in that it is sufficient that this Jew renounce his share in the common courtyard without the requirement that the remaining tenants rent it from him.[64] A Tannaic opinion quoted in BT Tractate Eruvin 69a states that, as distinct from the Jew who does not believe in the laws of *eruv*, a *meshumad* who deviates brazenly is also not entitled to simply renounce his share, and like the non-Jew, must rent it out before the others can erect their *eruv*. On the basis of this legal precedent, Maimonides offers the following ruling, which for the sake of clarity I will divide into three sections.

1. An Israelite who desecrates Shabbat publicly or worships idols is like a heathen for all purposes (*ke-goy lekol devarav*). He may not participate in an *eruv*, nor may he renounce his rights; rather, his domain must be leased from him as from a heathen.
2. If, however, the Israelite was one of the *minim* who does not worship idols or desecrate the Shabbat, such as the Sadducees and

Boethusians, and all who deny the validity of the Oral Law – in short, if he does not acknowledge the validity of the commandment to prepare an *eruv* – the rule is that he may not participate in an *eruv*, seeing that he does not admit its validity. In addition, his domain may not be leased from him, seeing that he is not a heathen. He may, however, renounce his rights in favour of a conforming Israelite, and this is the remedy in his case.

3.   Similarly, if one conforming Israelite and one Sadducee live in the same courtyard, the Sadducee renders the courtyard a forbidden domain unless he renounces his rights in favour of the conforming Israelite.[65]

Sections one and two represent Maimonides' elaboration of the law as outlined in Tractate Eruvin, with each depicting different forms of deviants, and thus leading to different legal consequences. Section one pertains to those classes of deviants who are given the same status as that of the non-Jew, with the accompanying statement that they are '*ke-goy lekol devarav*'. This status is here limited exclusively to the idolater and the *mehallel Shabbat befarhesia*. All other deviants, including those deemed in other cases by Maimonides as being intolerable, such as the Sadducee, are dealt with in section two. The difference between them is that the former need to rent their share, while the latter may simply cancel their share in order to enable the remaining Jewish residents to erect an *eruv*. The purpose of this more limiting condition for non-Jews, Jewish idolaters and public desecrators of Shabbat, as explained by Maimonides, was to make the erection of the *eruv* more difficult, 'in order to discourage Israelites from sharing their dwelling places with a heathen, lest they should learn from their ways'.[66] The comparison to the non-Jew in this instance serves to regulate the marginalization in the sphere of loyalty.

The important section for our purposes is found in section three. To reiterate, Maimonides there states:

3. Similarly, if *one* conforming Israelite and *one* Sadducee live in the same courtyard, the Sadducee renders the courtyard a forbidden domain unless he renounces his rights in favour of the conforming Israelite.[67]

The distinction between this case and the above case is that sections one and two deal with the situation of one non-Jew or deviant living with a number of Jews in good standing, while section three refers to the specific case of two people alone, *one* Israelite in good standing and *one* Sadducee, sharing the common courtyard. Here too the ruling is that the deviant in question, so long as he is not an idolater or a *mehallel Shabbat befarhesia*, may simply cancel his share.

The innovation and the radical implications inherent within this rule, however, only become apparent when Maimonides introduces the parallel law with regard to two partners in the courtyard, one a Jew in good standing and one a non-Jew as distinct from the Sadducee. In such a case, Maimonides argues, there is no need even to erect an *eruv* to render the courtyard private property. Maimonides explains the reason for this seemingly lenient ruling:

> If an Israelite resides in the same courtyard with a heathen or a
> resident alien, the courtyard does not become a forbidden domain
> (for carrying) because his sharing a residence with a heathen is not
> regarded as equivalent in this respect with another Israelite, but
> rather is similar to sharing it with cattle.[68]

The reason why no renting or cancelling of ownership is necessary is because the non-Jew is not perceived to generate legally significant ownership rights. Partnership with him resembles partnership in property with an animal. Consequently, from the perspective of the laws of Shabbat, a Jew may simply ignore the ownership of the non-Jew, and consider the courtyard his own private property. On the other hand, the Sadducee, as the model for the Israelite intolerable deviant who is not compared to the non-Jew, needs to renounce his share in the common courtyard because his ownership is consequential, rendering the courtyard a place which is not private.[69]

The importance of Maimonides' ruling in section three is now apparent. In the case of two partners who share the courtyard, only deviants such as Sadducees must cancel their ownership in the courtyard, while the idolater and the *mehallel Shabbat befarhesia*, by virtue of being *ke-goy lekol devarav*, do not. Thus the marginalization does not affect the sphere of loyalty but rather the sphere of basic membership. It is only fellow Israelites, even if intolerable, who create legally binding realities such as property ownership. As a part of Israel, the individual is 'considered', his actions have legal significance, and his hold on property creates property rights within the society. By equating the status of the idolater and *mehallel Shabbat befarhesia* with that of the non-Jew *lekol devarav*, and consequently removing from them the requirement of renouncing their share when living together with one Jew in good standing, their status as members, indeed as human beings, is altered. By defining them as '*ke-goy lekol devarav*', Maimonides is re-classifying them as outsiders, to put it mildly.

On this point of marginalization in the spheres of basic membership and even naming, the *Tur* diverges significantly from the Maimonidean position and sets a halakhic precedent that shaped the status of intolerable deviants henceforth. The *Tur*'s overall position regarding the status of deviants in these spheres is based on the single overriding principle of '*af al pi shehata yisrael hu'*, even though they sinned, they are still Israel. This principle is based on an Aggadic rabbinic statement,[70] and as stated above, first became a legal tenet in the writing of Rashi.[71] What is interesting is that it nowhere appears in Maimonides, either explicitly or by inference. '*Af al pi shehata yisrael hu*' bespeaks both a confirmation of the 'outsider-within' status of the intolerable deviant, naming him as a deviant while maintaining his status in the spheres of both membership and naming: 'Even though they sinned *they are still Israel.*'[72]

One of the more telling examples of the *Tur's* use of this rule applies to the charging and paying of interest on loans. The Torah teaches that it is permissible to charge interest on a loan to a non-Jew, restricting the prohibition on charging interest to Jews alone. This is due to the fact that the Biblical injunction in Lev. 25.36 states: 'Let him live by your side as your brother' (*ve-hai ahikha imakh*). It is only your brother towards whom there is a duty to facilitate his living by your side. Following this, the *Tur* rules regarding the *meshumad*:

> It is permissible to charge interest on a loan to a *meshumad* who denies the essence (Heb. *she-kafar be-ikar*), for we are not obligated to let him live by our side. However, it is forbidden to pay interest on a loan borrowed from him, for *af al pi she-hata yisrael hu*, and one who pays him interest violates the prohibition of not placing a stumbling block before the blind.[73]

The *Tur* distinguishes between borrowing and lending with interest. On the one hand, he permits charging the intolerable deviant interest on his loans for the general prohibition against this practice is based on the notion that one must take care of one's brother (*ahikha*). However, the intolerable deviant is not included under the category of *ahikha* when it comes to the sphere of loyalty, and consequently 'we are not obligated to let him live by our side'. When it comes to paying him interest on loans taken from him, however, the issue is not loyalty but his basic status as a Jew who is obligated by the laws of Torah. Making such a payment would imply that the intolerable deviant lender is not bound by the prohibition against receiving interest – an assumption that would categorize him as a non-Israelite, an outsider. The *Tur* rules that such a position is deemed untenable, for '*af al pi she-hata yisrael hu*'. Marginalization cannot affect the sphere of basic membership of the intolerable deviant as a member of Israel.[74]

Now, similar to Maimonides, there are a number of instances where the *Tur* specifically compares the status of intolerable deviants with that of the non-Jew.[75] However, as distinct from Maimonides, he makes very clear the limited scope of the comparison.

> It seems to me that his being like a non-Jew (*ke-goy*) is not
> applicable to all matters, for if he married an Israelite his marriage
> is binding. *Rather [the various prohibitions on eating his food] only
> apply to the issue of distancing him.*[76]

Being classified '*ke-goy*' is not meant to be understood as a complete
transformation in one's membership status to that of outsider, but rather
only impacts on issues of distancing him, i.e. the sphere of loyalty. The
intolerable deviant's status within the sphere of basic membership is not up
for discussion in the *Tur* – and it is this milder position, as we shall see, that
becomes accepted.

Moving from Intolerability to Tolerability: The Special Status of the Captive Child and the Karaites

One of the more significant and innovative shifts found in Maimonides'
writing on deviance and boundaries pertains to his discussion of the status of
the 'captive child' (*tinok shenishbah*) in Hilkhot Mamrim Chapter 3, and that
of the Karaites in his *Responsa* 449. Individuals who fall into these two
categories are considered throughout his writings to be intolerable deviants,
and are classified alternatively under the categories of *min*, *meshumad* or
apikorus. However, Maimonides then reclassifies them as tolerable, invoking
reasons that have far-reaching consequences for the definition and treatment
of tolerable and intolerable deviance in Jewish law.

    The category of *tinok shenishbah* refers literally to individuals who, in
their childhood, were captured by heathens and were not educated in the
ways of Judaism; they are possibly unaware that they are Jewish at all. In the
Talmud these individuals are treated as a paradigm for any Jew who is
unfamiliar with Jewish law and thus commits sin without an awareness that
he is sinning. Such a person is classified alternately as an accidental sinner
(*shogeg*)[77] or as one compelled to sin against his will (*anoos*).[78]

    In Hilkhot Mamrim, Maimonides suggests a more novel and
innovative application of this category. *Tinok shenishbah*, he says, includes
anyone whose deviant behaviour is not based on independent ideological
conviction, but rather has been shaped by his or her upbringing. This status
applies whether or not the person knows what Israel or its religion is.
Education is understood to be so powerfully formative that it diminishes the
notion of their free will and place them in the category of *anoosim*,[79]
individuals who are not responsible for their actions. Consequently, though
they incorporate delinquency or heresy that is otherwise intolerable, all
forms of marginalization are suspended in their case.

    As a result the blanket injunction for upstanding citizens to murder any *min, apikorus* or *meshumad* they come across, thus fulfilling a great *mitzvah*, is confined to:

> One who repudiates the Oral Law as a result of his reasoned opinion and conclusion, who walks light-mindedly after the capriciousness of his heart, denying first the Oral Law, and so applies to all who follow him. But their children and grandchildren, who were misled by their parents, and were born into *minut*, and were raised and trained upon its (*minut*) views, are like a *tinok shenishbah* amongst the heathens. The heathens raised him in their religion. He is like one compelled to sin against his will (*anoos*), for they raised and trained him according to their mistakes. So too is the case with those who hold to the teachings of their mistaken parents. Therefore efforts should be made to bring them back in repentance, to draw them near with paths of peace until they return to the strength-giving source of the Torah, and a person would not hurry to kill them.[80]

With this move, Maimonides effectively classifies all second-generation deviants, the vast majority of deviants out there, as tolerable deviants, i.e. individuals whose behaviour is deplored but who nevertheless are not subject to sanctions. They are not to be marginalized, and also every effort and kindness must be extended to them to encourage their return to the fold as members in good standing.[81] Instead of marginalization within the sphere of loyalty, their status within this sphere is not only maintained, but serves as the impetus for removing all other sanctions. As fellow members, society has the responsibility to do everything within its power to 'bring them back'. In contrast to the intolerable deviant, who, as seen above, is not even allowed to bring sacrifices so as to ensure that he will not repent, the status of *tinok shenishbah* reverses this rule and makes one's spiritual life and well-being the responsibility of the community.

This ruling in essence redefines the whole Maimonidean discussion of deviance, dramatically restricting the application of intolerability. Intolerability is now limited exclusively to those who, once members in good standing and living in the midst of members in good standing, rebel against their family, community and upbringing and make the decision to change their beliefs and practice. It is not the heresy or delinquency alone that generates intolerability, but this act of separation and rebellion. All other deviants are kept within the status of tolerable, in particular in the context of the sphere of loyalty. It seems that Maimonides was more interested in using boundary language and legislation to theoretically define the boundaries of the community's religious life than he was in actually marginalizing the deviants in question. With this move, Maimonides, to an even greater extent than even the Tannaim, limits the application of intolerability, and sets the foundation for the inclusion of most deviants. After all, who 'really' has parents who have given them all the education they need to be 'fully' responsible on their own, for the choices they make?[82]

The second sub-category of individuals towards whom Maimonides extends special treatment is the Karaites. This Jewish sect, characterized by its denial of rabbinic tradition, came into being at the beginning of the eighth century. In the twelfth century, their main centre was in Egypt, where Maimonides himself lived. In his *Responsa* 449, Maimonides treats at length the question of how those who adhere to rabbinic Judaism should behave toward Karaites. Should one circumcise the son of a Karaite on Shabbat? Should one inquire after and express concern for them, go to their homes, drink their wine, and the like? In his response, Maimonides ignores both his injunction in Hilkhot Mamrim to destroy anyone who adopts a heresy parallel to that of the Karaites, as well as his distinction between first- and second-generation deviants, and instead issues the following precedent-setting ruling:

> The Karaites living here in Alexandria and in the land of Egypt, and in Damascus, and in other places in Moslem lands and elsewhere, are worthy of respect. We should approach them honestly, and show decency when conducting our affairs with them, abiding by the ways of truth and peace, so long as they too behave toward us in good faith, and 'put away a dissembling mouth and perverse lips' (Prov. 4.24), refraining from slandering the rabbinic sages of this generation. All the more so, when they forgo mockery and ridicule when considering the words of our holy sages, the Tannaim of blessed memory, rabbis of the Mishnah and the Talmud whose words and rulings, as ordained by them, by Moses, and by God, we obey. If that occurs, it is incumbent upon us to respect them and inquire after them even at their homes, to circumcise their sons even on the Sabbath, to bury their dead, and to comfort their mourners.[83]

Maimonides rules that despite their deviance, Karaites are to be extended full rights in the spheres of loyalty and ritual[84] provided that they refrain from public verbal attacks against rabbinic Judaism and its leaders. Maimonides is in essence arguing, entirely without precedent, that so long as the Karaites cease to be enemy deviants, he can consider the abolition of marginalization procedures that their deviance may otherwise have warranted. In so doing, Maimonides is elevating enemy deviance to a central place in defining intolerability. The engagement in actively attacking and attempting to undermine others' way of life is that which transforms Karaite heresy from tolerable to intolerable deviance. Jewish collective space can allow for deviance, and different factions can extend rights towards each other in the spheres of loyalty and ritual, so long as this collective space is a safe one for those who abide there. Furthermore, Maimonides introduces a measure of reciprocity into the equation of intolerability: those who attack others and treat them as intolerable are themselves so defined.[85]

After his initial ruling, Maimonides then proceeds to offer further grounds for the classification of Karaites as tolerable. He refers to the Talmudic injunction to assist and conduct cordial relations with heathens in the interest of peace.[86] Maimonides extrapolates:

> If this is the case with worshippers of idols, how much more so should it be the case regarding one who rejects all the laws of the heathen and recognizes God, may His name be exalted.[87]

What Maimonides is arguing is that one cannot look at deviance in a vacuum and determine its status on its own merits alone. It is not simply that certain beliefs and practices are unacceptable and are thus classified as intolerable. Intolerability is a classification which affects a person and not a belief or act, and as a result, one must look at the deviant as a whole and measure his deviance in relation to his other beliefs and deeds. Similar to the *tinok shenishbah*, Maimonides here looks beyond the deviance itself to the larger reality of the person who is so believing or behaving. Though the Karaite rejects Maimonides' eighth principle of faith with regards to the authority of the Oral Law, he nevertheless accepts the first five, which involve belief in God and the rejection of idolatry.[88] What Maimonides here claims is that certain foundational types of fidelity to the law and faith of Israel – belief in God and the rejection of idolatry – mitigate the severity of a kind of deviance which otherwise would be viewed as intolerable.[89]

Beyond the argument itself, Maimonides displays here a particular largesse of spirit which is often difficult to come by, and in fact was absent in his own writing in the *Mishneh Torah*. It is not simple to overlook deviance and choose instead to focus on the positive, especially when it comes to a person who belongs to a competing ideology. Unlike the *tinok shenishbah* who is deemed tolerable by virtue of being considered irresponsible for his choices, the Karaite is so designated as a result of Maimonides being able to see not only the negative but also the positive. Perhaps it is for this reason that this move is made only after Maimonides' stipulation that the Karaites refrain from overt statements of aggression against the followers of rabbinic Judaism. Such largesse of spirit requires a particular social environment within which to develop. A climate of mutual de-legitimization will only breed greater mutual de-legitimization and hinder one's ability to see the positive in the other. The category of *tinok shenishbah*, on the other hand, works well in such an environment. In fact, it may even thrive there, for it entails a judgment of the other as a *tinok*, a child. Accommodation based on the inferiority of the other, on their not being responsible for their actions is much easier to make than one based on respect for the positive features that the deviant incorporates within his life.

This last line of reasoning points to a second and critical distinction between the two arguments. Maimonides' ruling regarding *tinok shenishbah*, in defining the deviant as a child, i.e. as one who is not capable of independent thought and thus not responsible for one's choices, is patronizing towards the deviant in question and at odds with his own self-perception. The Karaite model, on the other hand, upholds the agency and intellectual competence of the deviant. A self-respecting heretic can accept the kind of accommodation proposed in Maimonides' *Responsa* towards the Karaite, but will have more difficulty accepting classification as a *tinok shenishbah*. Consequently, the latter cannot function as a model of social accommodation between groups of hostile ideologies. Rather, it is primarily an internal tool of one group to justify their limiting the application of sanctions against other members. Conversely, the Karaite argument can serve as a model for some measure of mutual social accommodation even amongst groups who otherwise would classify each other as intolerable. What it requires, however, as stated above, is the will for such an accommodation and the environment to facilitate it.

On the issue of limiting intolerability, Joseph Karo, in his *Shulhan Arukh*, offers an additional consideration. He relates the case of a person who has divided his identity: in one city he is an idolater, while in another he joins '*beit yisrael* (the community of Israel) and says that he is a Jew'.[90] Which behaviour is understood to reflect the person's true convictions? At stake is the status of his wine: is it considered forbidden (*yein nesekh*), a status that would hinder day-to-day contact? Joseph Karo rules that his wine is not to be considered *yein nesekh*, reasoning that in cases of split loyalty or behaviour, one is to be assumed to be an *anoos* – the idolatrous beliefs and practices are faked, while the fidelity to Jewish practice is the authentic expression of the person's convictions. What is interesting is that Joseph Karo does not check the particulars of the case, but issues a general ruling for all such cases. He suggests that where there is room for doubt, we must choose to err on the side of designating the deviance tolerable.

Maimonides, and to a smaller degree the other mediaeval codifiers, add a number of seminal features to the overall discussion of boundaries. In terms of the definition of the intolerable, the mediaeval period witnesses the establishment of the Ammoraic position extending intolerability beyond the *meshumad lekol hatorah kullah* to include as well the *meshumad lehakhis*, though in Maimonides' case, with some additional limitations, such as requiring that the deviance be regular and that the deviant be notorious for this form of delinquency. This tendency to expand intolerability is further evidenced in what is one of the more dominant aspects of Maimonides' writing and is present, though to a lesser extent, in the *Shulhan Arukh*, i.e. the elevation of heresy devoid of delinquency to the status of intolerability. In addition, Maimonides also designates that which itself warrants tolerable classification as intolerable, when he believes that it may be the precursor to intolerable behaviour. This move, however, is limited exclusively to deviance which involves idolatry. Coupled with these two positions, in Maimonides we also witness the use of intolerable status in a prescriptive manner, i.e. the sanctioning as intolerable of those deviants who still view themselves as inside the community and generally loyal to its laws.

When it comes to the forms of marginalization, the major innovation is the Maimonidean move to include, in some cases, marginalization in the spheres of basic membership and naming. While he clearly also adopts this position in his halakhic codification, he is not consistent on this issue and also adopts the opposite stance, whereby the basic membership of the intolerable deviant is left intact. As distinct from Maimonides, the *Tur* articulates the ideological position rejecting any consequences in the sphere of basic membership on the basis of '*af al pi shehata yisrael hu*', a statement which does not appear in Maimonides' writing. In addition, while the severe sanction of *moridin velo ma-alin* is maintained, the extreme forms of shunning and marginalization in the sphere of loyalty directed towards the *min* as Jewish Christian generally disappear from the mediaeval codifications. This is accompanied by the tendency to apply all forms of marginalization equally to all forms of intolerable deviants.

Finally, with the theoretical expansion of the category of intolerability beyond the rabbinic and certainly the Tannaic notion, we also witness the introduction of mitigating factors which serve to limit the implementation of sanctions. These include the category of *tinok shenishbah* which forgives all second generation deviants; the notion that certain fundamental beliefs or practices can outweigh and generate a form of pardon for other intolerable beliefs or practices, as argued by Maimonides regarding the Karaites; and the *Shulhan Arukh*'s notion that when in doubt, assume that the deviance is either *leteiavon* or coerced and thus tolerable. The collective scope of the above considerations significantly limits the likelihood of the application of marginalization. It is as if the mediaeval codifiers were more interested in the theoretical assignment of the boundaries of Jewish collective space than in the actual sanctioning of those who have crossed these boundaries. What is decisive about these mitigating factors is that they require a halakhic figure with the will to implement them. One of the interesting features of the modern period to which we will now turn our attention is how the debate between the Orthodox, Conservative and Reform movements ultimately destabilized this will amongst contemporary Orthodox halakhic figures, leading, as we will see, to an unprecedented policy of marginalization so severe that it is almost entirely without precedent.

Notes

1 See Maimonides, *Introduction to Perek Helek*. See also A. Hyman, 'Maimonides' "Thirteen Principles"' in A. Altmann (ed.), *Jewish Medieval and Renaissance Studies* (Cambridge, 1967), pp. 119–44; and M. Kellner, *Dogma in Medieval Jewish Thought: From Maimonides to Abravanel* (Oxford, 1986), pp. 21–4.

2 In Hilkhot Teshuvah, Maimonides does not engage in a discussion of sanctions other than the impact of sin on one's share in the world to come.

3 In Maimonides, as in the Talmud, the term is always *meshumad*. See Y. Kapah, *Maimonides* Mishneh Torah, Hilkhot Shehitah 4.11 n. 14. This is also the case in the *Tur*. See *Tur* (Tel Aviv, Deborah Publishing, 2000), Oreh Haim 39.1 Hagahot ve-He-arot.

4 Thus the category of *kofer* disappears in his other halakhic writing, and its particular form of deviance divided amongst the other categories. Furthermore, in one instance he even refers explicitly back to the way a category is defined in Hilkhot Teshuvah, but does so inaccurately. See Maimonides, Mishneh Torah, Hilkhot Shehitah 4.14.

5 *Mishneh Torah*, Hilkhot Shehitah, 3.9.

6 *Ibid.*

7 *Ibid.*

8 *Mishneh Torah*, Hilkhot Teshuvah 3.6.

9 *Mishneh Torah*, Hilkhot Teshuvah 3.7.

10 *Mishneh Torah*, Hilkhot Teshuvah 3.8.

11 See, for example, *Mishneh Torah* Hilkhot Shehitah 4.14, Avodah Zarah 10.1–2, Yesodei Hatorah 6.8, Tefillin and Mezuzah and Sefer Torah 1.13; Maimonides, *Commentary on the Mishnah*, Sanhedrin 10.1 and Teshuvot ha-Rambam 263. See also M. Kellner, *Must a Jew Believe Anything?* (London, 1999), pp. 52–82.

12 Maimonides, *Introduction to Perek Helek*, translated by M. Kellner, in *Dogma in Medieval Jewish Thought*, p. 16.

13 *Mishneh Torah*, Hilkhot Mamrim 3.1. See also *Mishneh Torah*, Hilkhot Rotzeiah 4.10–11.

14 *Mishneh Torah*, Hilkhot Avodah Zarah, Chapter 1.2. Accordingly, not only intolerability, but membership itself is contingent on accepting these beliefs. See Maimonides' *Introduction to Perek Helek*, where membership in Israel is granted with acceptance of the essentials of faith (*emunah*), 'and when one believes in all of these fundamentals, and his belief in them is clear – *then* he enters into the Community of Israel'. (My emphasis.) See also *Mishneh Torah*, Hilkhot Isurei Biah, Chapter 12.2, where his belief in the centrality of faith for Jewishness gets

expressed in the conversion process. Breaking with rabbinic precedent, Maimonides innovates and adds an additional state that the potential convert must pass: 'And we inform him of the religious fundamentals (*ikarei hadat*), i.e. the unity of God and the prohibition against idolatry, and expound extensively about this matter.'

15 Maimonides, *Guide of the Perplexed*, 1.54. See also 3.27 and 3.51. See also Hilkhot Tehuvah 8.2 where one's place in the world to come is a function of the knowledge of God that one has attained.

16 See as well, *Mishneh Torah*, Hilkhot Ma-aseh Korbanot 3.4.

17 Now Maimonides has a specific category called *poresh min hatzibur* which is distinct from the *mumar lekol hatorah kullah*. A difference between the two as defined by Maimonides in Hilkhot Tehuvah 3.11 is that the *poresh min hatzibur* is an individual who does not sin, but simply separates himself from the fate of Israel. The *meshumad lekol hatorah kullah*, on the other hand, ceases to observe Jewish law when he converts, and it is through this change in practice that he expresses his rejection of the community.

18 See the comment of the Rabad (Rabbi Abraham Ben David of Posquieres, *c.* 1125–1198) on *Mishneh Torah*, Hilkhot Teshuvah 3.9, who does not make this distinction and argues that Maimonides is contradicting himself and that the *meshumad lekol hatorah kullah* should be defined as a *min*. See as well the Kesef Mishnah, who offers three solutions to the Rabad's comments, including the one offered here.

19 Rabad on Maimonides, *Mishneh Torah*, Hilkhot Teshuvah 3.7, translated by I. Twersky in his *Rabad of Posquieres* (Cambridge MA, 1962), p. 282. Twersky uses the term 'heretic' for *min*. For the purpose of this work, it is not important whether the Rabad himself subscribed to the principle of corporeality, or was defending either the legitimacy of those who did; or merely argued against their inclusion under the category of *min*. His statement is evidence of the fact that the issue was debated and that Maimonides uses the category of *min* in a prescriptive manner. For a discussion of the debate between Maimonides and the Rabad, and the Rabad's position, see Twersky, *Rabad of Posquieres*, pp. 282–6; M. Kellner, *Dogma in Medieval Jewish Thought*, pp. 89, 256, and *Must a Jew Believe Anything?*, pp. 20, 58; and M. Halbertal and A. Margalit, *Idolatry* (Cambridge MA, 1992), pp. 47–8, 108–12.

20 *Mishneh Torah*, Hilkhot Teshuvah 3.6.

21 *Mishneh Torah*, Hilkhot Avodah Zarah, Chapter 1. See also *Guide of the Perplexed*, 1.36.

22 A further example of such a move by Maimonides is found in the *Mishneh Torah*, Hilkhot Avodah Zarah 2.9, where he explains the applying of the sanction of shunning for the brazen and spiteful delinquent who violates some of the commandments and makes an ideology out of his deviance.

'The *minim* are those who run after the thoughts of their heart foolishly in the matters we discussed, until they find themselves transgressing the body of the Torah itself *lehakhis*, with disgust and a high hand, saying, "There is no sin in this." And it is prohibited to speak with them or to answer any question they ask, as it says, "Do not approach the entrance to her house ..." (Prov. 5.8). And the intent of the *min* is to idolatry.'

The sanction of shunning, one of the most severe in the legal arsenal, has not been applied hereto to such deviance, and in fact never appears again in Maimonides' writings. He justifies it with his closing remark: 'And the intent of the *min* is to idolatry.' The deviant in question is not guilty of idol worship, but of ideologically motivated delinquency, a sin of far less gravity. Given his desire to distance Judaism and the Jewish people as much as possible from exposure to idolatry, similar to his argument in Hilkhot Teshuvah, he includes under this ban forms of deviance which may either be founded on an idolatrous hidden agenda or possibly lead to it.

Another case is found in *Mishneh Torah*, Hilkhot Shehitah 4.14, where, in contrast to both the *meshumad ledavar ehad* and the Sadducee, the *meshumad* for idolatry, the *mehallel Shabbat befarhesia* and the *min* as heretic are barred from performing ritual slaughter under all instances, even if performed under the supervision of rabbis or authorities in the field, a status they hold in common with non-Jews. When it comes to the non-Jew, Maimonides explains that the invalidation derives from the prohibition on eating what is slaughtered for the purposes of idolatry, and there is a fear that at the moment of killing the animal, the idolater will intend the act to be done in the name of his god, something that is not given to inspection/supervision. As a further precautionary measure, the rabbis also invalidated the ritual slaughter of all non-Jews, to ensure that no errors will occur and accidentally we eat that which was slaughtered by an unknown individual, who was an idolater. See *Mishneh Torah* 4.9.

When the grounds for prohibiting ritual slaughter are the prevention of accidental participation in something that is associated with idolatry, Maimonides' invalidating of the ritual slaughter of the *meshumad* for idolatry and comparing him to the non-Jew is understood. There is no difference if a Jew or a non-Jew performs the idolatry; it is still idolatry. However, when the *mehallel Shabbat befarhesia* is included under this same rule, it begins to get more difficult. While the status of the *mehallel Shabbat* is often equated with that of the idolater, and both forms of deviance may be viewed as heresies, (see *Mishneh Torah*, Hilkhot Shabbat 30.16), it does not necessarily mean that the essence of their deviance or heresy is the same, particularly when the issue guiding the sanction is the suspicion that one may ritually slaughter in the name of one's idol. While the *mehallel Shabbat* may be viewed as a heretic, the assumption that he is also an idolater is a leap and extension of the nature of the deviance in question.

This issue becomes even more complex when one has to explain Maimonides' extension of the law to the *min* as heretic who denies the validity of the Torah and the prophecy of Moses. What Maimonides seems to be assuming is that one who rejects Torah, as well as one who rejects God as creator, will ultimately adopt idolatrous beliefs.

23 See Maimonides, *Mishneh Torah*, Hilkhot Teshuvah 3.10. One possible exception to this is Maimonides' statement in *Mishneh Torah*, Hilkhot Avodah Zarah

10.1–2, where he uses the notion of enemy deviance to justify the sanction of *moridin ve-lo ma-alin* to the *min* and *apikorus*.

'But as regards informers, *minim* and *apikorsim*, it is a *mitzvah* to take active measures to destroy them and cast them into a pit of destruction – the reason being that they persecute Israelites and turn them away from God, like Jesus the Nazarene and his students and Zadok and Boethus and their students, "the fame of the wicked rots" (Prov. 10.7).'

However, this same sanction is not unique to the enemy deviant. See *Mishneh Torah*, Hilkhot Rotzeiah 4.10–11 where both the non-enemy heretic as well as sinner *lehakhis* is also included; see also *Mishneh Torah*, Hilkhot Mamrim 3.1.

24 See *Tur*, Oreh Haim 547.9; Yoreh Deah, 2.7, 4.4, 145.8, 148.11, 155.1, 268.8 and 340.5; Even ha-Ezer 44.9, 123.2; and Hoshen Mishpat 283.2, 385.2.

25 See *Tur*, Oreh Haim 128.37; Yoreh Deah 266.12; Hoshen Mishpat 283.2 and 283.3; and Even ha-Ezer 157.4–5, where the deviant is called *meshumad*. See also Yoreh Deah 252.7, where the *Tur* speaks about a prisoner *shenishtamed*, but adds, 'even if only for one commandment such as to eat *neveilot lehakhis*'.

26 *Tur*, Oreh Haim 385.3; Yoreh Deah 2.7; and Even ha-Ezer 44.9 and 123.2.

27 See *Tur*, Oreh Haim 547.9; Yoreh Deah 2.5, 158.2, 252.7 and 340.5; and Hoshen Mishpat 266.2 and 285.10.

28 The *kofer* ceases to be an independent category, and the *apikorus* is only mentioned three times, all within general lists of deviants including the *min* and *meshumad*, without any specification of what offence it is meant to denote. See *Tur*, Yoreh Deah 158.2 and Hoshen Mishpat 34.22 and 266.2.

29 One exception to this unification of categories pertains to a deviant priest. In *Tur*, Oreh Haim 128.37, a priest who converted to another religion is disqualified from reciting the priestly blessing while deviance in other areas does not constitute grounds for disqualification. Another exception pertains to tefillin written by a *meshumad* or a *min*. The *meshumad*'s are deemed illegitimate, while the *min*'s must be burnt. See *Tur*, Oreh Haim 39.1–2.

30 *Tur*, Hoshen Mishpat 285.10. My emphasis. See also *Tur* Yoreh Deah 340.5 and 159.2, where in the latter, the *Tur* refers to the intolerable *meshumad* as *meshumad she-kafar be-ikar*.

31 See *Tur*, Yoreh Deah 2.2, 340.5, and Hoshen Mishpat 266.2 and 285.10. See also Yoreh Deah 251.2, where an opinion is presented that the *meshumad leteiavon* is also excluded from receiving *tzedakah* under the rationale that *tzedakah* is only distributed to one who falls under the category of *ahikha*.

32 For the idolater as *mumar* see *Shulhan Arukh*, Oreh Haim 128.37, 334.21, 385.3; Yoreh Deah 119.11, 130.6, 145.8, 148.11, 159.3, 268.2; Even ha-Ezer 17.3; Hoshen Mishpat 283.2–3 and 385.2. See also Oreh Haim 128.37, where idolatry is not explicitly mentioned but from the halakhah's source in the Mishnah Tractate Menahot 13.10 and Maimonides, *Mishneh Torah*, Hilkhot Tefillah 15.3, it is evident that the deviance intended is idolatry. For the idolater as *apikorus*, see *Shulhan Arukh*, Oreh Haim 53.18, 215.2; Yoreh Deah 12.2, 158.2; and Hoshen Mishpat 425.5. See also *Shulhan Arukh*, Yoreh Deah 155.1 and 381.1, where the *apikorus* is used to refer to the most ideological of idolaters. See also Hoshen

Mishpat 266.2, where the categories of *apikorus* and idolater are used as two distinct terms.

33 See *Shulhan Arukh*, Oreh Haim 385.1; Yoreh Deah 119.9, 228.43, 266.12, 345.6; Even ha-Ezer 44.9, 50.5, 123.2, 149.6; Hoshen Mishpat 283.2, 285.10.

34 *Shulhan Arukh*, Yoreh Deah 2.5 and Even ha-Ezer 17.3.

35 *Shulhan Arukh*, Oreh Haim 385.3 and Yoreh Deah 2.5.

36 *Shulhan Arukh*, Yoreh Deah 2.2, 5. See also Beit Yoseph, *Tur*, Yoreh Deah 159.2. See also *Shulhan Arukh*, Hoshen Mishpat 266.2 and 425.5, where he refers to him as an *apikorus*. See also *Shulhan Arukh*, Yoreh Deah 158.2. See also, Beit Yoseph, *Tur*, Yoreh Deah, 2.6, where Karo defines the *mumar ledavar ehad* as one who regularly and consistently violates the particular commandment in question and who sees himself as exempt from its obligation.

37 *Shluhan Arukh*, Yoreh Deah 158.2. See also Beit Yoseph, *Tur*, Yoreh Deah 2.6, where Karo defines the *mumar* as one 'who is *muad* to violate the commandment every time it occurs, and he has removed its obligation from himself'.

38 See for example *Shulhan Arukh*, Yoreh Deah 158.2, and Hoshen Mishpat 425.5.

39 Maimonides, *Mishneh Torah*, Hilkhot Ma-aseh Korbanot 3.4.

40 Here referred to as *min*.

41 *Mishneh Torah*, Hilkhot Shehitah 4.14.

42 See BT Tractate Gittin 45b.

43 *Mishneh Torah*, Hilkhot Yisodei ah-Torah 6.8. See also *Mishneh Torah*, Hilkhot Tefillin ve-Mezuzah ve-Sefer Torah 1.13.

44 See BT Tractate Gittin 45b and Rashi's Commentary.

45 Hebrew addition mine.

46 Maimonides, *Introduction to Perek Helek*, translated by M. Kellner, in *Drogma on Jewish Thought*, p. 16.

47 Maimonides, *Mishneh Torah*, Hilkhot Rotzeiah 4.10-11. See also *Mishneh Torah* Hilkhot Avodah Zarah, 10.1, where he limits the sanction to enemy deviants who actively persecute Israel and try to alter their faith system. This condition, however, neither appears in our source nor in the other instance where this sanction is mentioned, in Hilkhot Mamrim 3.1.

48 See BT Tractate Avodah Zarah 26b.

49 Maimonides, *Mishneh Torah*, Hilkhot Gezeilah ve-Aveidah 11.1–3.

50 *Mishneh Torah*, Hilkhot Teshuvah 3.14 (emphasis added).

51 *Mishneh Torah*, Hilkhot Isurei Be-ah, 13.17.

52 *Mishneh Torah*, Hilkhot Yibum ve-Halitzah 1.6. See also *Mishneh Torah*, Hilkhot Nahalot 6.12, where on the issue of inheritance rights Maimonides also rules that the *meshumad* still maintains his rights to inherit from his father, and the sons of the *meshumad* inherit from him, thus assuming his Israelite status. Unlike the convert to Judaism, whose conversion changes his family identity, and as a result does not inherit from his father and whose idolatrous son does not inherit from him, the *meshumad* is not perceived by Maimonides to have altered his status as a part of the family.

53 *Mishneh Torah*, Hilkhot Ma-aseh Korbanot 3.4. In addition to the above, see

Mishneh Torah, Hilkhot Yisodei Hatorah, 6.8, and Hilkhot Tefillin ve-Mezuah ve-Sefer Torah, 1.13, where the *min* is also distinguished from the heathen.

54 *Mishneh Torah*, Hilkhot Avodah Zarah 10.1.

55 Maimonides, *Introduction to Perek Pelekh*, p. 16. My emphasis.

56 For a discussion of Maimonides' position, see M. Kellner, *Must a Jew Believe Anything?*, pp. 52–65. There Kellner also takes the position that the above statement is Aggadic and not intended to halakhically contradict the notion of Jewishness as a condition of descent.

57 Maimonides, *Mishneh Torah*, Hilkhot Avodah Zarah 2.5.

58 *Mishneh Torah*, Hilkhot Shabbat 30.15. Here again, as was the case in Hilkhot Shehitah, and as distinct from Hilkhot Teshuvah, Maimonides follows the distinction in BT Tractate Hullin 5a between the *mehallel Shabbat* and idolater on the one hand, and all other deviants on the other. Intent, such as *lehakhis* or *teiavon*, is not a factor in distinguishing between types of deviants.

59 *Mishneh Torah*, Hilkhot Mamrim 3.1. See also Maimonides, *Commentary on the Mishnah*, Hullin 1.2, where he states that this punishment is to be applied despite the general ban on capital punishment in the times of exile. As an explanation, Maimonides classifies the *minim*, and the followers as Zadok and Boethus, i.e. the Karaites, as enemy deviants who endanger the faith of Israel.

60 See Maimonides, *Mishneh Torah*, Hilkhot Avodah Zarah 10.1.

61 *Mishneh Torah*, Hilkhot Isurei Biah 13.17. My emphasis.

62 Rabbi Yom Tov Vidal, the fourteenth-century author of the Maggid Mishneh, the important commentary on Maimonides' *Mishneh Torah*, attempts to resolve this contradiction by defining the apostate convert as a *meshumad leteiavon*. See Maggid Mishneh, *Mishneh Torah*, Hilkhot Isurei Biah, 13.17. It is only the *meshumad lehakhis*, who deviates out of an ideological consciousness that ceases to be either brother or friend.

63 Mishnah, Tractate Eruvin 6.1.

64 See Tosefta Eruvin 7.18.

65 Maimonides, *Mishneh Torah*, Hilkhot Eruvin 2.16.

66 *Mishneh Torah*, Hilkhot Eruvin 2.9.

67 *Mishneh Torah*, Hilkhot Eruvin 2.16. Emphasis mine.

68 *Mishneh Torah*, Hilkhot Eruvinm 2.9.

69 Now, the difference between the need for the renting of the share of a non-Jew who is a partner with numerous Jews, as distinct from when there is only one Jewish partner, does not stem out of his status as an owner, which as stated, does not exist. Rather, as stated above, it was designed as a measure to deter living in close proximity with non-Jews. Maimonides explains that this measure was not instituted in the case of one Jew dwelling in a shared courtyard with a non-Jew for the following reason: 'Because this is uncommon, out of fear that he will be alone with him and he will murder him, and (the rabbis) already forbid being alone with a non-Jew.' (*Mishneh Torah*, Hilkhot Eruvin 2.9.)

Given the existing dangers, at that time, which a Jew would face when living alone in close proximity with a non-Jew, such a case was too rare to require a special rabbinic enactment. Multiple Jewish partners would not be afraid, and consequently might try to rent property with a shared courtyard with a non-Jew, a reality that the rabbis felt compelled to try to prevent.

70 BT Tractate Sanhedrin 44a.

71 See Jacob Katz's article 'Af Al Pi Shehata Yisrael Hu' in his book *Halakha and Kabbalah* (Jerusalem, 1986), 255–69.

72 As argued by J. Katz, *ibid.*, pp. 255–69, it was Rashi who introduced the use of this statement as the source and foundation for disallowing marginalization in the sphere of basic membership. See for example Teshuvot Rashi 171, 173 and 174.

73 *Tur*, Yoreh Deah 159.1–2. My emphasis. See also *Shluhan Arukh*, Hoshen Mishpat 283.2, where the *Tur* uses the category to uphold a deviant's inheritance rights. As stated above, Maimonides in the *Mishneh Torah*, Hilkhot Nahalot 6.12 rules in a similar fashion, even though he does not accept the premise of '*af al pi shehata yisrael hu*'. This issue was the subject of debate in the Gaonic period. See O. Ir-Shai, 'Meshumad ke-Yoresh be-Teshuvot ha-Gaonim', *Shenaton ha-Mishpat ha-Ivri* 11–12 (1984–6) pp. 435–61.

In addition to the above cases, there are a number of other instances in which the *Tur* argues for the status of the *meshumad* within the sphere of basic membership without specifically mentioning the principle of *af al pi shehata yisrael hu*. These involve the issue of marriage, *halitzah* and *yibum*. See *Tur*, Even ha-Ezer 44.9 and 157.4–5.

74 The *Tur*'s position on this issue differs from Rashi who, in Teshuvot Rashi 175 employs the argument of *de-af al pi shehata yisrael hu* to also prohibit the charging of interest. Rashi thus does not distinguish between being considered *ahikha* in the sphere of basic membership from *ahikha* in the sphere of loyalty. Once one is *ahikha*, it applies throughout. See also *Tur*, Hoshen Mishpat 266.2, where the *Tur*, similar to Maimonides, exempts community members at large from their obligation to return the lost property of various intolerable deviants. In doing so, however, unlike Maimonides, he does not exclude them from the category *ahikha*.

75 See for example *Shulhan Arukh*, Yoreh Deah 2.7; Oreh Haim 385.3; and Even ha-Ezer 123.2.

76 *Shulhan Arukh*, Yoreh Deah 268.12. Emphasis mine.

77 See BT Tractate Shabbat 68a-b. Following this use, Maimonides rules that a deviant such as the *tinok shenishbah*, who was raised among heathens and 'does not know what Israel or its religion is' (*Mishneh Torah*, Hilkhot Shegagot 2.6), even though he sins intentionally, has the legal status of *shogeg* and may bring the offering for involuntary sin. From this ruling it is reasonable to infer that one who subsequently becomes aware of his Jewish identity, and of the legal obligations attendant on it, sheds his *tinok shenishbah* status and is subsequently considered an intentional sinner (*meizid*). Maimonides, as stated, refrains from making this argument.

78 R. Yohanan and R. Shimon ben Lakish, BT Tractate Shabbat, 68a–b and Rashi, *Shulhan Arukh*, Patur. See also BT Tractate Shavuot 5a.

79 See G. Bildstein, 'ha-Gisha la-Karaim be-Mishnat ha-Rambam', *Tehumin* 8, (1988) 502–3, who argues that according to Maimonides the correct association for the *tinok shenishbah* is *shogeg*.

80 Maimonides, *Mishneh Torah*, Hilkhot Mamrim 3.3. See also Maimonides, *Commentary on the Mishnah*, Tractate Hullin 1.2, where this qualification is repeated. See also n. 16, p. 174, in the Kapah edition, where Kapah points out that this addition was absent from earlier versions of the *Commentary* and only added by Maimonides later in his life. See also G. Bildstein, 'ha-Gisha la-Karaim be-Mishnat ha-Rambam', p. 504.

81 Compare Maimonides' ruling in his *Mishneh Torah*, Hilkhot Mamrim, with his ruling in the *Guide of the Perplexed* 1.36, whereby *shegagah* or lack of knowledge of any kind is not grounds for leniency. See M. Kellner, *Must a Jew Believe Anything?*, pp. 82–6, who distinguishes between different forms of heresy in Maimonides, and thus attempts to explain this seeming inconsistency. I will return to Kellner's claim in the discussion of the Karaites in Maimonides' *Responsa* below.

82 The *Tur*, while not referring explicitly to the category of *tinok shenishbah*, does refer to those who were taken captive and subsequently converted as *anoosim*, i.e. individuals who were coerced and, as a result, were not culpable for their actions. As a result they are not subjected to the punishment of *moridin ve-lo ma-alin* and their property is to be preserved. See *Tur*, Hoshen Mishpat 285.10. In an interesting move, he grounds the leniency of the person taken captive not on his being *anoos*, but rather on his being motivated by definition by *teiavon* and not *lehakhis*.

83 Maimonides, Teshuvot ha-Rambam, *Responsa* 449.

84 In Teshuvot ha-Rambam, *Responsa* 365, Maimonides expands on the issue of the Karaites' participation in the sphere of ritual. He rules that their participation is to be determined on a case-by-case basis, depending on whether they believe in or accept the obligatory nature of the law in question. Where their Karaite ideology parallels rabbinic Judaism's, they can participate. When it does not, for example regarding the requirement of a *minyan* for a *davar shebekedushah*, or three for *zimun*, they cannot.

'Any area (of our laws) that they believe to be obligatory and accept its application, it is permissible for us to be included together with them, and anything that they do not believe it to be obligatory or accept its application, it is forbidden for them to be included together with us ... for then the fulfilment of the law is based on someone who does not believe in it.'

The issue of inclusion or exclusion in the sphere of ritual is not based on sanctions resulting from their deviance, but rather on the formal issue of not including individuals in rituals which they do not accept as valid and binding. This is similar to Maimonides' position in Hilkhot Eruvin 2.16, where the Sadducee is not allowed to participate in the *eruv* only because he does not accept it as valid, and not because he is a deviant.

85 See G. Bildstein, 'ha-Gisha la-Karaim be-Mishnat ha-Rambam', pp. 505–7, who similarly argues and explains that, for Maimonides, the sanctioning of the *min* and

consequently the Karaite, was not the result of their heresy, but of the social dangers they posed. The *min* is an enemy and not merely a sinner. When the *min* agrees to conduct himself with restraint in public, he ceases to be an enemy who threatens the Jewish community and can be exempt from the sanctions associated with the enemy.

86 The fact that Maimonides makes an argument for basing the treatment of Jewish deviants on precedent which applies to the treatment of non-Jews is interesting. The deviant is always, at least initially, an insider, and it is because of this dual status as both insider and deviant that the law which applies to him sanctions him as well. As distinct from the insider, an outsider cannot be a deviant, for there is no mutually accepted system from which he or she deviates. As a result, they do not threaten the system to the same degree, often resulting in a greater amount of tolerance. In fact, this is precisely what Maimonides states in *Mishneh Torah*, Hilkhot Edut 11.10, where he classifies the *min*, *apikorus* and *meshumad* as deviant outsiders who are on a lower level and subject to more severe sanctions than non-Jewish idolaters. Thus the fact that there are areas of accommodation which apply to outsiders might be considered irrelevant in determining the treatment of outsiders-within. Maimonides ignores this distinction.

87 Maimonides, Teshuvot ha-Rambam, *Responsa* 449.

88 See M. Kellner, *Must a Jew Believe Anything?* pp. 82–6, where he argues that the distinction between the first five principles of faith and the remaining eight are the grounds for Maimonides' acceptance of the Karaite who is a *tinok shenishbah*, despite his position in the *Guide of the Perplexed* 1.36, where lack of knowledge is not considered an extenuating circumstance. Kellner explains that with regard to the first five principles of faith there is no room for compromise, and one who rejects them, regardless of motivation or circumstances, has no place in the world to come. The Karaite who is a *tinok shenishbah* rejects parts of principles 6–8 which define the community of Israel. One who rejects them, however, may still have a place in the world to come and if there are extenuating circumstances may not be excluded from Israel. In his *Responsa*, however, Maimonides goes even further and in direct contradiction to the *Introduction to Perek Helek*, is willing to include the Karaites in the spheres of ritual and loyalty solely on the basis of their acceptance of God and rejection of idolatry.

89 Following Maimonides, the *Shulhan Arukh* too grants a unique status to the Karaites, and, unlike other intolerable deviants, it is even forbidden to charge them interest on loans. See *Shulhan Arukh*, Yoreh Deah 159.3. What is interesting is the debate around this ruling, evidence of which he provides in his Beit Yoseph. On the issue of the Karaites, it seems to me that, according to Maimonides in his *Commentary on the Mishnah* in Hullin, where he classifies them as *tinok shenishbah*, they do not have the status of *meshumadim* and it is forbidden to charge them interest on loans. This is despite what the Nimukei Yoseph wrote, that one is only given the status of *tinok shenishbah* if one was never acquainted with the Torah of Israel. However, one who resides among Israel and nevertheless goes and cleaves to the laws of the nations may be charged interest on loans. However, we do not set aside the explicit words of Maimonides for the

sake of the words of the Nimukei Yoseph. (Beit Yoseph, *Tur*, Yoreh Deah 159.3.)

The Nimukei Yoseph (Joseph Ibn Haviva, 15th century) attempts to limit the applicability of *tinok shenishbah* to its literal meaning: those who, like the infant who was taken captive, never had access to or even basic familiarity with Judaism and its attendant obligations. Those who live in the midst of Jews, however, cannot continue to use the prior fact that when they began to sin they did not know better. Now that they do know and have the ability to change, their continued deviance ought to be classified as intolerable. Faced with this option, Karo chooses to follow the precedent of Maimonides.

90 *Shulhan Arukh*, Yoreh Deah 119.11. See R. Yonah in Teshuvot ha-Rashbah 7.719.

CHAPTER FOUR

The Hatam Sofer and the
Boundaries of Orthodoxy

Orthodoxy, like Judaism itself, is diverse and multi-faceted, and thus it is
difficult to speak of it as one coherent movement. There are right-wing and
left-wing, Zionist and non-Zionist, haredi, centrist, nationalist, modern and
liberal Orthodoxies. However, one area where there is a broad measure of
agreement, albeit no unanimity of opinion, is the movement's appraisal of
the diverse religious expressions that emerged in the Jewish community as a
result of modernity and enlightenment. Seeing itself as the sole heir of
traditional Judaism over the centuries, Orthodoxy in general perceives the
other denominations as having deviated from the core principles and
directions essential to what Orthodoxy refers to as a 'Torah-true' Jewish life.
As a result, the diversity that these other denominations have engendered is
almost never assessed under the categories of pluralism or even tolerance,
leaving the only range of flexibility between the areas of tolerable and
intolerable deviance.

The boundary policies that Orthodoxy has produced reflect this
attitude. Instead of serving to further clarify the collective identity of the
Jewish people as a whole, they essentially serve to demarcate the boundaries
of Orthodoxy alone, often leaving all others, at least theoretically, outside.
As self-appointed protectors of the tradition, the vast majority of Orthodox
thinkers take the position that the innovations which characterize Jewish life
ought to have no place in defining the content of Judaism. What Jews do
may be of sociological significance, but it must have no impact on the
definition of Judaism itself.

These next two chapters will explore two of the leading and
precedent-setting exemplars of these marginalization policies: Rabbi
Moshe Schreiber, who was known as the Hatam Sofer (1762–1839) and
Rabbi Moshe Feinstein (1895–1986). The Hatam Sofer lived at a time when
the impact of modernity on tradition was just beginning to be felt and its
outcome was not yet clear. In Moshe Feinstein's lifetime, in contrast, the full
extent of the impact of modernity was already complete, and non-traditional
approaches to Jewish life had become the majority. Nonetheless, each in his
own era and context strove to respond to the challenges of diverse non-
traditional approaches to Jewish life by developing comprehensive boundary
policies which, at least with regards to non-Orthodox denominations, were

extreme and exclusionary. In examining their halakhic writing on the subject, special care will be paid to their relationship to the rabbinic and mediaeval precedents on the boundaries of intolerable deviance and the way one responds to these deviants. This analysis of their positions will in turn serve as the foundation for the concluding chapter, where I will propose a different direction for contemporary Jewish boundary policies.

With the onset of the Enlightenment and the political emancipation of the Jews in Western Europe at the end of the eighteenth and throughout the middle of the nineteenth centuries, Jewish individual and collective identity in Western Europe faced an unprecedented challenge.[1] Everywhere the Enlightenment penetrated, it deeply influenced Jews' understanding of themselves and their sense of religious duty and belonging. Jewish identity became susceptible to religious, cultural and political assimilation as well as open to non-traditional and non-religious ideas and aspirations. Various identities, like various ideas and customs, took on growing prominence within Jewish consciousness as Jews began to integrate into the social and cultural environments that were now open to them for the first time. As a result Jewish principles and orientations did not always take precedence. As historian David Ellenson puts it, 'If the approach of pre-modern tradition-alists is crystallized in the verse, "I place God before me always," the paraphrase that arises from modern religious traditionalists is, "I place God before me, but not always." '[2]

This new reality generated two new religious phenomena that significantly challenged the boundaries that defined and delineated Jewish collective life. The first was the reality of growing, unprecedented numbers of Jews for whom fidelity to the halakhah was not the defining factor of their Jewish identity. While non-observance of *mitzvot* has been a common factor throughout the course of Jewish history, at the end of the eighteenth and beginning of the nineteenth centuries it became both more prevalent and significant. Beyond the pressures placed on halakhic observance as a result of the fact that Jewish life was more attuned to and integrated with the broader non-Jewish social atmosphere, this period also witnessed a change in the sense of the role of halakhah in the definition of both private and public Jewish life. Thus, for example, where in the past the *mehallel Shabbat befarhesia* was clearly separating himself from the community and constituted a *meshumad lekol hatorah kullah*, now such a breach in halakhah was not perceived to necessarily entail either a rejection of the community, nor would it necessarily cast doubt on one's personal fidelity to the remainder of Torah.

The second religious phenomenon was the birth of the Reform movement, which carried out reforms in both Jewish custom and ideology and attempted to adapt aspects of Jewish law and customs to the ideas and reality of modernity.[3] Starting in Germany in the early nineteenth century, in its early stages Reform Judaism still had not suggested a coherent philosophical or ideological framework in general, nor for the fulfillment of *mitzvot* in the modern world in particular. At the beginning of the nineteenth century, the primary focus of the movement's rabbis and leaders was on the development of texts, rituals and customs for synagogue worship that would be acceptable, both ideologically and culturally, to Jews integrated to various degrees into aspects of secular and Christian life.[4]

Despite the relatively benign nature and limited focus of the debate between Reform and traditional notions of Judaism, the political reality of this period served to transform what might have been a moderate debate about synagogue customs into a broader, more contentious altercation. In nineteenth-century Europe, religion and state had not been fully disassociated from one another; a person's religious beliefs and affiliation were believed to shape their ability and credibility to function as a citizen. All citizens were required to belong to a recognized and/or officially sanctioned religious system. Prior to Emancipation, when Jews were barred from citizenship and Judaism remained a non-sanctioned faith, the involvement of the state in internal Jewish religious affairs was limited. However, after the French Revolution, as Judaism began to be elevated to the status of state-sanctioned religion in parts of Western Europe, debates between Jews were no longer the domain of rabbis alone. These debates could and often did become the affair of the government, with each side aspiring to receive from the state acknowledgment of and support for its positions. Furthermore, the fact that at this time there was only one state-recognized Judaism and Jewish community made it impossible for clashing groups to break off from one another and establish their own community institutions, as was the case for Jews in America. Factionalism was generally frowned upon and was often illegal. There was room for only one understanding of Judaism, and the two conflicting ideologies, Orthodox and Reform, struggled to establish their positions as determinant of *the* state-sanctioned Judaism. As a result, each side threatened the existence of the other. To use the language of boundary politics, each side perceived the other as an enemy deviant, for one's opponents not only disagreed, but also actively adopted policies that threatened the ability of the other to exist.[5]

The structure of the community also contributed to the worsening of this tension. Membership of the community was not a voluntary matter. For both financial and political reasons, there was only one community rabbi and in most cases also only one synagogue and one community school, which were financed and supported by taxes levied on community members. Therefore the dispute, despite its primary focus on the synagogue service, was often transformed into the question of who would determine the religious leadership and identity of communal institutions.

Intolerable Deviance

The Hatam Sofer's work is the product of a time in which the effects of Enlightenment were just beginning to generate tension between traditional and Reform Jews. In response both to traditional precedent and to the new realities prevalent within the Jewish community, the Hatam Sofer categorized four primary forms of deviance as intolerable. They are the apostate, i.e. the convert to Christianity (an increasingly common phenomenon in the post-Emancipation era); the *mehallel Shabbat befarhesia;* the idolater and the Reform Jew. The first two are classified exclusively under the category of *mumar,*[6] while the Reform Jew is solely a *min*[7] or *apikorus.*[8] The idolater, by which the Hatam Sofer means either the contemporary apostate or the classical idolater, is categorized as either a *mumar* or a *min.*[9] The *mumar ledavar ehad lehakhis,* while in theory intolerable,[10] ceases to be a significant category in his discussion of intolerability.[11] The Hatam Sofer thus functionally returns to the Tannaic position, whereby intolerable deviance is reduced to very particular and limited forms of delinquency.

In analysing the Hatam Sofer's discussion of these forms of deviance, one can isolate three primary characteristics of his notion of intolerability. The first parallels the rabbinic notion of *mumar lekol hatorah kullah* and involves the complete rejection of all of Jewish law coupled with a separation of the self from the community.

> The *mumarim* of our times, the majority of them become absorbed
> amongst the nations of the world and they take it upon themselves
> to be separated and distinguished from the community of Israel
> and reject the Torah of Moses and *all* its laws.[12]

The second characteristic, emanating from his discussion of the *mehallel Shabbat befarhesia,* and growing out of the Maimonidean precedent, is that intolerability is activated as a consequence of the heretical implications of the desecration of the Shabbat. Similar to Maimonides, the Hatam Sofer defines the *mehallel Shabbat befarhesiah* in terms of the heresy indicated by the delinquency and not the implied separation from the community, as is the sense in rabbinic sources. Thus he calls him a *kofer,* and *kofer bekol hatorah,*[13] and adopts the position of Rashi discussed above, whereby the *mehallel Shabbat befarhesia* is considered a *mumar lekol hatorah kullah* by virtue of his being a *kofer* in the act of creation.[14]

This position regarding the *mehallel Shabbat befarhesia,* as stated, is not original to the Hatam Sofer. However, due to the particular historical context within which it was articulated, it has a far-reaching implication for the boundaries of intolerability. It was not that the Hatam Sofer disregarded the rabbinic comparison between the *mehallel Shabbat befarhesia* and the *mumar lekol hatorah kullah* in which both entail being a *poresh min hatzibur*. Rather, by the time of the Hatam Sofer, the *mehallel Shabbat befarhesia* could no longer be comparable to the apostate, for in fact he was neither a *poresh min hatzibur* nor one who rejects the covenant. While in the Hatam Sofer's age the desecration of the Shabbat was still rare and the exception to the rule,[15] nevertheless, the community contained ever-increasing numbers of individuals who saw themselves as members of the community and loyal to Torah in general, despite desecrating the laws of Shabbat in public. The Hatam Sofer recognized this fact as well as the different but comparable reality of Jews who, while members of the community, simultaneously attended Christian liturgical services:

> The apostates of our time, who assimilate amongst the nations, certainly violate all of the commandments. However, he who lives amongst Israel, and who follows her practices, *only* being a *mumar* to worship idols or to desecrate the Shabbat, while being a *mumar lekol hatorah*, nevertheless, is not a *hashud lekol hatorah* [i.e. suspected of violating all the precepts of the Torah].[16]

In the language of the Hatam Sofer their sin is '*only* being a *mumar* to worship idols or to desecrate the Shabbat', with the qualifier 'only' not intending to diminish the severity of the deviance, but rather to define its parameters. The Hatam Sofer is acknowledging that by the beginning of the nineteenth century there is an individual, in the language of the Hatam Sofer, 'who worships idols or who desecrates the Shabbat and still observes the *whole* [i.e. all the rest of the Torah]'.[17]

While his recognition of this reality has implications for the scope of marginalization to which the *mehallel Shabbat befarhesia* and the idolater who is not an apostate are subjected, as will be seen below, nevertheless, they are both still classified by the Hatam Sofer as intolerable.[18] In doing so the Hatam Sofer, similar to Maimonides, expands the boundaries of intolerability far beyond the strict Tannaic criterion that activates intolerable status only when one is a *poresh min hatzibur* and completely rejects the covenant. In the terms of the Hatam Sofer, the *mehallel Shabbat befarhesia*, and possibly even the idolater, are *mumarim ledavar ehad* of a particular kind that are deemed intolerable due to the heresy vis-à-vis God and God's role as creator. Put in more general terms, there are certain central beliefs in Judaism, the rejection of which, when founded on delinquent behaviour, warrants intolerable classification even though one maintains one's connection to the remainder of the system.

The Hatam Sofer's third feature of intolerable deviance is to be found in his discussion of the status of Reform Jews. As stated, he classified Reform Jews exclusively under the categories of *min* or *apikorus*, categories that place greater emphasis on the heretical nature of the deviance in question. By consistently abstaining from using the category of *mumar* for the Reform Jew, the Hatam Sofer is indicating that his essential opposition to Reform Judaism is not based on their halakhic behavioural innovations or delinquency, but rather on the belief system which founded the movement and which served as the ideological basis for these halakhic innovations.[19]

In accordance with Reform halakhic practices in his time, the Hatam Sofer formally locates the essence of the dispute with these Jews around synagogue rituals and the prayer book. He attacks them for moving the *bimah* from the centre to the front of the synagogue, praying in the vernacular and not in Hebrew, using an organ (played by a non-Jew) during prayers on Shabbat, abolishing the requirement of communal prayer with a *minyan* during the week, reading the Torah without *ta-amei mikrah* (the traditional ritual incantation), and abolishing the prayers which call for the coming of the messiah and the redemption of Israel.[20]

All these charges (except perhaps the latter) more aptly warrant the classification of *mumar ledavar ehad*. After all, they involve neither idolatry nor the desecration of Shabbat in public.[21] They should have been viewed as either tolerable or merely marginally intolerable, and by and large ignored, as was the case with all other expressions of deviance of this form. Furthermore, from a purely legal perspective, most of the positions taken by the Reform movement were at least plausibly halakhic, with precedents in the Talmudic and halakhic literature. In fact, the position taken by the Hatam Sofer prohibiting prayer in the vernacular, for instance, is in many ways far more innovative and difficult to justify halakhically than the Reform position that legitimizes it.[22]

But it was not issues of delinquency that motivated the Hatam Sofer's designation of Reform Judaism as intolerable, but rather his perception of them as heretics of a new and particularly dangerous nature. In one of his most poetic attacks, he frames his perspective on the nature of their heresy.

> How is it that words which emanated out of the mouths of the knowledgeable and wise, whose understanding is as wide as the opening of the universe and which were sifted and refined again and again over hundreds of years by thousands of rabbis and became permanent fixtures amongst the people for close to two thousand years, with no one even contemplating and raising a

word or moving a finger in objection, there then rise these 'little foxes',[23] the darkness of exile, to breach the rabbis' wall and destroy their fence and alter the form of their prayers and blessings?[24]

The Hatam Sofer's difficulty with Reform innovations is simply that they are innovations. For him, tradition, that which was a 'permanent fixture amongst the people for close to two thousand years', cannot be removed or changed, especially not by 'little foxes', a phrase he adopts from the Song of Songs (2.15). To fail to commit to the authority of tradition is *the* heresy that is intolerable. Thus the Hatam Sofer restates over and again:

> Why should we rise and change a custom of our ancient fathers?[25]

> How could they permit in public, in their houses of worship, that which our fathers and fathers' fathers deemed forbidden?[26]

> We do not have the authority to innovate from our hearts a *mitzvah* that our predecessors did not envision.[27]

> Anyone who changes is inferior (lit. his hand is on the bottom) and anyone who holds on to the words of the rabbis and the custom of his fathers is superior (lit. his hand is on the top).[28]

> Heaven forbid changing from that which was.[29]

> May a thousand of these (Reformers) be destroyed and let not a single dot of the customs of Israel be moved from its place.[30]

According to the Hatam Sofer, the past must even define the parameters of current halakhic practice through its omissions, that is, even if in the past the rabbis merely refrained from doing something, or something was simply not done, it follows that it is our halakhic duty to continue to refrain from doing so as well.

> If it were permitted to translate the Torah into other languages (during the reading of the Torah in the services), the men of the Great Synod would have done it. If they refrained from doing it, it follows that for us (to do so) is also forbidden.[31]

> In all these matters, since our fathers and father's fathers did not act as if it was allowed, it constitutes a forbidden custom.[32]

This conception of faithfulness to tradition as a core, if not *the* core of Jewish faith, is encapsulated most powerfully in what has become the Hatam Sofer's most notable statement, one which he reiterates over and again in his *Responsa*:

> Whatever is new is forbidden by the Torah (*hadash asur min hatorah*).[33]

As Jews began to leave the physical and intellectual ghetto and embrace ideas, values and culture from a world that for the first time began to open its doors to Jews, the Hatam Sofer understood that at issue were not some minor matters of synagogue ritual. Modernity did not simply challenge particular aspects of Jewish law; it was beginning to create a competing system of loyalty, authority and subsequently, identity for the Jews of his generation. The Hatam Sofer believed that the only way to withstand the ideological temptation and onslaught of modernity was to make Judaism impervious to it, an idea that ultimately became the foundation of ultra-Orthodoxy. As he stated in his will:

> May your mind not turn to evil and never engage in corruptible partnership with those fond of innovations ... Be warned not to change your Jewish names, speech and clothing – God forbid ... Never say 'Times have changed' ... We have an old Father – praised be His name, who has never changed and never will change.[34]

By exhorting Jews to keep their names, speech and dress distinct, the Hatam Sofer aspired to recreate a portable ghetto which would ensure separation from the larger world and thus protect Jewish life and identity from the influence of modernity. Accordingly, he created a new boundary, a new definition of intolerable deviance, i.e. change. *Hadash asur min hatorah* was a radical innovation created at a time when the foundations were being laid for the possible marginalization of the role of Jewish tradition in determining the shared cultural space of the Jewish people. While Reform Judaism was not calling for such a radical overhaul, the Hatam Sofer envisioned it as setting the foundation for this position. Judaism and the Jewish people would be safe, the Hatam Sofer believed, only to the extent that they regrouped around the traditional practices and were willing to live in accordance with a mythic past that was disconnected from the contemporary reality. Change of any form became the declared enemy, and its advocates were labelled heretics and intolerable deviants. Ironically, of course, in designating Reform as intolerable in the name of fidelity to the past, the Hatam Sofer was in fact instituting one of the most significant innovations of the modern era. If 'what is new is forbidden under Jewish law', then the ruling of the Hatam Sofer regarding Reform Jews itself ought to have been designated as forbidden.

If any precedent can be found for the Hatam Sofer's designation of Reform Jews as intolerable deviants, it may possibly be found in the rabbinic classification of Jewish Christians. In both cases there was a perception of being attacked, a perception that warranted enemy deviant classification and the status of intolerability. The one significant difference is that in the case of the Jewish Christian, from the rabbinic perspective, the deification of Jesus also involved idolatry, thus grounding their intolerability status on strong halakhic grounds. Such grounding is totally lacking with regards to Reform Jews. As stated above, the nature of Reform delinquency was at best marginal, and coupled as it was with their continued commitment to halakhah and the Jewish people, should have warranted, on the basis of legal precedent, the status of tolerable deviant.

In summary, the reality of secularism and the beginning of Reform Judaism profoundly affected the Hatam Sofer's notions of intolerability. While maintaining the central classic condition of intolerability, i.e. being a *meshumad lekol hatorah kullah*, which applies essentially to the apostate, he adds two individuals to the classification of intolerability. The first is the *mehallel Shabbat befarhesia* as the delinquent heretic who is still loyal to the law and a part of the community, and the second is the individual not bound by a sense of tradition and who believes that change is the way to integrate Judaism and modernity.

Modes of Marginalization

Some of the most significant innovations and contributions of the Hatam Sofer to the issue of intolerable deviance are to be found in his marginalization policies. As was the case with regard to his classification of Reform Judaism as intolerable, here too, his assessment of the meaning and impact of the modern world on Jewish life played a significant role in the radical form and degree of marginalization for which he calls. As stated above, there are four primary forms of intolerable deviants: the apostate; the idolater; the *mehallel Shabbat befarhesia*; and the Reform Jew. While his treatment of the idolater generally follows rabbinic and mediaeval precedent, in his marginalization of the other three, the Hatam Sofer breaks new ground. As a result this analysis will focus on them alone.

The Apostate

For the Hatam Sofer, the apostate was not an ideologue ('the majority of them do not believe in idolatry, but rather are motivated by simple *teiavon*[35]). As a result he classifies them under the category of *mumar* and not *min*. Nevertheless, he subjects these converts to an array of marginalizing sanctions which far exceed those associated with the category of *mumar* in both the rabbinic and mediaeval writings. The primary location of these sanctions is in the sphere of loyalty as manifested in the areas of property and compensation. Thus, if one is in possession of an apostate's property, one can take it or destroy it and one is under no obligation to return it.[36] In general, all obligations that arise towards one who is categorized as being either *ahikha* (kin) or *amitekha* (friend) are suspended. With regard to *amitekha*, the Hatam Sofer follows the reading in BT Tractate Baba Metziah 59a in which this term refers to *am she-itkha be-mitzvot*, (a people that shared with you in the practice of *mitzvot*), and on the basis of this excludes the *mumar*. In his *Responsa*, this provides the basis for the suspension of many of the *mumar*'s rights. For example, the laws of *ona-ah*, which require and regulate fair, honest and non-hurtful conduct and speech in everyday and business settings, do not apply to the *mumar* apostate.[37] Furthermore, one is to distinguish between Israelites who observe the *mitzvot* and the *mumar* in giving preference, priority and first choice to the former when buying or selling items.[38]

Similarly, the Hatam Sofer removes the ban on interest payments and classifies the apostate in this context similarly to a non-Jew. In doing so he does not make any distinction, similar to that found in the *Tur*, between interest payments as they pertain to lending and borrowing.[39] While the *Tur* allowed one to charge interest to the *mumar*, he retained the prohibition on borrowing from him with interest - a reflection of the *Tur*'s core sense that this individual is still a Jew, and one should therefore not facilitate his violation of the law. However, even that minimal sense of loyalty to help protect him from further deviance is removed.

A general lack of concern for the religious welfare of the apostate is manifested in other aspects of the Hatam Sofer's system. Even after death, the apostate is to be further distinguished from Israelites in good standing by segregating his burial plot from theirs. Furthermore, family and friends are not to mourn in accordance with the halakhic customs of mourning.[40]

One of the more severe and significant sanctions imposed against the apostate by the Hatam Sofer is a ban on the marrying of an apostate's children:

> With regards to his daughters, one must also distinguish. The *mumar*, who is assimilated amongst the non-Jews, is to be considered similar to an actual non-Jew.[41]

The exclusion of the possibility of marriage is the ultimate expression of the fact that the community does not want to have anything to do with him or his family. This ban creates an irreparable boundary that over time will also lead to the assimilation of the family into the non-Jewish world. It is important to state that this ban on marriages constitutes a significant legal innovation, applying to the *mumar* a measure of shunning only associated in the rabbinic sources with the *min* as Jewish Christian. Then, as argued above, the shunning is associated with the perception of the *min* as enemy deviant who threatens the faith and fidelity of Israelites in good standing. In applying this ruling to the apostate, the Hatam Sofer gives testimony to this same fear, but with an interesting variation.

> One must take into account the danger involved (in marrying an apostate) and that he will take the children who will be born and raise them in the tradition of false religion ... there is the apprehension that he will turn his children away from God.[42]

The difference between the *min* in the rabbinic sources and the apostate *mumar* involves the scope of the fear. The *min* of the rabbis is an enemy deviant who threatens the wholeness of the community; hence the general ban on all contact. With regard to the apostate *mumar*, the fear of negative influence only pertains to his wife and children. Consequently the ban of the Hatam Sofer does not apply to all contact but only to the realm of marriage where the negative influence of the apostate may be expressed. The fact that the Hatam Sofer did not perceive the apostate as being an ideologue also influences the scope of danger. He is an 'enemy deviant' only to those over whom he has authority, for his apostasy, regardless of its motivation, will shape, and consequently influence, the actual conduct of his family.

The *Mehallel Shabbat Befarhesia*

In the Hatam Sofer's treatment of the *mehallel Shabbat befarhesia* one can again see the way the changing reality of Jewish life in the modern world influenced his position on marginalization. As stated above, the *mehallel Shabbat befarhesia* in this period remained a member of the community and, in general, still felt bound by halakhah. As a result, the Hatam Sofer was willing to accept that the individual in question could be trusted to observe the law. To justify this ruling despite the clear precedent to the contrary,[43] the Hatam Sofer creates a new distinction between one who is a *mumar lekol hatorah* and one who is a *hashud lekol hatorah*, i.e. one who is suspected of violating all the commandments of the Torah.

> The apostates of our time, who assimilate amongst the nations, certainly violate all of the commandments. However, he who

lives amongst Israel, and who follows her practices, *only* being a *mumar* to worship idols or to desecrate the Shabbat, while being a *mumar lekol hatorah*, nevertheless, is not a *hashud lekol hatorah*.[44]

Rabbinic precedent, the Hatam Sofer argues, when using the category of *mumar*, in fact applies only to those who are *hashud lekol hatorah*, such as the apostate. It is they and they alone who are assumed to have completely rejected all aspects of the covenant and its laws. With regard to the *mumar lekol hatorah kullah* there is no such assumption. Consequently, the Hatam Sofer rules that a woman who is merely an idolater or a desecrator of the Shabbat can marry a Cohen (member of the priestly tribe)[45] or continue conjugal relations with her husband,[46] as one assumes that she has not had sex with other men, including non-Jews. However, one who is an apostate, given the fact that there is a presumption that she has violated all of the laws, cannot do so.[47]

Similarly, the Hatam Sofer refrains from imposing the ban on intermarriage on the children of the *mehallel Shabbat befarhesia* and idolater, a ban that, as seen above, he enforced on the apostate and his children.

> With regards to his daughters, one must also distinguish. The *mumar*, who is assimilated amongst the non-Jews, is to be considered similar to an actual non-Jew. However, if he is an Israelite and worships idols (or is a *mehallel Shabbat befarhesia*) it is possible that his children will not follow in his path.[48]

Given the fact that Jewish law may be generally observed in the home of the *mumar lekol hatorah kullah* who is an idolater or *mehallel Shabbat befarhesia*, there is no presumption that the children will necessarily follow in the sinning ways of their father the *mumar*, making a general ban on intermarriage unjustifiable. Furthermore, given the possibility that there is a chance that righteous offspring will ensue from the *mumar lekol hatorah*, for their benefit, the *mehallel Shabbat*'s property must be given the same protection as that of any other Israelite in good standing. In the case of the apostate, on the other hand, where there is no such assumption, the property may be harmed.[49]

The above accommodation towards the *mehallel Shabbat befarhesia*, however, does not influence the severity of the sanctions to which he is subjected. The opposite is the case. In the writing of the Hatam Sofer we witness some of the most severe forms of marginalization levelled against the *mehallel Shabbat*, sanctions that far exceeded those levied against him in both rabbinic and mediaeval writings.

> The punishment of the public desecrator of the Shabbat: It is not in our hands to implement the laws of capital punishment. All we

can do is compel him, with the help of the ministers (of the government) to observe the laws of Israel. If they (the ministers) will not listen, and we cannot compel him, he is to be *segregated* from the community of Israel and judged as one who has left the religion. He is neither an Israelite nor a Christian nor a Muslim. Therefore, it is forbidden for anyone from Israel to eat in his house. His ritual slaughter is forbidden to us, as is stated in the Shulhan Arukh Yoreh Deah 2.5. We do not accept testimony from him, nor do we accept his oath. As a general rule, it is as if his name has been erased from Israel until he returns to God who will have compassion on him ...

It may be concluded from all this that it is forbidden upon anyone who *bears the name of Israel* to open his store or to conduct business from his store or for his business, or to load or unload from his wagon on the Shabbat and holidays. If he does not listen and it is beyond our authority to coerce him to do so with the help of the ministers of the country, he is *separated and distinguished from the community* of Israel and he has no religion at all. He is not trusted as a witness, to give an oath or for any other thing. His ritual slaughter is forbidden and all his food and drinks have a status of being forbidden since he lost his trustworthiness.[50]

From the perspective of both the spheres of ritual and loyalty the *mehallel Shabbat befarhesia* is to be severely marginalized. As customary with respect to a *mumar lekol hatorah*, he is not trusted to participate in any of the ritual functions that require a level of trustworthiness. As a result both his ritual slaughter, and food and wine in his possession, are deemed not kosher. Incidentally, it is worth noting that this statement that 'all his food and drinks have a status of being forbidden', is reminiscent of Tosephta Hullin's shunning of the *min*:

The meat which is slaughtered by the *min* (is regarded as) intended for idolatry, their bread is the bread of Cutheans, their wine is considered as wine used for idolatrous libation, and their fruit is *tevel*.[51]

When adding to the above his more general statements whereby the *mehallel Shabbat befarhesia* is to be 'segregated from the community of Israel',[52] and 'he is separated and distinguished from the community of Israel',[53] the Hatam Sofer is effectively applying to the *mehallel Shabbat befarhesia* the type of segregation associated by the rabbis exclusively with the category of *min*, a move which itself is unprecedented.

This prescription of separation is especially telling in light of the Hatam

Sofer's recognition that the *mehallel Shabbat befarhesia* is not separating himself from the community, but rather remains a loyal member and even partially loyal adherent to Torah and its *mitzvot*. I would suggest that it is precisely this fact that may have served as the catalyst for the Hatam Sofer's innovative ruling. At a time when the *mehallel Shabbat* was perceived as a *poresh min hatzibur*, given his realignment of himself outside the community's shared identity, the *mehallel Shabbat* was not feared, and as a result was not shunned. However, when individuals saw it as possible to simultaneously both belong to the Jewish people and desecrate the Shabbat, and when the battle lines as to what was and was not permissible for Jews on the Shabbat were being waged most fiercely, the impact and influence of the *mehallel Shabbat* on the future practices of the community was seen as decisive. Such an individual was to be feared as never before, leading to a reassessment of the forms of marginalization to which he was to be subjected.

In addition to the above sanctions on the sphere of loyalty, the Hatam Sofer continues Maimonides' policy of also marginalizing the *mehallel Shabbat befarhesia* in the sphere of naming. In his extensive discussion of the status of the *mehallel Shabbat* in Hoshen Mishpat 195, quoted above, the Hatam Sofer specifically refers to the consequence of bearing the name 'Israel'. 'It is forbidden upon anyone who bears the *name* of Israel', and 'as a general rule, it is as if his *name* has been erased from Israel'. The *mehallel Shabbat befarhesia* loses his basic right to bear the name Israel, until, as the Hatam Sofer states, 'he returns to God Who will have compassion on him'.

The Reform Jew

The Reform Jew, as stated above, is classified as a *min*. While the category of *min* generally brings with it the widest and most extensive array of sanctions, it is precisely here that the Hatam Sofer refrains from explicitly instituting formal sanctions.[54] Sanctions against Reform Jews, as the Hatam Sofer surely realized, were politically problematic. Given the fact that Reform Jews were arguing that they were not sinners and were petitioning the authorities for recognition of their authenticity as Jews, a recognition that they often received, sanctions against them were often outside the authority of Jewish courts and remained more of an aspiration than a policy that could be implemented.

Given this political reality, the Hatam Sofer refrains from explicit sanctions, and instead calls for marginalization of the Reform Jews in a more subtle if not surreptitious manner. A case in point is found in one of his *Responsa* where he debates Reform practice and ideology. With regard to rabbis who are willing to change the ruling of a prior court without fulfilling the pre-requisite condition of being greater than them in both number and wisdom, he states:

> If they state thus, then they subject their necks to the burden of the words of the Rambam at the beginning of Chapter Three of Hilkhot Mamrim.[55]

And again, with regard to the removal of the prayers for redemption from the liturgy:

> Maybe these people do not expect and await or do not believe at all the words of the prophets regarding the rebuilding of the temple and the coming of the messiah and all that was said on this issue in the words of the rabbis. If so we return to the words of the Rambam at the beginning of Chapter Three from Mamrim.[56]

The Hatam Sofer does not explicitly indicate the sanction to which such deviants are to be subjected, but rather alludes to 'the beginning of Chapter Three' of Maimonides' Hilkhot Mamrim.[57] As discussed in the previous chapter, Chapter Three of Hilkhot Mamrim states:

> Whoever repudiates the Oral Torah is not the rebellious elder mentioned in the Torah, but rather is one of the *minim*, whom any person has a right to put to death. Once it is made clear that he indeed repudiates the Oral Torah, he is cast into (a pit) and not rescued from it (*moridin ve-lo ma-alin*), similar to the other *minim*, *apikorsim*, those who the say that the Torah is not from heaven, informers and *mumarim*. All of the above are not a part of Israel, and do not require witnesses, prior warning, or judges (before being put to death). Rather anyone who kills one of them has fulfilled a great *mitzvah* and removed a stumbling block.[58]

Continuing this policy of speaking indirectly about sanctions, in what has become his most famous statement regarding Reform Jews he asserts the following:

> If their fate were in our hands, I would be of the opinion to separate them from our midst, to desist from giving our daughters to their sons and their sons to our daughters so as to prevent our being drawn after them. Let their community be like that of Zadok and Boethus, Anan and Saul, they living their lives and we ours. All of this is what I believe should be the law, in theory but not in practice, so long as we do not have the approval and permission of the king, without which may my words be void and inconsequential.[59]

From the perspective of the Hatam Sofer, Reform Jews are enemy deviants who threaten 'our' existence, and there is a need to prevent intermarriage with them so as to protect 'us' from their influence. As such, they are given the same treatment reserved by him for apostates alone. In both cases, he yearns to institute a complete separation of the two groups: 'they living their lives and we ours'.[60] There is, however, a significant difference between the deviance of the apostate and the Reform Jew, one which on the basis of rabbinic precedent ought to have lent greater lenience towards the Reform Jew. The apostate has self-defined himself as an 'outsider', rejecting all of Jewish law as well as his or her association with the community, a fact which makes his process of marginalization descriptive. The Reform Jew at the time of the Hatam Sofer, on the other hand, has made no such move. While rejecting certain aspects of the law and the authority of certain rabbis, he still sees himself as bound by other portions of Jewish law and locates his identity firmly within the Jewish community. In this, he is more similar to the *mehallel Shabbat befarhesia* or even the idolater of the Hatam Sofer's generation. Such consideration, however, is not present in the Hatam Sofer's 'theoretical' sanctions vis-à-vis Reform Jews. Instead he is 'theoretically' willing to locate Reform Jews beyond where they saw themselves, i.e. outside of the community.

Marginalization in the Sphere of Basic Membership

Within the overall discussion of marginalization, the Hatam Sofer's position regarding the status of the intolerable deviant within the sphere of basic membership warrants special attention. On this issue the Hatam Sofer is, at times, unequivocal and at others ambiguous. On the one hand he explicitly rules that all forms of deviance do not affect one's status in the sphere of basic membership. Thus in the case of the apostate, where there might have been most grounds for questioning the individual's status in the sphere of membership, the Hatam Sofer definitively classifies this individual as a Jew, adopting Rashi and the *Tur*'s position of *af al pi shehata yisrael hu.*[61] Similarly he states:

> It seems in my humble opinion, that it is clear that *the apostate is a complete Israelite.*[62]
>
> [A non-Jew cannot serve as an emissary for an apostate] for they are distinguished from each other in the essence and are only equal in the absence [of a shared quality]. [*They are distinguished from each other in the essence in that*] one is an Israelite and the other is not an Israelite, while they are equal only in the absence [of a shared quality] in that both lack the covenant, and the equality

which emanates out of the absence [of a shared quality], is not comparable to the distinction between the inequality in the essence.[63]

Following this position, on one of the key indicators of Jewishness, i.e. the legality of marriages, the Hatam Sofer rules that the *mumar*'s marriages are legally binding.[64] In addition, the Hatam Sofer reaffirms the status of deviants not merely as *ahikha*, but also as a *ben brit*, i.e. participants and members of the covenant of the Jewish people with God.[65] Finally, as seen above, while the *mehallel Shabbat befarhesia* is banned and shunned, and 'it is as if his name has been erased from Israel',[66] nevertheless, if he wants to return, all that is needed is his decision.[67] No reconversion process is necessary, thus reaffirming his status as an insider in the sphere of basic membership.

On the other hand, one also finds in the Hatam Sofer's *Responsa* statements that seem to alter the basic membership status of the intolerable deviant. One example is the above-quoted statement pertaining to the public desecrator of Shabbat whereby the Hatam Sofer asserts that he is neither an Israelite nor a Christian nor a Muslim.[68] While this was interpreted above as pertaining to the sphere of naming, it may also be read as applying to the sphere of membership. When one is considered to be neither an Israelite nor a Christian nor a Muslim, the implication is that there has also been a change in one's membership affiliation.

The most compelling evidence for arguing that intolerable deviance affects the sphere of basic membership for the Hatam Sofer are his statements regarding Reform Jews.

> If their [Reform Jew's] fate were in our hands, I would be of the opinion to separate them from our midst, to desist from giving our daughters to their sons and their sons to our daughters so as to prevent our being drawn after them.[69]

Membership in its most basic sense both implies and entails a minimal sense of loyalty, a minimal level of care on the part of the community to which one belongs. The meaning of the saying '*af al pi she-hata yisrael hu*' is that sin, while generating sanctions, does not sever the basic connection between the sinner and membership in the community. When the Hatam Sofer aspires to the ultimate removal of Reform Jews and their becoming separate and distinct from the community of Israel, he is thus violating their core rights under the sphere of basic membership. The fact that political realities prevented him from implementing this wish does not mitigate the conceptual significance of his statements. Even though he subscribes to the belief that '*af al pi she-hata yisrael hu*', there are members of *yisrael* whom the Hatam Sofer is apparently willing to banish. If they truly maintained their status in the sphere of basic membership, there would be no grounds for the hope for their assimilation amongst the non-Jewish nations. For the Hatam Sofer there are certain sins that, in theory, cancel or override the principle of *af al pi she-hata yisrael hu*. All that is needed is a different political environment in which the theory can become a reality.

Not all contradictions can and need to be resolved, and it is possible that the two positions outlined above are indicative of ambivalence on the part of the Hatam Sofer as to certain deviants' status in the sphere of membership. We have seen a similar inconsistency in the writing of Maimonides, who both argues that the intolerable deviant maintains his status as a member, as evidenced in the fact that his marriages are binding, but nevertheless still institutes marginalization in other areas pertaining to this sphere. In the case of the Hatam Sofer, however, the above duality may be two sides of an innovative and more complex position whereby certain deviants, while not losing their status in the sphere of basic membership, nevertheless, have their status temporarily suspended. While sin cannot transform an Israelite into a non-Israelite, for *af al pi she-hata yisrael hu*, it can move one into an uncertain state wherein one's membership status is ambiguous and not resolved. Evidence of this may be found in the Hatam Sofer's statement regarding the *mehallel Shabbat befarhesia*: 'He is neither an Israelite nor a Christian nor a Muslim.'[70] It is not that the *mehallel Shabbat* ceases to be Israel. He has no identity at all. It is as if the Hatam Sofer is placing him in a marginal state wherein he is neither considered member nor a non-member, neither Israelite nor heathen. His membership has not been cancelled, for then returning would require a conversion. His status, however, has been put on hold, and remains contingent on his return and repentance.

Descriptive vs. Prescriptive Marginalization

One of the more important facets of the Hatam Sofer's treatment of deviants pertains to the parameters of instituting intolerable deviance status. In the rabbinic and mediaeval writings previously analysed, intolerable status generally confirms the previous social status that the deviant has already shaped for himself, i.e. it is generally descriptive. This is the case in particular when it comes to deviance contained under the category of *meshumad/ mumar*. As to the *min* as enemy deviant in Rabbinic sources, or as to the *min* as heretic in Maimonides, in particular in areas which may result in idolatry, there is evidence of a willingness to institute intolerable status in these cases in a way that imposes a new social status not necessarily aligned with the deviant's self-understanding. Nevertheless, prescriptive use of marginalization is the exception to the rule, with the core marginalization of intolerable deviants being descriptive; that is, the imposed status conforms to the opinion that the deviant already has of himself.

What characterizes the boundary policy of the Hatam Sofer is not that prescriptive marginalization is used for the first time, but rather that the rule and its exception have reversed roles: prescriptive marginalization now becomes the rule, and descriptive marginalization the exception. Amongst the four primary forms of deviance marginalized by the Hatam Sofer, i.e. the apostate, the *mehallel Shabbat befarhesia*, the idolater (the Jew who participates in Christian worship), and the Reform Jew, only the apostate clearly removes himself from the Jewish community and its legal system. The idolater, *mehallel Shabbat befarhesia* and Reform Jew still maintain both their communal identity and adherence to the majority of the legal system. However, in these cases, this fact does not lead to a classification as tolerable; instead it engenders prescriptive marginalization of unprecedented severity.

At the same time, as prescriptive marginalization becomes predominant, the Hatam Sofer still allows for some measure of the deviant's self-perception to play a role in determining both the *extent* and *areas* of marginalization. Thus, while prescribing for the *mehallel Shabbat* and the idolater severe sanctions in the sphere of loyalty, where the sanctions are contingent on a factual assessment of the scope of the deviance in question, such as whether Jewish law is in fact observed in the home (affecting, for example, issues of intermarriage with the deviant's children and their inheritance rights), the Hatam Sofer rules in a descriptive manner. Here he takes into account the changing reality of the relationship of the *mehallel Shabbat* and idolater with the community and Jewish law, and he does not classify them in accordance with similar deviants in previous eras. This accommodation, however, is not afforded to Reform Jews. While still viewing themselves as insiders and bound by Jewish law, often to a greater extent than the other deviants, they are nevertheless prescriptively marginalized in the spheres of loyalty, ritual, and possibly basic membership as well.

The prescriptive marginalization of Reform Jews, however, involves a number of particular factors that distinguish it from the other intolerable deviants. The first, which is time-specific, pertains to their functioning at the beginning and middle of the nineteenth century as enemy deviants of the Hatam Sofer and the community he represented. As stated above, Orthodox and Reform Jews both competed for the exclusive right to regulate the collective life and institutions of the Jewish community. As a result, prescriptive marginalization in this case may follow the rabbinic precedent with regard to Jewish Christians. The Hatam Sofer's stated hope for the separation of Reform Jews from 'us', is evidence of this parallelism, as he in essence aspires for them to follow the path of Jewish Christians outside of both normative Judaism and ultimately the Jewish community.

The second factor distinguishing the intolerable deviant emanates out of the modern environment wherein one common collective Jewish identity is superseded by individual denominational affiliations. This is especially acute in the period when the various denominations are first being formed, attempting to define their identity and borders, and more significantly, fighting over the right to be the exclusive representative of the community. In this reality, it is not that the opposing sides are merely enemy deviants, but much worse. They are outsiders to each other. In this context, while Reform Jews still see themselves as Jewish insiders, from the Hatam Sofer's perspective, they have chosen to leave his denomination and collective affiliation. As such, his decision to marginalize them within his communal setting maintains, from his perspective, a distinct descriptive quality.

The interesting question, which will be explored in the next chapter, pertains to the period that begins a century later, when the various denominations in fact lived side by side within the same community. Will the same prescriptive/descriptive use of marginalization continue once the initial denominational battles are over, the lines between them set, and the need to battle for exclusive communal representation removed? And if they do, then one can no longer say that it is still somehow following precedent, but rather is in fact creating a new rule for implementing marginalization.

Notes

1 For a more detailed analysis of this period, see J. Katz, *Out of the Ghetto* (Cambridge, 1973); *ha-Halakhah be-Meitzar* (Jerusalem, 1992); *A House Divided: Orthodoxy and Schism in Nineteenth-Century Central European Jewry* (Hanover, 1988); *Tradition and Crisis* (New York, 1993), pp. 214–36; *Jewish Emancipation and Self Emancipation*, pp. 3–19; and 'Orthodoxy in Historical Perspectives', in P. Medding (ed.), *Studies in Contemporary Judaism* II, (Bloomington, 1986), pp. 3–17; Y. Greenwald, *Sefer Mekorot ha-Torah ve-ha-Emunah be-Hungariah* (Budapest, 1921), pp. 21–56; M. Samet, 'Halahkah ve-Reformah' (Doctoral Thesis, Hebrew University, 1967), and 'The Beginning of Orthodoxy', *Modern Judaism* 8, 3 (1988) 249–69; D. Ellenson, *Tradition in Transition: Orthodoxy, Halakha and the Boundaries of Modern Jewish Identity* (Lanham 1989) pp. 161–84; P. Mendes-Flohr and J. Reinharz, *The Jew in the Modern World* (New York, 1980), pp. 101–81; M. Meyer, *Response to Modernity* (New York, 1988), pp. 10–61; *Jewish Identity in the Modern World* (Seattle, 1990), pp. 3–32; *The Origins of the Modern Jew* (Detroit, 1967); M. Silber, 'Shorshei ha-Pilug be-Yahadut Hungariah' (Doctoral Thesis, Hebrew University, 1985); D. Philipson, *The Reform Movement in Judaism* (New York, 1907), pp. 3–56; J. Bleich, 'Rabbinic Responses to Nonobservance in the

Modern Era' in J. Schachter (ed.), *Jewish Tradition and the Non-Traditional Jew* (Northvale, 1992), pp. 37–115. See also M. Meyer, 'Where Does the Modern Period of Jewish History Begin?', *Judaism* 24, 3 (1975), 329–38, who discusses the question of when to locate the turning point of modernity; as well as A. Shohet, *Im Hillufei Tekufot* (Jerusalem, 1960), who identifies the transformation as already occurring from the beginning to the middle of the eighteenth century.

2 D. Ellenson, 'German Jewish Orthodoxy: Tradition in the Context of Culture', in J. Wertheimer (ed.), *The Uses of Tradition* (New York, 1992), pp. 5–22.

3 For the birth and history of the Reform Movement, see M. Meyer, *Response to Modernity* (New York, 1988); D. Rudavsky, *Modern Jewish Religious Movements: A History of Emancipation and Adjustment* (New York, 1972), pp. 156–85; W. G. Plaut, *The Rise of Reform Judaism – A Sourcebook of its European Origins* (New York, 1963).

4 See M. Meyer, *Response to Modernity*, pp. 62–99. For a background on the early debates between Reform and Traditionalist as well as the primary contributors, see Eliezer Liebermann, *Nogah ha-Tzedek* (Dessau, 1818); *Or Nogah* (Dessau, 1818); *Eleh Divrei ha-Brit* (Altona, 1819), (commissioned by the Hamburg Rabbinic Court); 'Chorin, Aaron', *Encyclopedia Judaica* (Jerusalem, 1975), Vol. 5, p. 495; Greenwald, Y., *Sefer Mekorot ha-Torah ve-ha-Emunah be-Hungariah* (Budapest, 1921), pp. 41–4; J. Katz, *ha-Halakhah be-Meitzar* (Jerusalem, 1992), pp. 43–72; M. Samet, 'Halahkah ve-Reformah' (Doctoral Thesis, Hebrew University, 1967), pp. 188–203; 'Hashinuim Bessidrei Beit Haknesset', *Asufot* 5 (Jerusalem, 1991), 345–404; D. Philipson, *The Reform Movement in Judaism* (New York, 1907, pp. 41–56; P. Mendes-Flohr and J. Reinharz, *The Jew in the Modern World* (New York, 1980), pp. 140–85; A. Guttman, *The Struggle over Reform in Rabbinic Literature*, (New York, 1977), pp. 5–47; M. Meyer, *Response to Modernity*, pp. 50–1, 53–61; J. Bleich, 'Rabbinic Responses to Nonobservance in the Modern Era', in J. Schachter (ed.), *Jewish Tradition and the Non-Traditional Jew* (Northvale, 1992), pp. 40–53; J. J. Petuchowski, *Prayerbook Reform in Europe* (New York, 1968), pp. 49–58.

5 For the use of the category of *mumar* to refer to the apostate in the writing of the Hatam Sofer, *Responsa Hatam Sofer*, Yoreh Deah 253, 342; Even ha-Ezer 1.3, 1.21, 1.22, 1.43, 1.104, 2.24, 2.38, 2.60, 2.73, 2.74, 2.88, 2.89, 2.99, 2.174; Hoshen Mishpat 134,154; Likutei She-eilot ve-Teshuvot 56, 83 and Kovetz Teshuvot 21. For his use of the *mumar* to refer to the *mehallel Shabbat*, see, Hatam Sofer, Orekh Haim 99; Yoreh Deah 120; Even ha-Ezer 1.22, 1.93, 2.1; Likutei She-eilot ve-Teshuvot 39,56 and 83. See especially J. Katz, *A House Divided*.

6 For the apostate as *mumar*, see *Responsa Hatam Sofer*, Yoreh Deah 253, 342; Even ha-Ezer 1.3, 1.21, 1.22, 1.43, 1.104, 2.24, 2.38, 2.60, 2.73, 2.74, 2.88, 2.89, 2.99, 2.174; Hoshen Mishpat 134, 154; Likutei She-eilot ve-Teshuvot 56, 83; and Kovetz Teshuvot 21. For the *mehallel Shabbat* as *mumar*, see *Responsa Hatam Sofer*, Orekh Haim 99; Yoreh Deah 120; Even ha-Ezer 1.22, 1.93, 2.1; Likutei She-eilot ve-Teshuvot 39, 56 and 83.

7 *Responsa Hatam Sofer*, Hoshen Mishpat 162; Likutei She-eilot ve-Teshuvot 84, 86, 89, 94.

8 *Responsa Hatam Sofer*, Orekh Haim 81; Yoreh Deah 162; Likutei She-eilot ve-Teshuvot 61, 81, 84, 89. See also Yoreh Deah 322, where the *apikorus* is linked to the *min* and used to denote a general heretic.

9 For the idolater as *mumar*, see *Responsa Hatam Sofer*, Orekh Haim 208; Yoreh Deah 1, 341; Even ha-Ezer 1.21, 1.22, 1.93; Likutei She-eilot ve-Teshuvot 56, 83; Kovetz Teshuvot 21. For the idolater as *min* see *Responsa Hatam Sofer*, Yoreh Deah 322; Even ha-Ezer 2.60; Kovetz Teshuvot 68.

10 See for example *Responsa Hatam Sofer*, Even ha-Ezer 2.60.

11 With the exception of *Responsa Hatam Sofer*, Even ha-Ezer 2.115, where he states that the *mumar* to eat *neveilot lehakis* is disqualified from serving as a witness and Kovetz Teshuvot 9, where he states that the *mumar's terumah* is not valid.

12 *Responsa Hatam Sofer*, Even ha-Ezer 1.21. Emphasis mine.

13 *Responsa Hatam Sofer*, Oreh Haim 99.

14 *Responsa Hatam Sofer*, Likutei She-eilot ve-Teshuvot 83. See Rashi, BT Tractate Hullin 5a.

15 See M. Silber, 'Shorshei ha-Pilug be-Yahadut Hungariah' (Doctoral Thesis, Hebrew University, 1985), pp. 18–48, 83–92. See also *Responsa Hatam Sofer*, Hashmatot 195, where even in 1829 he bears witness to the fact that in the community of Pressburg the public desecration of the Shabbat was not to be found.

16 *Responsa Hatam Sofer*, Likutei She-eilot ve-Teshuvot 83. My emphasis. See also *Responsa Hatam Sofer*, Even ha-Ezer, 1.21, 1.22.

17 *Responsa Hatam Sofer*, Likutei She-eilot ve-Teshuvot 56. Emphasis mine.

18 See A. Ferziger, 'Hierarchical Judaism in Formation: the Development of Central European Orthodoxy's Approach to Non-Observant Jews (1700–1918)' (Doctoral Thesis, Bar Ilan University, 2001), pp. 193–8, who argues that this latter feature is indicative of the Hatam Sofer's lenient approach towards the *mehallel Shabbat*. This is due, according to Ferziger, to their being merely non-observant Jews and not apostates or deviants who adopted ideological positions that endanger Judaism's elementary principles, such as the Reform Jew. The problem with this theory is that it fails to properly assess the severe and innovative nature of the marginalization of the *mehallel Shabbat* on the part of the Hatam Sofer. Second, nowhere does the Hatam Sofer negate the ideological nature of the deviance of the *mehallel Shabbat befarhesia*. Quite to the contrary, he calls him a *kofer*, and *kofer bekol hatorah* (Oreh Haim 99), and adopts Rashi's position in BT Tractate Hullin 5a in which the *mehallel Shabbat befarhesia* is considered a *mumar lekol hatorah kullah* by virtue of his being a *kofer* in the act of creation (Likutei She-eilot ve-Teshuvot 83). Third, the Hatam Sofer treats the *mehallel Shabbat* as he does the idolater, as deviants who clearly adopt heresies which endanger Judaism's elementary positions. Fourth, according to the Hatam Sofer, it is precisely the apostate who is a non-ideologue. For the position Ferziger ascribes to the Hatam Sofer, one has to look to R. Moshe Feinstein, whose position is analysed below.

19 See D. Ellenson, *Traditional Reactions to Modern Jewish Reform: The Paradigm of*

German Orthodoxy, pp. 733, 735, 737. See also M. Samet, *ha-Shinuim be-Sidrei Beit ha-Knesset: Emdat ha-Rabbanim Keneged ha-Mihadshim ha-Reformim*, p. 392.

20 *Responsa Hatam Sofer*, Orekh Haim 28; Hoshen Mishpat 192, 193; Likutei She-eilot ve-Teshuvot 84, 85, 86, 89, 90, 94, 95, 96. For the background and sources of this debate and of its major protagonist see E. Liebermann, *Nogah ha-Tzedek* and *Or Nogah, Eleh Divrei ha-Brit*; D. Philipson, *The Reform Movement in Judaism*, pp. 41–56; Y. Greenwald, *Sefer Mekorot ha-Torah ve-ha-Emunah be-Hungariah*, pp. 41–4; J. Katz, "Pulmus ha-'Heikhal" be-Hamburg ve-Aseifat Beranshvieg – Avnei derekh be-Hit-havut ha-Ortodoxia' in J. Katz, *ha-Halakha be-Meitzar* (Jerusalem, 1992), pp. 43–72; M. Samet, 'Halakha ve-Reforma', pp. 188–203 and 'ha-Shinuim be-Sidrei Beit ha-Knesset: Emdat ha-Rabbanim Keneged ha-Mihadshim ha-Reformim', pp. 341–404; A. Guttman, *The Struggle over Reform in Rabbinic Literature*, pp. 5–47; P. Mendes-Flohr and J. Reinharz, *The Jew in the Modern World*, pp. 145–81; M. Meyer, *Response to Modernity*, pp. 50–1, 53–61; 'Chorin, Aaron' *Encyclopedia Judaica*; J. J. Petuchowski, *Prayerbook Reform in Europe*, pp. 49–58; J. Bleich, 'Rabbinic Responses to Nonobservance in the Modern Era', pp. 40–53.

21 J. Katz, "Pulmus ha-'Heikhal" be-Hamburg ve-Aseifat Beranshvieg – Avnei derekh be-Hit-havut ha-Ortodoxia', p. 52, argues that the Hatam Sofer could find a plausible reason for rejecting Reform practice in their removal of the prayers from the liturgy which refer to the Messiah and redemption, for the belief in the Messiah was one of the *ikarei emunah*. However, the Hatam Sofer, *Responsa Hatam Sofer* Yoreh Deah 356 specifically states that the belief in redemption is not one of the *ikarei hadat* and that one can envision a Judaism without it. Rejecting it, however, involves being a *kofer be-ikar shel ha-amanat ha-Torah ve-hanevi'im*, for the Torah, Prophets, and the majority of the rabbis all speak of it. This, however, is a heresy of a different kind, a heresy which is not unique to the issue of redemption but rather, as we will see, pertains to the Reform enterprise as a whole, as understood by the Hatam Sofer.

22 See Mishnah Sotah 7.1; Maimonides, Peirush Hamishnayot Sotah 7.1 and Teshuvot ha-Rambam 254; *Tur*, Orekh Haim 101; *Shulhan Arukh*, Orekh Haim 101.4. See J. Katz, "Pulmus ha-'Heikhal" be-Hamburg ve-Aseifat Beranshvieg – Avnei derekh be-Hit-havut ha-Ortodoxia', p. 51.

23 See Song 2.15, 'Catch us the foxes, the little foxes that ruin the vineyard'.

24 *Responsa Hatam Sofer*, Likutei She-eilot ve-Teshuvot 84.

25 *Responsa Hatam Sofer*, Hoshen Mishpat 192.

26 *Responsa Hatam Sofer*, Likutei She-eilot ve-Teshuvot 84.

27 *Ibid.*

28 *Ibid.* See as well, *Responsa Hatam Sofer*, Orekh Haim 28.

29 *Ibid.*

30 *Responsa Hatam Sofer*, Likutei She-eilot ve-Teshuvot 85.

31 *Ibid.*, 86. See also *ibid.*, 89.

32 *Ibid.*, 86.

33 *Responsa Hatam Sofer*, Orekh Haim 28, 148, 181; Yoreh Deah 19; Even ha-Ezer 1.69, 1.130, 2.29; Kovetz Teshuvot 58. See M. Samet, 'ha-Shinuim be-Sideri

Beit ha-Knesset: Emdat ha-Rabanim Keneged ha-'Mehadhsim' ha-Reformim', p. 401 n. 305.

34 Quoted in P. Mendes-Flohr and J. Reinharz, *The Jew in the Modern World*, p. 156.

35 Teshuvot Hatam Sofer, Yoreh Deah 341.
See also *Responsa Hatam Sofer*, Even ha-Ezer 2.60 and Likutei She-eilot ve-Teshuvot 56. As such they resemble Maimonides' category of *mumar lekol hatorah kullah* in Hilkhot Teshuvah 3.9.

36 *Responsa Hatam Sofer*, Hoshen Mishpat 154. The only question is whether there is a chance that he will produce righteous offspring to whom we have obligations. Harming his property has an adverse effect on them. In the case of the convert, however, the Hatam Sofer assumes that they will follow in the ways of their father. As will be seen below, this consideration also impacts on the question of marrying a *mumar*'s children.

37 For the scope of the issues covered under the law of *ona-ah*, see the *Tur* and the *Shulhan Arukh*, Hoshen Mishpat 227 and 228.

38 *Responsa Hatam Sofer*, Hoshen Mishpat 134. See *Sifra*, Bahar, Parshah 3 and Rashi, Leviticus 25.14.

39 *Responsa Hatam Sofer*, Hoshen Mishpat 134. See also *Responsa Hatam Sofer*, Even ha-Ezer 93, where in his explanation of the debate between the Mordechai and Rabbi Mordechai from Rotenberg he states that in every case where *ah* is mentioned with regard to *mitzvoth*, the *mitzvah* only applies to *ahikah be-mitzvot*. See also, *Responsa Hatam Sofer*, Likutei She-eilot ve-Teshuvot 67, where only the *mumar leteiavon* is included under the category of *ahikha be-mitzvot* and thus cannot be lent money with interest. By implication the *mumar* who is not a *mumar leteiavon* can be charged interest.

40 *Responsa Hatam Sofer*, Yoreh Deah 341. See also *ibid.*, 326, where the father is allowed to mourn because he did not merit raising a child to the worship of God.

41 *Responsa Hatam Sofer*, Likutei She-eilot ve-Teshuvot 83. It is interesting to note that for the Hatam Sofer, this ban should not only affect marriages with the apostate's children, but in theory ought to affect marriages with the apostate himself, requiring, for example, the cessation of any marriage between an Israelite in good standing and an apostate. Here, however, the Hatam Sofer's refusal to innovate and change traditional precedent makes him distinguish between theory and practice. With regard to existing marriages, the Hatam Sofer admits to the compelling nature of the argument to obligate a divorce in the case of the *mumar* apostate.
'The truth is that logically I would say that with regard to a *mumar* about whom one must take into account the danger involved, and that he will take the children who will be born and raise them in the tradition of false religion and erroneous shelter, it is forbidden for her to have sexual relations with him. Consequently she cannot fulfil the requirement of *onah*. Under these conditions, he is to be compelled to release here, even more than if he refuses to fulfil his conjugal duties. Furthermore, the *poskim* (who rejected the position that the *mumar* be coerced to divorce his wife) did not refer to a *mumar* with regard to whom there is the apprehension that he will cause his children to deviate away

from God'. (*Responsa Hatam Sofer* Even ha-Ezer 2.60.)

Nevertheless the Hatam Sofer, refuses to obligate coerced divorces in these cases.

'I am not inclined to be lenient and coerce the *mumar* to divorce' (*ibid.*). What stayed his legislative hand was the question of the legality of coerced divorces and the precedent disallowing coercing *mumarim* to divorce. (See Beit Yoseph, *Tur*, Even ha-Ezer 134.) Despite his recognition that the halakhic authorities, suspicious of the validity of forced divorces, 'were not speaking of a *mumar*, in which case there is the concern that he may turn his children away from God' (*Responsa Hatam Sofer*, Even ha-Ezer 2.60), the Hatam Sofer was not prepared to be the one to innovate on this matter, and instead hoped to bring about a divorce by getting the authorities to obligate the husband to support his wife, an obligation which would influence him to give her a *get* (*Responsa Hatam Sofer*, Even ha-Ezer 2.60).

In a similar vein, in *ibid.*, 2.73, regarding the laws of *yibum*, the Hatam Sofer argues for the legitimacy of the claim that a *yabam* who is a *mumar* does not have to give the widow a *halitzah* on the grounds that, given the fact that he will influence her and her children, both she and her former husband would not have married in the first place, thus annulling the first marriage and consequently removing the need for *yibum*. Here too, however, at the end the Hatam Sofer refrains from making the innovative ruling and states: 'It is not in our hands to release (the women to marry). Let someone whose knowledge is broader than ours open the gate to free her from her shackles. We, however, cannot.' See also *ibid.*, 2.88.

42 *Ibid.*, Even ha-Ezer 2.60.
43 See for example BT Tractate Hullin 5a.
44 *Responsa Hatam Sofer*, Likutei She-eilot ve-Teshuvot 83. My emphasis. See also *Responsa Hatam Sofer*, Even ha-Ezer 1.21, 1.22.
45 *Ibid.*, 1.22.
46 *Ibid.*, 2.1.
47 See *ibid.*, 1.21.
48 *Responsa Hatam Sofer*, Likutei She-eilot ve-Teshuvot 83.
49 *Responsa Hatam Sofer*, Hoshen Mishpat 154.
50 195, my emphasis. See also *Responsa Hatam Sofer*, Orekh Haim 99, where the Hatam Sofer states: '(The observance of the Shabbat) is for us one of the central commandments and one who does not abide by its laws is a *kofer* and a *mumar* in all the Torah ... and his treatment is to be as that of a *kofer* in all the Torah and like one who exited the religion of Israel.'

See also *Responsa Hatam Sofer*, Yoreh Deah 120, where the public desecrator of the Shabbat's wine is deemed *yein nesekh*, and Hoshen Mishpat 99, quoted above, where he or she is defined as being a *mumar lekol hatorah kullah*.
51 Tosefta Hullin 2.20.
52 See *Responsa Hatam Sofer*, Orekh Haim 99.
53 *Responsa Hatam Sofer*, Hoshen Mishpat 195.
54 One exception to the Hatam Sofer's general rule of not sanctioning Reform Jews

is his ruling with regard to the treatment of the collection of *Responsa* entitled *Nogah Tzedek*, which promulgates and outlines Reform practice and ideology. The Hatam Sofer classifies it as *sifrei minut* and following the Talmud both prohibits bringing it into one's house and obligates that it be burnt. See *Responsa Hatam Sofer*, Likutei She-eilot ve-Teshuvot 94.

55 *Ibid.*, Likutei She-eilot ve-Teshuvot 84.

56 *Ibid.*

57 The historian Jacob Katz argues that the mere indirect reference to Maimonides indicates that the Hatam Sofer is not calling for the implementation of the sanction. But if this were the case, why make any reference to Hilkhot Mamrim in the first place? And why would he then go into such detail, as will be seen below, about the type of sanctions he would institute were it politically feasible? See J. Katz, *ha-Halakhah be-Meitzar*, p. 45.

58 Maimonides, Hilkhot Mamrim 3.1. It is important to notice that the deviance mentioned by Maimonides in Hilkhot Mamrim pertains to one who rejects the authority of the Oral Law in total, i.e. the Karaite. It does not apply to one who refuses to accept a specific ruling of the rabbis, like the rebellious elder specifically mentioned by Maimonides, or, for that matter, Reform Jews either.

59 *Responsa Hatam Sofer*, Likutei She-eilot ve-Teshuvot 89. See also *ibid.*, 86, where the Hatam Sofer states that the fate of Jews who incline towards Reform practice 'are not our responsibility'. Compare too the status of Reform Jews with that of the followers of Shabbtai Zvi, whom the Hatam Sofer also categorized as *minim*.

'The cursed sect, the believers in Shabbtai Zvi, may his name be erased, may they die and their bones be crushed if heaven forbid they do not turn their hearts to good. May they be persecuted with their sons and daughters, for they are all cursed by God. *Minut* is embedded in their hearts and there is no idolatry in the world that they have not incorporated amongst their false beliefs. It would be better, and would be considered as a great *mitzvah*, if they would separate from the Diaspora community and assimilate amongst the idolatrous nations, they and their sons. Yet, while still amongst the Jews, their bread is considered the bread of Cutheans and their wine *yein nesekh*.' (*Responsa Hatam Sofer*, Yoreh Deah 322.)

60 This statement by the Hatam Sofer became over the years the founding text for the position which favoured a complete break between Orthodox and Reform Jewry, in particular after the Hungarian Jewish Congress of 1868–9 and the permission granted in 1876 to German Jewry to establish two distinct national organisations. Thus, for example, Rabbi Moshe Schick (Maharam Schick; 1807–79), the leading disciple of the Hatam Sofer, rules in his *Responsa*, Oreh Haim 305, as follows:

'Even though the power and authority of the Torah scholar derive from the king, I see no reason to refrain from making the truth known regarding the law that applies to these people. According to our Holy Torah, since they have denied the heavenly ordained Torah, as many of their utterances and heretical literature will testify, they are therefore not Jews, and are as complete Gentiles ... And not only are they not trustworthy regarding any matters of ritual law, and other legal and religious matters pertaining to the Holy Torah, they are certainly not trustworthy to be teachers and rabbis ... and they are disqualified to serve as witnesses and count in a *minyan*, and in any case their divorces and marriages are void, and as Maimonides writes in Hilkhot Edut Ch. 11, and therefore because they are utter Gentiles, they are forbidden to us, as are their daughters and their sons ...

Furthermore, these *apikorsim* have removed themselves from the religious collective and come together as a sect unto themselves, and in their arrogance also decided in matters of *halitzah* and divorce to replace good with bad. Therefore, their progeny may be of *mamzer* status, and we shall not mingle with them, even if they should return from their ways and take on the true faith.'

Likewise, in *Responsa* 306, the Maharam Schick inveighs against Seligman Baer Bamberger, who ruled that if the Reform Jews would pledge that it was not their desire to separate themselves, and that they agreed to conduct community matters according to the Torah, then it would be permissible to remain united with them:

'And in truth, I did not know what came over the great Torah scholar, may his light shine, because in my opinion, it is simple and clear that we are forbidden by the Torah and the writings and the words of our Sages and convention and also from experience ... And it is written in the Torat Kohanim "if you separate from the other peoples, you will be unto me, and if not ..." Now, even though this text referred to the (non-Jewish) nations, certainly those who desecrate the Sabbath in public and deny the Lord's commandments from the Torah, which our Sages of blessed memory said are like utter Gentiles, are also included under this ruling. We are therefore cautioned by the Torah to remain separate from them by reason of *a fortiori* since while one is permitted to accept sacrifices, vows and voluntary offerings from heathen, it is prohibited to accept them from *mumarim*. And we have said that in so doing one might lead to their *teshuvah*, which is why it was made permissible to accept sacrifices from the transgressors, that they might repent, but from a *mumar* and a desecrator of the Sabbath in public and *apikorsim* one must not accept them. And it is written, "Do not come near the doorway of her house" (Prov. 5.8), which refers to *minut* and *apikorsut*, since "*minut* is distinguished in that it is alluring ... And experience and that which is generally accepted teaches us on the basis of that which is already well known, that one who associates with them, even if the adults do not become corrupted, the future generations become corrupt like them ... do not be inclined to listen to them so as not to let "the staff of the evil rest on the portion of the righteous" (Ps. 125.3). Furthermore, I received instructions from the great rabbi, the Hatam Sofer of blessed memory, to distance ourselves from them as much as possible and that we should refrain from joining them in any common association.'

Rabbi Samson Rafael Hirsch (1808–88) in his *Responsa* Shemesh Marpe 10.46, in his dispute with R. Bamberger, rules similarly:

'That which the Hatam Sofer wrote, "without permission and divine authority" is already outdated, due to the issuing of *hok haprisha* of 5 Av 1876. The aforementioned ruling, issued as a theoretical guidance by our rabbi, the

Hatam Sofer, has now become practice. And based on this ruling, together with a similar ruling issued a short time ago in Vienna by Rabbi Zalman Spitzer, the head of the Bet Din in Vienna and signed by 389 rabbis from three countries, his honour among them – I reiterate my ruling of 18 Shvat 1877. At the end I "commented": Every God-fearing Jew has only one way to keep clean of the prohibition, and that is "to separate from the community" (of Frankfurt-am-Main) according to the *hok haprisha* of 5 Av 1876, and anyone who tempts his God-fearing brethren to do otherwise is misled and misleading.'

Hirsch indeed makes an interesting distinction that appears neither in the writings of the Hatam Sofer nor in those of the Maharam Schick, in distinguishing between separating from the Reform community, and separating from Reform individuals:

'Indeed I did not prohibit associating with individual Reform [Jews] who cast off the yoke of Torah, but rather I prohibited joining together with the Reform community.' (*ibid.*)

Moreover, he emphasizes that separation does not include ordinary business and daily contact with Reform Jews. As a basis for this position, Hirsch invokes Maimonides' view in Hilkhot Mamrim of *tinok shenishbah* – a legal category which applies only to deviants as individuals.

'The Reform Jews of today are already the second and third generation of those who instigated this betrayal and made it widespread, and to them applies Maimonides' view of the *apikorus* and the Karaites of his generation, in Hilkhot Mamrim Ch. 3, 5.3. And just as we have a responsibility not to push them away but rather to draw them in with words in order to restore them to goodness by our exemplary behaviour, and by showing them the light of the Torah, so are we obligated to distance ourselves completely from their methods and institutions and the *apikorsut* and *minut* in which they were raised.'

The position of the Hatam Sofer on the matter of the obligatory disassociation between Orthodox and Reform, the Orthodox position that developed in response to this position, and the dispute between Hirsch, the Maharam Schick and Bamberger, have been topics of extensive study. See J. Katz, *A House Divided*; D. Ellenson, 'For the Heretics Have Arisen: Maharam Schick and the 1876 Controversy over Orthodox Secession from the General Jewish Community in Germany', in his *Between Tradition and Culture: The Dialectics of Modern Religion and Identity* (Atlanta, 1994), pp. 41–58, and 'Germany Jewish Orthodoxy: Tradition in the Context of Culture', in J. Wartheimer (ed.), *The Uses of Tradition* (New York, 1992), pp. 7–11; M. Silber, 'The Emergence of Ultra-Orthodoxy: the Invention of a Tradition', in J. Wartheimer (ed.), *The Uses of Tradition*; A. Ferziger, *Exclusion and Hierarchy: Orthodoxy, Nonobservance and the Emergence of Modern Jewish Identity* (Philadelphia, 2005), pp. 90–185; L. Trepp, 'The Controversy between Samson Raphael Hirsch and Seligman Bar Bamberger and its Significance' in S. F. Chyet and D. H. Ellenson (eds), *Bits of Honey* (Atlanta, 1993), pp. 289–310.

61 *Responsa Hatam Sofer*, Even ha-Ezer 1.131 and 2.60. See also *ibid.*, Even ha-Ezer 1.93.

62 *Responsa Hatam Sofer*, Hoshen Mishpat 134. Emphasis mine.

63 *Responsa Hatam Sofer*, Orekh Haim 116. Emphasis mine.

64 *Responsa Hatam Sofer*, Even ha-Ezer 1.93.

65 See *Responsa Hatam Sofer*, Yoreh Deah 1 and Hoshen Mishpat 134, where he distinguishes between two forms of covenants, *brit torah* and *brit basar*, the covenant of Jewish law and the covenant of circumcision. Despite the fact that due to his deviance, one may classify the *mumar* as not being a *ben brit*, the Hatam Sofer argues that this only pertains to the *brit torah*. There is a different sense of *brit*, that which pertains to *brit basar*. In this latter covenant the status of the *mumar* is like the rest of Israel.

66 *Responsa Hatam Sofer*, Hoshen Misphat 195.

67 *Ibid.*

68 *Ibid.* See also *Responsa Hatam Sofer*, Orekh Haim 99, where the Hatam Sofer states, '(The observance of the Shabbat) is for us one of the central commandments and one who does not abide by its laws is a *kofer* and a *mumar* in all the Torah ... and his treatment is to be as that of a *kofer* in all the Torah and like one who exited the religion of Israel.'

69 *Responsa Hatam Sofer*, Likutei She-eliot ve-Teshuvot 89.

70 *Responsa Hatam Sofer*, Hoshen Mishpat 195.

CHAPTER FIVE

Moshe Feinstein and the Boundaries
of Orthodoxy

The North American milieu in the mid-twentieth century, within which
Moshe Feinstein developed his halakhic writing, was in many ways
unprecedented, and certainly very unlike that of the Hatam Sofer. As noted
above, the Hatam Sofer's halakhic writings were formulated in nineteenth-
century Germany and Hungary, in which the majority of Jews still by and
large observed the traditional boundaries of Jewish identity and life. In
addition, before the Orthodox move towards official separation within the
Jewish community at the Hungarian Jewish Congress of 1868–69, there was
room for only one official ideological representative of the Jewish
community, adding an element of competition to denominational disputes.

By contrast, the Jewish community of North America in the period
between 1940 and 1980 was clearly not traditional in the Orthodox sense.[1]
Despite the Orthodox identity of the vast majority of the nearly two million
Jews from Western Europe who arrived in America between 1880 and
World War I, these immigrants did not preserve their traditionalism upon
settling in America. Already by the end of the 1920s and 1930s, most of their
children exhibited hostility or indifference towards the traditional Judaism of
their parents and grandparents – as evidenced by the steep decline in
Orthodox schools and in ritual baths, both hallmarks of observant Jewish
life. Although the American Jewish community underwent a dramatic
Jewish awakening in the 1940s and 1950s, this did not involve a return to
traditional Orthodoxy, but rather a strengthening of Reform and
Conservative affiliation.[2] By the middle of the century, Orthodoxy had
become a minority. And so, in contrast to the Hatam Sofer, Rabbi Moshe
Feinstein was not engaged in a battle to curb the influence of Reform
Judaism. In America that battle was already over, and as far as Rabbi
Feinstein was concerned, the other side had won.[3]

Beyond religious affiliation, the American reality in which Rabbi
Feinstein operated was profoundly different from that of the Hatam Sofer in
at least four significant ways. First of all, Conservative and Reform Jews no
longer functioned as enemy deviants – they did not attack the status,
existence or even legitimacy of Orthodoxy. As distinct from the mid-
nineteenth century German and Hungarian Orthodox, who needed to
obtain legal permission to be represented in the community, in America the

separation of church and state was more fully in operation. Each denomination had independent authority and the freedom to appoint its own rabbis and to establish its own synagogues and schools. Orthodoxy did not need to fight for its political and legal status in order to subsist.

The second distinction, mentioned above, was the fact that Orthodoxy now functioned as a minority. As such, the danger facing Orthodoxy was not with regard to its place within the larger community, but in terms of its efforts to prevent its members from assimilating. The statistics showing that only twenty per cent of Orthodox Jews at the end of the 1950s planned to remain Orthodox are more than sufficient evidence of this danger. By the 1960s, however, Orthodoxy succeeded in stabilizing itself. The columns of what the sociologist of American Jewry Charles Leibman referred to as 'committed' Orthodox, grew in comparison with those who were merely affiliated and non-observant. There was significant growth in enrollment in Orthodox educational organizations, as well as a rise in halakhic observance. From a movement uncertain of its survival, by the beginning of the 1960s Orthodoxy began to demonstrate strength, stability, and growth. Nevertheless, its position as a minority was a constant characteristic of its standing in American Jewish life.

The third distinction was the need for Orthodoxy to deal not only with the influence of non-Orthodox factions, but also with those within Orthodoxy who did not observe halakhah. While the Hatam Sofer was able to boast that there was no *hillul Shabbat* in Pressburg, Rabbi Feinstein found himself within an Orthodoxy in which a large percentage were *mehallelei Shabbat befarhesia*. Again in the language of Charles Leibman, halakhic loyalty to all aspects of the commandments was often part of the 'religion of the elite', as opposed to the 'popular religion'.[4] Many Jewish communities were composed of great numbers of members who came to synagogue on Shabbat, and then went downtown to open their stores. While the Hatam Sofer confronted a reality of individuals who were *mehallelei Shabbat befarhesia* but nonetheless maintained their *Jewish* identity, Rabbi Feinstein had to deal with a reality of masses of people who were public desecrators of the Shabbat but nonetheless maintained their *Orthodox* identity.[5]

Finally, Reform and Conservative Judaism,[6] the two denominations with whom Moshe Feinstein contested, had ceased to be movements which merely called for minor reforms in synagogue ritual. While significantly different from one another, in particular with regard to their commitment to halakhah, both Reform and Conservative Judaism were now coherent, cohesive movements, which worked to comprehensively incorporate the beliefs and customs of Judaism within the ideas and understanding of the modern world.[7] As a result, while the initial battle over the identity of Jewish life was by now over, leading, potentially, to a less contentious form of co-existence, the lines between the denominations were now also clearer and the differences far more pronounced.

Intolerable Deviance

Of all the figures analysed above, Moshe Feinstein has the clearest and most concise definition of the boundary between the tolerable and the intolerable. For Feinstein, there is only one central feature that determines intolerability and that is heresy, *kefirah*. While still generally requiring that the heresy be accompanied by delinquency, he explicitly states over and again that it is the presence of heresy that activates the status of intolerability. In doing so, Moshe Feinstein follows the path essentially charted by Maimonides, who elevated issues of creed and belief to the centre of Jewish shared collective space. This clarity, however, is restricted by the fact that, as distinct from Maimonides, Feinstein does not outline in any comprehensive manner the nature of the beliefs that are essential to Jewishness, the rejection of which cannot be tolerated. Instead he uses general terms such as belief in God; belief in the essential principles of faith (*ikarim*), the content of which he does not specify; and a total and unquestioning acceptance of the authority of the laws of Torah.

Furthermore, for Feinstein, there are no minor or partial heretics. Once any measure of heresy is deemed by Feinstein to be present, one is classified as a *kofer* (heretic) and assumed to have adopted all forms of heresy. Thus, for example, Feinstein rejects the validity of the blessings made by the *mumar lehakhis*, the one who violates the law out of spite.

> To be called to the Torah, if he is only a sinner motivated by *teiavon*, there is no prohibition, since he is not a *kofer*. However, a *kofer* and *mumar lehakhis* are prohibited (to be called to the Torah) since they have no intention of teaching God's Torah in their reading. As a result, when reading (the Torah) their words are like words in general and not like the reading of the words of the Torah, the Torah of God.[8]

While the individual in question is merely violating one law, for Feinstein, regardless of the sin involved, he is considered a general and complete *kofer*, an individual who has no concern for Torah or God.

The lack of regard for the specific content of the heresy that generates intolerability, coupled with the absence of gradations of heresy, creates a dangerous situation whereby intolerability can be assessed in an extremely broad and unprecedented manner. Instead of being the rare occurrence that the category socially prescribes, in Feinstein's hands almost anyone can be so classified, if one so desires. It is not by accident that, as will be seen below, Feinstein is able to marginalize the majority of the Jewish people.

Returning to Feinstein's definition, intolerable status is warranted when one fails to accept any of a set of generally stated beliefs, regardless of the nature of the delinquency through which it is expressed. In fact, the nature of delinquency becomes insignificant, with severe and less severe forms of delinquency compared by virtue of the heresy that is either present or lacking.[9] Thus the *mumar lehakhis* resumes his status as intolerable by virtue of the heresy involved,[10] while at the same time the reverse is also the case: even a delinquent as severe as the *mehallel Shabbat befarhesia*, if his deviance is perceived to be devoid of heresy, is classified as tolerable.[11]

As evidence of the centrality of heresy in his writing, Feinstein resurrects the Maimonidean category of *kofer* as a category of intolerable deviance, but in Feinstein's case, without the focused definition placed on it in Hilkhot Teshuvah. For Feinstein it is a general category for all forms of heresy and is the most prevalent and widely used of the deviance categories. All major intolerable deviants, regardless of their classification under one of the other deviance categories, are also referred to as *kofrim*, and all of the categories of deviance are explicitly associated with the attribute of *kefirah*. Thus one can be a *mumar* and a *kofer*, a *min* and a *kofer*, and an *apikorus* and a *kofer*.

In Moshe Feinstein's writing one finds reference to four primary forms of intolerable deviance. They are the *mumar ledavar ehad lehakhis*,[12] the 'apostate/idolater',[13] the *mehallel Shabbat befarhesia*[14] and the Reform and Conservative Jew and rabbi, with no distinction made between the rabbi and the average Jew vis-à-vis sanctions.[15] Where Moshe Feinstein's discussion of intolerability is most innovative is with regard to the status of the *mehallel Shabbat befarhesia* and Reform and Conservative Jews, and this analysis will thus focus primarily on them. As is the case with the Hatam Sofer, the first is denoted exclusively by the category of *mumar*[16] while the latter is referred to as a *min*[17] or *apikorus*.[18]

Despite Feinstein's unification of the categories of intolerability under the umbrella of heresy, there is still a subtle but critical distinction between the category of *mumar* on the one hand, and *min* or *apikorus* on the other. While all may be used to denote the heretic, the *mumar* can also be used to denote delinquency devoid of heretical motives, while the categories of *min* and *apikorus* always entail heresy. Thus, given Feinstein's stand on intolerability, the *mumar* can be used for deviance that is also tolerable, while the *min* and *apikorus* cannot. Furthermore, the category of *min* is associated with a unique array of sanctions, in particular in the sphere of loyalty. These sanctions are absent from the *mumar*. By categorizing the *mehallel Shabbat* as *mumar* and the Reform and Conservative Jew as *min*, as will be seen below, Feinstein is thus setting the stage for the possible tolerability of the former and the necessary intolerability of the latter.

Mehallel Shabbat Befarhesia

In delineating the category of *mehallel Shabbat befarhesia*, Moshe Feinstein presents the radical notion of a *mehallel Shabbat befarhesia leteiavon* who, like all *mumarim leteiavon*, is classified as tolerable. This is a radical break from the traditional classification schemas. As seen in the previous chapters, the motivations of desire or spite had previously not played any role in determining the intolerability of the Shabbat desecration – the crucial determining factor was always whether the act was performed in public or private. Moreover, the *mehallel Shabbat*, like the idolater, was the only type of sinner for whom *teiavon* was not a mitigating factor: regardless of one's motivation, these two sins were always seen as an expression of a more comprehensive deviance. For Feinstein, however, even in the case of the *mehallel Shabbat*, *teiavon* served as a mitigating factor. Thus, it is possible to view Feinstein as extending a trend that had already begun with the Hatam Sofer. The Hatam Sofer observed that in the modern context, being a *mehallel Shabbat befarhesia* no longer necessarily means that one intends at the same time to be either a *poresh min hatzibur* or one who completely rejects the authority of halakhah. While the Hatam Sofer took this new reality into account and limited the scope of sanctions, Moshe Feinstein takes the next step and creates a category of the tolerable *mehallel Shabbat befarhesia*.

> Clearly there is no necessity to assume that everyone who desecrates the Shabbat out of *teiavon* is a *kofer* in the acts of creation, for it is possible that even though he believes (in the acts of creation), he cannot control his desire for making money and other passions ... There is serious cause not to designate them as similar to non-Jews and they do not have the status of *mumar lekol hatorah*. This is even more the case with regards to those about whom it is known that they observe the laws of the Shabbat in those areas which do not have bearing on their livelihood that they are not to be designated as *mumarim*. However, those who are not known to be observers of Torah (and desecrate the Shabbat), they have the status of *mumarim lekol hatorah* and have the status of non-Jews.[19]

Feinstein bears witness to individuals who are otherwise pious Jews and who, due to financial pressures, go to work after the Saturday morning prayer services are over. Instead of attacking this phenomenon, as did the Hatam Sofer, Feinstein is willing to incorporate them within the boundary of tolerability so long as the acts are motivated by desire and thus devoid of heresy. However, when heresy is present, then the *mehallel Shabbat befarhesia* resumes his status as intolerable and is considered a *mumar lekol hatorah kullah.*

In order to justify his iconoclastic move, Feinstein creates a parallelism between the classic distinction with regards to violating the laws of Shabbat, i.e. public (*befarhesia*) and private (*betzina*), and *lehakhis* and *teiavon.*[20] Feinstein argues that the distinction between public and private determines the intolerability of the act not because it is a sign of one's connection to the community, but rather because it influences a person's presumption of innocence. When violations are done in private, the presumption of innocence places the deviance within the category of *teiavon*, unless proven otherwise, and as such tolerable. However, when the act is a public one, the public perception of the act overrides this presumption and determines its meaning independent of the intent of the individual who performs the act. Here the differences between the traditional and modern context come into play. In traditional times, when violation of the Shabbat in public was generally a flagrant indication of a larger heretical outlook vis-à-vis God and the authority of law, the public assessed the act accordingly, rendering the act intolerable. In the modern context, however, when the public is well aware of financial motivation behind many of the Shabbat violations, the public nature of the act does not change the presumption of innocence. Quite to the contrary, it reinforces the presumption that the sin was motivated by *teiavon*. Consequently, in the modern context the public desecration of the Shabbat has the status that private desecration had in the past.

Feinstein's motivation for this innovative move becomes more apparent when one takes into account those who are its primary beneficiaries. He does not attempt to ameliorate the status of all cases of *mehallel Shabbat befarhesia*, but rather only that of those who are otherwise faithful and loyal to halakhah. He explicitly refers to individuals who, in areas not pertaining to work, observe Shabbat laws and go to synagogue. In other words, Moshe Feinstein is referring to the *hillul Shabbat befarhesia* of Orthodox-affiliated Jews, and it is their Shabbat desecration alone that ceases to have the status of the *mumar lekol hatorah kullah*. Those Jews who are generally non-observant, even though they see themselves as part of the Jewish people, and even though they may be partially committed to halakhah, would not qualify. Once their motivation for *hillul Shabbat* is not limited to areas pertaining to making a living, the motivation is no longer assumed to be *teiavon* and consequently is assumed to be heretical and intolerable.[21]

This move towards the inclusion of Orthodox-affiliated deviants and the removal of their deviance from the status of intolerability is a prevalent

move in Feinstein's responsa. In the case of halakhic Orthodox Jews who
want to rent a room in a non-halakhic Orthodox synagogue, Feinstein offers
the following ruling.

> But these synagogues of the Orthodox that are not proper, in that
> they pray without a *mehitzah*, or use a microphone [on the
> Shabbat], they are not, heaven forbid, *kofrim* with regards to these
> commandments. They simply are making light of them even
> though they are believers in all the commandments of the Torah.
> It has come to be perceived by them as permissible (*na-asah lahem
> ke-heter*) as a result of the fact that they repeatedly violated the law
> on an ongoing basis over time. They are upstanding (*ksherim*) Jews
> and are often merely completely inadvertent sinners (*shogegim*).
> Regarding protesting about their behaviour, it depends. If there is
> room to hope that they will listen, it is a requirement to notify
> them [that they are violating the law], and if not, it is preferable
> that they remain inadvertent sinners.[22]

What is important about the above analysis is that, unlike working on
Shabbat, one cannot claim that the motivation for a synagogue's use of a
microphone during Shabbat service and the lack of *mehitzah* separating men
and women during worship is *teiavon*. This would leave their motivation as
lehakhis and thus render them as intolerable deviants, a status which would,
as we will see below, necessitate the maintaining of distance and would
prohibit the renting of a room. Feinstein, however, rejects this line of
thought and refuses to associate heretical motivation when it comes to the
deviance of Orthodox-affiliated Jews. Instead he classifies the causes for their
deviance as either being inadvertent or as being the product of innocent
ignorance – they do not know better, and they have come to believe that
such behaviour is permitted (*na-asah lahem ke-heter*). It is interesting to note
that he does not make this claim on the basis of a first-hand familiarity with
the community, nor is the ruling contingent on an investigation on a case-
by-case basis. Rather it is simply by virtue of their formal affiliation.

Further evidence for this denominational motivation may be found at
the end of the above-quoted ruling, when he prohibits instructing the
members of the synagogue as to the error of their ways. If the sinning
Orthodox were in fact merely inadvertent sinners whose deviance was the
result of their being unfamiliar with the law, then informing them of the
error of their ways should lead to an immediate change in their behaviour.
Yet Feinstein openly admits that, at least in some cases, this will not be the
case. Nonetheless he does not change their status as non-heretics. It seems
that the fact that their affiliation is Orthodox serves to remove them, as if by
definition, from the status of *kofrim* regardless of the empirical reality to the

contrary. Furthermore, this affiliation generates a bond of loyalty which requires that one investigate on a case-by-case basis if the community will be ready to face up to their deviance, for one must take care not to push them into a position of being intentional sinners, *meizidim*. When a case-by-case policy serves to protect, it is used; when it may not, as is the case with assessing their intolerability, it is set aside for the sake of an *a priori* determination in accordance with their affiliation.

What further strengthens the argument for denominationalism as a key factor in Feinstein's assessment of tolerability is the fact that every one of the above arguments could be applied towards Reform and Conservative Jews, especially when one considers that Feinstein assumes that the Orthodox will not cease to deviate even when made familiar with the law. There is nothing stopping Feinstein from applying the categories of *shegagah* or *na-asah lahem ke-heter*. Given their education and upbringing, it would require far less interpretive ingenuity to claim that Reform and Conservative Jews in fact do not know that their practices are contrary to the law, as their familiarity with halakhah as understood by Feinstein is marginal at best. This is the core meaning of being a *tinok shenishbah*, a status that Feinstein readily admits applies to them, as will be seen below. He nevertheless refuses to permit the renting of a room in a Conservative synagogue, asserting instead that by virtue of their heresy, it is forbidden.

As a result, it is necessary to amend Feinstein's definition of intolerability. It is not just heresy, but heresy coupled with non-Orthodox affiliation, that renders one intolerable. Whereas heresy is that which activates intolerability, it is one's denominational affiliation that activates the assessment of one's motives as heretical.

While the Hatam Sofer was still campaigning against the phenomenon of *hillul Shabbat* and still hoping to win the battle against its expansion, Feinstein lived in a time when not only had Shabbat desecration become a commonplace practice for Jews, but it had in fact even penetrated into the Orthodox community. While he could have continued the Hatam Sofer's fight and worked to remove the Orthodox desecrators of the Shabbat from the community, he chose otherwise. Instead of marginalizing them, he uses his halakhic authority and ingenuity to enable them to remain members in good standing.

Reform and Conservative Jews

The significance of Feinstein's attention to denominational affiliation in assessing heresy and intolerability becomes even more apparent when analysing his position vis-à-vis Conservative and Reform Jews and their rabbis. They, as distinct from Orthodox deviants, are always classified as heretics and intolerable.[23] Unlike the Hatam Sofer, however, theirs is not a unique or new form of heresy, but is similar to the generic heresy of all intolerable deviants, from the apostate, to the *mumar ledavar ehad lehakhis*, to the *mehallel Shabbat befarhesia*. Like all of these individuals, the Conservative and Reform are designated by Feinstein as *kofrim* in God, God's Torah and the principles of faith (*ikarim*).[24]

What is interesting about this designation is that, as distinct from the *mehallel Shabbat*, it has no exceptions. The affiliation with any one of these non-Orthodox movements designates one by definition as a heretic. Thus he states with regard to Conservative rabbis:

> Given the fact that he belongs to the Conservative Rabbinate whose position it is to revoke some of the commandments of the Torah, including Biblical ones and most of the rabbinic prohibitions, all of which involves *kefirah*, they are invalid as witnesses. This is the case even if we have not heard anything about [his *kefirah*] ... for [being designated a *kofer*] is dependent on publicity and legal presumption (*hazakah*) and there is no greater publicity or *hazakah* [of being a *kofer*] than holding by the principles of the Conservative to deny many of the laws of the Torah and to even possibly deny the essence of receiving the Torah at Sinai than him serving as a Rabbi in their synagogue.[25]

The grounds and ramifications for this *a priori* designation will be analysed at greater length below in the section on models of marginalization. What is important to note at this point is the role that denominational affiliation plays in Feinstein's designation of intolerable status.

An excellent example for the centrality of denominational affiliation for assessing intolerability may be found in the way Feinstein reworks the category of *tinok shenishbah* to ensure that it does not mitigate the intolerability of Conservative and Reform Jews. As seen in Maimonides' writing in the previous chapter, this category serves to remove the heretic and consequent intolerable status of all second-generation deviants. Instead of sanctions, being designated as *tinok shenishbah* requires that 'efforts [should] be made to bring them back in repentance, to draw them near with paths of peace until they return to the strength-giving source of the Torah'.[26] On the basis of this ruling, were Conservative and Reform Jews to be classified under the category of *tinok shenishbah*, all forms of marginalization would have to be suspended. Now, were Moshe Feinstein interested in adopting this approach, as he obviously was in the case of the Orthodox *mehallel Shabbat*, the Maimonidean precedent would have been sufficient. However, he was not; yet because of the role that Maimonides plays in his halakhic rulings, he could not simply ignore Maimonides' position on this issue. In order to uphold the comprehensive designation of Conservative and Reform Jews as intolerable, he needed to neutralize the halakhic implications of the category of '*tinok shenishbah*'.

> Even though they are *shogegim* like *tinokot shenishbu* among the heathens, due to the fact that their parents and the environment in which they were raised led them astray and the laws pertaining to punishments do not apply to them ... nonetheless, they are *kofrim*, and it is necessary to distance oneself from them as in the rule of 'keep yourself far from her', and what Maimonides wrote, that it is appropriate to bring them back in repentance and to draw them with friendly words until they return to the strength of Torah, this is not relevant to their gatherings, i.e. their synagogues, which are not an appropriate place for this, nor is every person suitable for this.[27]

While accepting the classification of Conservative Jews as *tinok shenishbah*, Feinstein posits that the classification does not override the obligatory sanction of 'keep yourself far from her'. In doing so he uses a three-step argument. First he contends that one must separate the obligation of 'keep yourself far from her' from the issue of sanctions. He accepts that it is indeed forbidden to marginalize the *tinok shenishbah*; however, separation is not a sanction against the deviant. It is rather a self-protective measure for the righteous, protecting them from the dangerous influences of the deviants. The *tinok shenishbah* might be an inadvertent sinner who is not responsible for his deviance, but he nevertheless is a carrier of dangerous ideologies that can negatively influence those with whom he comes into contact.

Now, the problem with Feinstein's argument is that Maimonides explicitly mandates that outreach efforts be made to draw near those classified as *tinok shenishbah* to bring them back into the fold. This is not possible if one is obligated to 'keep yourself far from her'. Feinstein is aware of this, and therefore he adds a second and third argument. The second is that outreach efforts, while obligatory, cannot be performed 'in their places of communal gathering, like the synagogue, for that place is not fitting for this'. The third is that 'not everyone is suited to do this'. Under the second argument, one-on-one contact and interaction with Conservative Jews is allowed and possibly even required. However, no effective outreach is possible, Feinstein argues, in communal settings, especially in their places of communal gathering, such as their synagogue. Under the third argument, regardless of location and setting, the obligation to reach out to the *tinok shenishbah* is not incumbent on everyone, but only on those who have the required skills. Feinstein does not specify who they are, but by issuing this general rule forbidding entrance into Conservative synagogues, it can be inferred that this work is not generally appropriate except for a select few.

These last two arguments limiting the implications of *tinok shenishbah* status, while not mentioned in Maimonides, are at least plausible, in particular at a time when Orthodoxy is ideologically challenged as the minority position and is struggling to maintain the loyalty of its members. It is interesting to note, however, that Feinstein uses these arguments only when it comes to Conservative and Reform Jews, and he is not consistent with his reasoning in other seemingly parallel instances where the deviants in question are Orthodox. Take for example, his position on membership and participation in an Orthodox synagogue, many of whose members are halakhically non-observant.

> Regarding one who wants to cease being a member in a synagogue where many of the members do not act properly, my opinion is that one should not leave so that there should remain one who will protest. And one should not get dejected and say that they will certainly not listen, for a small light illuminates a great darkness and therefore the protest may have influence on many prohibitions. All of this applies only so long as the synagogue abides by proper halakhic norms. If they deviate, however, from the rules of synagogue practice, such as removing the divider between men and women, or they change even in a minor way the prayer services or the reading of the Torah, all who fear God are obligated to cease being members there.[28]

Feinstein rules that where one is not put in a position of violating halakhah, one is to be encouraged to not only have episodic contact, but in fact to maintain full membership, so as to have a positive influence on the deviant members. Nowhere does he argue that not everyone is qualified for this type of work. Absent as well is the distinction between reaching out to individuals and attempting to influence them in the context of a communal organization. Quite to the contrary, all are obligated to stay, and Feinstein's assumption is that by preserving the connection with these sinning Jews, anyone can be a force for change, for indeed 'a small light illuminates a great darkness'. To serve as such a light towards Conservative and Reform is not considered, for it is their denominational affiliation which serves as the foundation of their intolerability, a status that Feinstein is interested in perpetuating. Thus he also prohibits a teacher, who presumably would fall under the category of one who is 'suited to do this', from teaching in a Reform or Conservative school, unless he has no other way of supporting himself.

> If [the teacher] is allowed to teach them the Torah of God [may
> He be blessed], and to pray appropriately, and also that it will be
> in a different place, not their synagogues; then therefore we will
> not prevent those who need a livelihood from receiving such a
> job, for indeed there is also a benefit to this, that the children of
> the Conservatives need to learn the Torah of God [may He be
> blessed], and perhaps they will grow up in Torah and *mitzvot*, like
> kosher Jews. But to say that, because of this benefit, the spirit of
> the Sages rests well with this, does not follow at all, because
> against this [benefit] there is a concern for the teacher himself, that
> he should not be drawn after them, since through this [position]
> he will have closeness and connection with the heretics, and the
> Sages were very concerned to keep distance from them, as it says
> in Avodah Zarah, page 17 ... and therefore, only because of the
> need for a livelihood we don't prevent this.[29]

This ruling establishes that the obligation to keep one's distance from the
intolerable deviant completely negates the special obligation that exists vis-
à-vis the *tinok shenishbah*. Even teachers who should be at the vanguard of
the effort are forbidden to come close.

It is, furthermore, important to note the only exception Feinstein is
willing to make to the prohibition. It is 'only because of the need for a
livelihood we don't prevent this'. It is not for the sake of the children's
Jewish education, but out of loyalty to the Orthodox teacher. The children,
by virtue of their being Reform or Conservative, are intolerable deviants
and as such outside of Feinstein's sphere of loyalty with their needs of no
concern to him. This is what he explicitly claims when he states:

> And if a person desires, for pure motivations, to educate children,
> there is plenty of work to do with the children from the
> synagogues of those who behave properly.[30]

It is only the children of those who behave properly, i.e. the Orthodox-
affiliated that are his concern, together with the adults of the same
denomination. The rule of 'keep yourself far from her', while seemingly
overpowering, even to the extent that it nullifies the laws of *tinok shenishbah*,
can be set aside when one towards whom Moshe Feinstein feels responsible
is in need. It seems ironic, but the financial needs of the single Orthodox
teacher move Feinstein to a greater extent than the future association of the
majority of Jews with Judaism. It is clear that Moshe Feinstein chooses to
nullify the Maimonidean obligation towards deviants defined as '*tinok
shenishbah*', and his extenuating arguments are but a façade. His point is not
the fear of influence from relationship or the inefficacy of efforts to reach

out to those who are not members of the Orthodox community. It is the classification of Conservative and Reform Jews as intolerable that he wants to maintain. Through the category of '*tinok shenishbah*', Maimonides attempts to ensure that all those who are not to be held responsible will remain within the classification of tolerability. Moshe Feinstein takes the opposite tack. On the basis of one's denominational affiliation he determines one's intolerability, thus requiring the nullification of the protection afforded by the classification of *tinok shenishbah*.

Modes of Marginalization

The marginalization of both the *mumar ledavar ehad lehakhis* and the intolerable *mehallel Shabbat befarhesia* are primarily, though not exclusively, in the sphere of ritual,[31] while marginalization in the sphere of loyalty is generally reserved for Reform and Conservative Jews, a product, as will be seen below, of his desire to essentially break off all contact.

With regard to the sanctions directed towards the intolerable *mehallel Shabbat befarhesia* who is a *kofer*, Feinstein rules that such an individual cannot to be trusted to observe Jewish law,[32] his testimony is invalid,[33] he cannot serve as either a *mohel*[34] or as a *shohet*. In this latter capacity, his status is similar to that of a non-Jew: even when someone is supervising him, his ritual slaughter is still invalid.[35] He is barred from being called up to the Torah,[36] and should not to be appointed as a *gabbai* in a synagogue.[37] Despite the above sanctions in the sphere of ritual, Feinstein nevertheless rules that the *mehallel Shabbat* can in a situation of urgency be counted as part of a *minyan*. This is because being considered part of the community for the purposes of prayer does not involve the sphere of ritual, but is contingent upon validation in the sphere of basic membership in the Jewish People, a status, as will be seen below, that Feinstein still accords to deviants even if they are *kofrim* and *mumarim*.[38] The one sanction in the sphere of loyalty that he does ascribe to the *mehallel Shabbat* relates to the issue of whether to erect an *eruv* in a city. Those in favour argue that since many Jews violate the laws of the Shabbat and carry, the existence of an *eruv* would render such actions permissible. But Feinstein disagrees. He argues that it is not the responsibility of halakhic authorities or the community to prevent the wicked from sinning or to assist them in observing halakhah. Rather, he argues, let them sin and suffer the consequences.[39] In this ruling, there is something of a resemblance to the rabbinic ruling in BT Hullin 5b, where the *meshumad lekol hatorah kullah* is prohibited from bringing a sacrifice, in order to prevent him from repenting.

When it comes to Feinstein's marginalization of Conservative and Reform Jews, following the rabbinic sanctions applied to the *min*, he argues for the adoption of a policy that involves a prohibition on almost all contact and association with these groups, who constitute the majority of the Jewish people in America. He thus calls for the broadest application of this sanction in Jewish history. In this context he rules that it is forbidden to rent a room in a Conservative or Reform synagogue for the purposes of housing an Orthodox *minyan*,[40] or in a school for Orthodox children,[41] on the grounds of 'keep yourself far away from her'.

> There is, in addition, also the fear that there will be someone who will hear that the Rabbi is giving a sermon, which is usually made up of words of *kefirah* and *minut*. Given the close proximity, he will be inclined to enter and listen to the sermon, while if he is far away he will never be in a situation to go in and listen. See in Avodah Zarah page 17, which states: 'Keep yourself far away from her', referring to *minut*.[42]

The erection of a boundary separating Orthodox from Reform and Conservative does not stop at the prohibition on entering or renting space in the latter's buildings. A person who is a teacher in an Orthodox school cannot work at the same time in a Conservative or Reform school. This prohibition remains in place even if the school functions according to halakhah, and the teacher is never required to teach the students something that is not in accordance with Orthodox practice. Feinstein bases the prohibition on the fear that the students in the Orthodox school might mistakenly assume that it is legitimate to learn in the Reform or Conservative schools given the fact that their teacher teaches there as well.[43] Furthermore:

> It is self-evident that it is forbidden to take such a position, for even though he might have a positive influence, on the other hand there is an even greater fear that the opposite will occur, for *minut*, heaven forbid, attracts, and 'keep yourself away from her' refers to *minut*. See Avodah Zarah page 17.[44]

In one of the strongest expressions of marginalization in the sphere of loyalty, quoted above, he turns to the teacher who wanted to take a job in a Conservative school and states:

> And if the individual has the desire to do so [teach], motivated to educate children for the sake of heaven, there is yet much work that has to be done with the synagogue youth of those who act appropriately.[45]

As an Orthodox Jew, one's loyalty is first and foremost to fellow Orthodox Jews and their children. Conservative and Reform children are not

Feinstein's concern, and as a result, he does not have to allow for teachers who will contribute to their educational and spiritual well-being.

The legislated separation from Conservative and Reform Jews does not only affect circumstances that involve going into 'their' space. Feinstein further extends it to exclude all cooperations in Jewish communal institutions, such as Federation, which serves the social welfare, educational, religious and political needs of the community as a whole, and Jews worldwide:

> By law it is required to distance as much as possible from those Conservative who are also *kofrim* in many principles of religion and in many of the commandments of the Torah, and most of their rabbis are deceivers and enticers (*mesitim* and *medihim*) to heresy and to the desecration of the Shabbat and to many other severe sins ... In no way is one permitted to join a committee together with *kofrim* of any type. It is required to institute a separate community constituted by Torah observant alone, which will oversee all matters that pertain to the welfare of Jews.[46]

Here Feinstein comes close to the type of position advanced by the Hatam Sofer. The conclusion of the ban on all contact is ultimately the recognition that Orthodoxy must set up its own distinct community, without the participation of those who are not affiliated with it. It is not simply that we cannot pray together. Building a community involves too many issues under contention, and he sees no common ground with non-Orthodox Jewry. But of course Feinstein, as distinct from the Hatam Sofer, did not need the permission of the state in order to implement such a ruling.

All of the above sanctions prescribed by Feinstein are in line with the rule 'keep yourself far from her'. But what is the basis for associating this rule with Conservative and Reform Jews? It is important to notice that in his writing, though he reiterates the fear associated with the *minim*, nowhere does he make the claim that Reform and Conservative Jews are proactive enemy deviants like the Jewish Christian in the times of the Talmud, or as he views Christians in his time.[47] Rather, he simply testifies to the dangerous tendency of Reform and Conservative ideology and practice to attract and influence through mere contact and exposure.

Feinstein relies on several sources to justify his marginalization of Reform and Conservative Jews. The first is cited in the Responsa regarding renting a room in a Conservative synagogue for an Orthodox *minyan*. Feinstein attempts to justify the application of the sanctions of 'keep yourself far from her':

In a synagogue of the Conservative it is forbidden to hold services, even in a separate room since it is public knowledge that they are a group that are *kofrim* in a number of the laws of Judaism. It says in Avodah Zarah 17a: 'Keep yourself far from her'. This is stated with regard to *minim* and *minut* and even those who are *kofrim* with regard to one thing are still considered as *kofrim* in the Torah as it is stated in Maimonides, Laws Pertaining to Repentance, Chapter 3.8 and they are to be treated as *minim* as it is stated *ibid.*, halakhah 6.[48]

The above argument is divided into a number of distinct steps. First, he classifies Conservative Jews as '*kofrim* in a number of the laws of Judaism'. Second, he argues that one who is found to be a *kofer* in even one thing warrants the status of '*kofer* in the Torah' on the basis of Maimonides Hilkhot Teshuvah 3.8, which states that 'one who says that the Torah is not from God, even one verse – even one word – if he said, "Moses said this on his own": behold, he is a *kofer* in the Torah'. The third, and most crucial step of his argument, is that once individuals are *kofrim* in the Torah, 'they are to be treated as *minim* as it is stated *ibid.*, halakhah 6', and *minim* are subject to the sanction of 'keep yourself far from her'. Feinstein knows that this sanction only applies to the *min* and, as a result, he argues from Hilkhot Teshuvah that one is to make the leap from *kofer* to *min*.

The first step of his argument, in which Conservative Jews are defined as '*kofrim* in a number of laws of Judaism' is empirically correct, in that Conservative Judaism does formally reject certain traditional aspects of halakhah as understood by Feinstein. The second step, whereby the status of '*kofer*' is ascribed to one who is merely a *kofer* in some issues, is in essence the view posited by Maimonides in Hilkhot Teshuvah, even though the issue there is the divine authorship of the Torah. However, the third step, whereby the sanctions associated with the category of *min* are extended to the *kofer* as well, is in no way justified by Hilkhot Teshuvah 3.6, the source upon which Feinstein relies. In 3.6, Maimonides merely lists all those who have no place in the world to come, including the *min* and *kofer* in the Torah. He does not claim that all deviants are subject to the same sanctions. Furthermore, as seen above, while Maimonides unifies the various deviance categories, he at the same time essentially eliminates the unique status of enemy deviant and its sanction of 'keep yourself far from her' which, with one exception, is never mentioned by him. Moshe Feinstein attempts to find a basis for his ruling in Maimonides, but it is important to realize that Maimonides simply does not provide him with the precedent he seeks.

Feinstein's marginalization of Reform and Conservative Jews, particularly with regard to the sphere of ritual, is grounded also in the

Maimonidean ruling that a scroll of Torah written by a *min* or *apikorus*[49] should be burnt. As seen in the previous chapter, Maimonides states:

> A *min* from amongst Israel who wrote a Sefer Torah – it should be burnt together with the names of God within it, for he does not believe in the sanctity of the name [of God] and did not write it to His name. Rather he assumes that [God's name] is like all other things. Since this was his intent, the name [of God in the Sefer Torah] was not sanctified; it is a *mitzvah* to burn it so as not to leave a remembrance for the *min*, nor for his work.[50]

The Maimonidean argument is made up of two steps. The first is the claim that what a *min* or *apikorus* writes has no sanctity, for given their heresy, the writing of God's name is equivalent for them to the writing of any other word or name. If not written by a religious scribe, God's name as it appears in the scroll has neither religious significance nor sanctity. The second stage of the argument is that once the Sefer Torah is deemed to be devoid of holiness, it is not only permissible, but is a *mitzvah* to burn it, in order to ensure that no memory remains of *minim* or *apikorsim* or of what they produce.[51]

Feinstein extends the application of Maimonides' ruling and uses it to shape the status of all blessings made by *minim*, *apikorsim* and *kofrim*.[52] At issue is the nature of the role these individuals can play in the sphere of ritual, such as whether they may be called up to the Torah, and whether they are permitted to recite blessings in public community gatherings, thereby exempting others from their responsibility.

Thus, in response to the question as to whether it is permissible in the context of communal events to honour a Reform or Conservative rabbi with the blessing over bread or the like, Feinstein rules as follows:

> We have seen from Maimonides that for one who does not believe in the holiness of God, the letters of God's name are similar to all other things, it is therefore self evident that when he mentions God's name (in a blessing), it is also like words in general.[53]

Consequently, Feinstein rules:

> It is in my humble opinion clear that even if he (a Reform or Conservative rabbi) would recite the blessing properly, without delaying between the recitation and eating, since he is a *kofer* in God and His Torah, as are most of their rabbis, the recitation of God's name is for him similar to words in general, with no intent

to God; his blessings do not have the status of blessings for they are without the mention of God's name and His kingship.[54]

From a relatively minor sanction which excludes the *min/apikorus* from serving as a scribe of sacred scrolls, Maimonides' ruling becomes, in the hands of Feinstein, the foundation for a complete ban on any leadership or public role in the sphere of ritual for anyone classified as *min*. Conservative and Reform Jews and rabbis, once classified under the category of *min*, are determined by Feinstein to be *kofrim* in God and His Torah, and thus their recitation of God's name is an act devoid of religious value.

It is important to note that Conservative and Reform Jews are subjected to this extreme exclusionary sanction seemingly by definition, i.e. by virtue of their classification as *minim* and *apikorsim* who are *kofrim*. Maimonides' ruling is addressed towards a particular *min* who in fact does not believe in God, or at least not in the God of Judaism as defined by Maimonides. Feinstein applies it to anyone whom he categorizes as a *min/kofer*. While it is evident that Reform and Conservative halakhic innovations are unacceptable to Feinstein, this in no way justifies the claim that they do not believe in God, and this type of claim, at the very least, is in need of empirical justification or verification. Feinstein, however, makes no attempt at such verification.

This is not the case, however, with the status of the blessings of one who is a *mehallel Shabbat befarhesia*. Here, as distinct from above, Feinstein rules that their blessings are not disqualified by definition, but rather must be assessed on a case-by-case basis.

But if it is known that his desecration of the Shabbat is motivated by *teiavon*, for example if he prays and puts on *tefillin*, his blessing is a valid blessing and should be answered with 'amen' for his intention [when mentioning God's name] is directed to God. In this case the prohibition [against giving him an aliyah] is removed, even though in other matters, such as ritual slaughter and wine and the like, there is no such distinction [between the *mehallel Shabbat* who prays and puts on *tefillin* and the *mehallel Shabbat* who does not] since he is a *mehallel Shabbat befarhesia* he is similar in status to the non-Jewish idolater, even though he fulfills other commandments. In any event, with regard to issue of blessings it is different, for once we see that he believes in God, his blessings qualify as legitimate blessings and one is to answer 'amen'. Consequently, there is no prohibition against him reading the Torah.[55]

Feinstein explains that on the issue of the validity of blessings, the only question is whether one in fact believes in God. Now, while Feinstein defines both the *mehallel Shabbat befarhesia* and the Conservative and Reform Jew and rabbi as *kofrim*, it is only with regard to the former that he is willing to consider if in fact this applies to all individuals who deviate in this manner. If the *mehallel Shabbat* prays and puts on *tefillin*, thus indicating that he is a person of faith, his blessings are valid and he can be called up to the Torah. But with regards to Conservative and Reform, no such exceptions are made. Despite the fact that they may pray regularly and put on *tefillin*, he is unwilling to create exemptions.[56]

It seems, then, that if one goes to an Orthodox synagogue, even if one is a *mehallel Shabbat befarhesia*, one is within Feinstein's sphere of loyalty, and thus he will look for ways to include one in his community's sphere of ritual. When an individual is outside of his area of solidarity, then exclusion is mandated by definition, and no attempt is made, even when possible, to find a halakhic solution that would allow his inclusion on the ritual plane.

In addition to the rabbinic dictum to 'keep yourself far away from her' and the Maimonidean ruling about the Torah scroll written by a *min*, a third textual source that significantly shaped Feinstein's writing on the marginalization of the Reform and Conservative Jews, and in particular their rabbis, is the law of *moridin ve-lo ma-alin*. In Feinstein's legislative hands, the issue was not the actual sanction itself, which in its classic sense, affected the sphere of loyalty by basically forfeiting the life of the *min* and *mumar* in an extra legal manner: it allowed citizens to take the law into their own hands, and, without any need for witnesses, classify others as intolerable and then surreptitiously bring about their death. According to Feinstein, the application of the law to the area of capital punishment is conditional on the existence of a functioning Sanhedrin.[57] Rather, he focuses on the aspect of the law of *moridin ve-lo ma-alin* that pertains to the ability to classify someone as a *min/mumar/kofer* without due process of witnesses and outside a court of law. Such a classification means that their testimony is automatically disqualified without the need for corroborative testimony of witnesses to their heresy.

> ... It is clear that one does not require the testimony of witnesses in the presence of the defendants in front of a court of law to the effect that they are *kofrim*. Once it is publicly known that they are *kofrim*, they are disqualified as witnesses, even without the corroborating testimony of witnesses. For with regard to the law of *moridin ve-lo ma-alin* the testimony of witnesses is not necessary, as is seen in Maimonides, Chapter 3 of Hilkhot Mamrim, Halakhah 2 ... And if we allow capital punishment simply on the

basis of the fact that the deviance is publicly known, all the more so we can base ourselves on public knowledge [of the deviance in question] to disqualify witnesses.[58]

In general, the process of disqualifying the testimony of a witness is a legal procedure that requires a formal hearing in front of a court, witnesses, and prior warning. Feinstein argues, however, that with regard to anyone about whom the halakhah is willing to say *moridin ve-lo ma-alin*, it is essentially saying that their guilt does not have to be substantiated in a court of law, 'for with regard to the law of *moridin ve-lo ma-alin* the testimony of witnesses is not necessary'. Consequently, Feinstein surmises that such an individual's testimony can also be invalidated without having to substantiate his deviance in a court of law.

On the basis of this contention, Feinstein nullifies all the marriages performed by Reform or Conservative rabbis, as their testimony to the legal propriety of the proceedings is invalid.

> Given the fact that he belongs to the Conservative rabbinate whose position it is to revoke some of the commandments of the Torah, including Biblical ones and most of the rabbinic prohibitions, all of which involves *kefirah*, they are invalid as witnesses. This is the case even if we have not heard anything about [his *kefirah*]... for [being designated a *kofer*] it is dependent on publicity and legal presumption (*hazakah*) and there is no greater publicity or *hazakah* [of being a *kofer*] than holding by the principles of the Conservative to deny many of the laws of the Torah and to even possibly deny the essence of receiving the Torah at Sinai than him serving as a rabbi in their synagogue.[59]

> It is clear that the Reform rabbis are extreme *kofrim*, and are worse than regular Reform [Jews] in that they are deceivers and enticers (*mesitim ve-medihim*) and are all disqualified to serve as witnesses, even if testimony to this was not received in a *Bet Din* in their presence.[60]

Being disqualified from serving as a witness also delegitimizes, by definition, all conversions performed by Reform and Conservative rabbis, for once they cannot serve as witnesses, they are also disqualified to constitute or serve on a *Bet Din*.

> A *Bet Din* of the Conservative is disqualified from serving as a *Bet Din* given the fact that they are *kofrim* in many of the essential principles of the religion and transgress many of the prohibitions ... It is a certainty that they violate some of the Biblical

prohibitions. And even though no testimony regarding them has not been received, there is a legal assumption (*anan sahadei*) that anyone who bears the disgraceful name of Conservative, has a legal presumption (*hazakah*) of being *a* delinquent with regards to many prohibitions and to *kefirah* in many principles, and I have already clarified in one Responsa that one who has a *hazakah* of *kefirah* is disqualified [from serving as a witness] even without receiving testimony about him ... It is therefore self-evident that the conversion performed by a Conservative rabbi is nothing.[61]

Through the utilization of the law of *moridin ve-lo ma-alin*, Feinstein is able to effect the above disqualification *a priori*, and en masse, with no need for an investigation as to the actual practices of the rabbi in question, and with no room for exceptions. The label of Reform and Conservative is sufficient to disqualify regardless of whether the rabbi is observant, and regardless of whether the ceremony is performed in accordance with halakhah as understood by Feinstein.

While the invalidation of all wedding ceremonies performed by Reform and Conservative rabbis marginalizes them in the sphere of ritual, it paradoxically serves to maintain some relationship in the sphere of loyalty. If Feinstein in fact wanted to achieve the type of separation from Conservative and Reform Jewry as called for by the Hatam Sofer, and as indicated by him throughout his Responsae, an ideal vehicle for this would be to undermine the possibility of intermarriage between Orthodox Jews and Conservative and Reform Jews. Given the absence of *gittin*, or at least Orthodox-perceived valid *gittin*, in Reform and Conservative divorces, there exists a legal foundation for arguing for the preponderance of *mamzerim* in non-Orthodox circles; with rising divorce rates, this situation would be exacerbated over the course of time, making the status of the non-Orthodox increasingly questionable, and rendering intermarriage between them and the Orthodox increasingly difficult. This would not be a sanction, but simply a legal consequence of their ambiguous personal status. In this way, the Hatam Sofer's yearning 'to separate them from our midst, to desist from giving our daughters to their sons and their sons to our daughters',[62] would become a halakhic necessity. What is interesting, however, is that it is precisely the disqualification of Conservative and Reform rabbi's marriages by Feinstein that prevents this from occurring. Once it is deemed that no marriage occurred in the first place, the union could simply be annulled without the woman requiring a *get* from her former husband.

This position, however, requires firm halakhic grounding, as even a couple without a formal marriage and who live in public in a relationship of husband and wife, can only dismantle their bonds through a *get*. The reason for this is the halakhic principle that a person does not make his sex licentious (*ein adam oseh be-ilato be-ilat zenut*), which makes the following argument: since no one would want to be a part of a marriage relationship characterized as licentious (*zenut*), couples intend their sexual relations to serve as a legal consummation of their marriage relationship. Consequently, according to Jewish law, they too require a *get*.[63] In a bold legal move, Feinstein rules that the only exceptions to this halakhic principle are those marriages performed by Reform and Conservative rabbis.[64] For them the sexual act, he rules, does not constitute *kiddushin*. To justify this position, he offers the following argument:

> In any event, it seems that we don't have to worry [about the lack of a *get*] even if they maintained their marriage for a number of years, for this [i.e. a marriage performed by a Reform rabbi] is worse than a civil marriage. In the case of a civil marriage, most people, even those who do not observe the laws of the Torah, know that there exists a requirement of marriage according to Jewish law that was not fulfilled by the civil marriage. Therefore, there is a ground to state that he did not count on the first marriage that was performed in the civil courts, and intended his sexual relations to constitute an act of *kiddushin*. However, in the case of Reform marriages, those who go there believe that it constituted an act of *kiddushin* and marriage in accordance with the laws of Israel. As a result, all consequent sexual relations are deemed as legitimate on the basis of this first act of marriage, for they do not know that there is anything missing from this *kiddushin* [performed by Reform rabbis] which would then necessitate that he intend his sexual relations to serve as the act of *kiddushin*.[65]

It would be difficult to argue conclusively that Feinstein's intent behind this ruling was to ensure that a barrier would not be erected prohibiting intermarriage between Jews of different factions. It is likely that the significant issue from his perspective in each case was freeing women from potential *agunah* status, and children of subsequent marriages from being considered *mamzerim*. However, the possible consequences of requiring a *get* were obviously known to him. By preferring to cancel the necessity of a *get*, he chose to enable the continuation of marriage among different communal factions, thus validating bonds of loyalty and fellowship among different factions within the community.

An interesting exception to the above unconditional marginalization of Reform and Conservative and the rejection of their status in the sphere of ritual appears when the issue is a *get* arranged by a Conservative rabbi who also served as one of the signatory witnesses. In the particular case that Feinstein is adjudicating, the rabbi in question is known as one who prays regularly, puts on *tefillin*, observes the Shabbat, and keeps the Jewish dietary laws. His only known deviance is that he violates the prohibition of carrying on Shabbat. This is only known, however, from the rabbi's self-testimony. Feinstein renders the latter issue inadmissible as evidence under the rule prohibiting self-incrimination. Feinstein then raises the point of the rabbi's testimony being disqualified by definition, given the fact that he studied in the Conservative Rabbinic seminary and holds a position in a Conservative synagogue, and is thus a *min* and *apikorus* and disqualified by definition without requiring any corroboratory testimony as to his deviance. The logical consequence of this chain of reasoning would be the disqualification of the *get*. Feinstein, however, proceeds to argue:

> There are however grounds to say that since there are some who learn [in the Conservative rabbinical seminary] for a period of time [solely] motivated by the increased salary they will attain afterwards from the position of rabbi in a [Conservative] synagogue, their presumption of innocence [of being neither a *min* or *apikorus*] is not changed, and they are not to be suspected of heresy.
>
> Even though it is forbidden [to learn in their seminary and serve in their synagogues] on the basis of the verse 'keep yourself far away from her' which refers to *minut* ... in any event, one is not to disqualify his [testimony] because of this prohibition, for [learning in their seminary] is not a negative prohibition the violation of which requires lashes, and one who is suspected of violating something minor is not suspected of violating something major.
>
> As a result, such an individual retains his presumption of innocence of not being a *kofer*. Therefore I am in doubt as to whether the rabbi should be disqualified from serving as a witness, and I am even more inclined to not disqualify him.[66]

There are two interesting aspects to this ruling. The first is the fact that Feinstein contradicts his other ruling and removes the *a priori* ban and disqualification of at least Conservative rabbis. The second is his argument to justify this ruling by removing the rabbi from the category of *min*, *apikorus* and *kofer*, and defining him instead as a *mumar leteiavon*, motivated by profit, and consequently one who retains his presumption of innocence. Only if there is explicit testimony that the Conservative rabbi deviates in such a way as to disqualify him from testimony, then and only then is his testimony invalid. In the absence of this explicit testimony, he is allowed to serve as a witness, and in this case, both to arrange the *get* proceedings and serve as a witness. This argument stands in direct contradiction to his statements in the following Responsa.

> There is no greater publicity or *hazakah* than his holding by the principles of the Conservative to deny many of the laws of the Torah and to even possibly to deny the essence of receiving the Torah at Sinai than him serving as a Rabbi in their synagogue. And even if he does this to make a living, he still has the status of *kofer* who is disqualified from serving as a witness, for when it comes to *kefirah* there is no distinction between an actual *kofer* and one who is a *kofer* as a result of the fact that he profits and makes a salary from it. Moreover, if the motivation is to make a living, regarding validity to testify he is even more problematic, for a *mumar leteiavon* is disqualified according to all, while the *mumar lehakhis* is not disqualified according to the opinion of Rava.[67]

In one instance Feinstein validates the testimony of a Conservative rabbi on the grounds that the motivation for his deviance is *teiavon*; in the other instance he argues that there is no category of *kofer leteiavon*, and even if there were it would not help, for *teiavon* does not mitigate deviance when it comes to testimony. Furthermore, in the latter case the mere fact that one serves in a Conservative synagogue makes one by definition a *kofer*, while in the former, *kofer* status is only rendered if there is explicit testimony to his heresy.

To understand the reason for this contradiction in Feinstein, one has to understand the particulars of each case. The testimony of the Conservative rabbi is accepted in a case in which to fail to do so would invalidate the *get*, rendering the women an *agunah*. In the case where the testimony is rejected, the first marriage, which ended without a *get*, is annulled, making the women's second marriage valid and her subsequent children legitimate, thus avoiding the issue of *mamzerut*. It is thus clear that as a *posek*, Feinstein has taken it upon himself to do anything possible to ameliorate the personal status crises of *agunot* and *mamzerim*. Those individuals who turned to him for a ruling, and thus also accept or recognize his authority, fall within his sphere of loyalty, and as a result, they benefit from his halakhic courage and ingenuity. Reform and Conservative Jews and rabbis, on the whole, do not. As a result, they are subjected to consistent attempts at disqualification and de-legitimization. What is evident, however, is that the labelling of Reform or Conservative rabbis as *kofrim* is not a necessary conclusion. Feinstein has the ability to legitimize their marriages and conversion, not to mention their blessings and religious functions; what he lacks is the desire to do so. This willingness to accommodate the other is an essential by-product of the sphere of loyalty. In Moshe Feinstein's case, this loyalty is never applied to Reform and Conservative Jews in the first place.

Marginalization in the Sphere of Basic Membership

On the issue of the sphere of membership, Feinstein's verdict is clear. Nowhere does he even consider changing the membership status of deviants.[68] Even the most severe deviants maintain their status as 'Israel',[69] are described as maintaining '*kedushat yisrael*' (the sanctity of Israel), and are clearly distinguished from the non-Jew.[70]

Despite the above, throughout Feinstein's Responsae, there is extensive evidence of a legislative policy calling for a total separation from certain deviants, in particular Conservative and Reform Jews. If all contact and cooperation is forbidden, separate communal institutions are required, and even educators are forbidden to reach out to them (not to mention regular individuals who are not 'qualified'), the question is in what sense are Orthodox, Conservative and Reform Jews members of the same collective. This separation is most evident in the sphere of loyalty. By this I do not merely mean the prohibition to support a Federation which funds Conservative and Reform institutions, or the permission to charge them interest. Rather, I am referring to Feinstein's creating a distinction between 'our' children and 'their' children when it comes to education, even though Feinstein himself defines them under the category of *tinok shenishbah*. Furthermore, his consistent effort to ignore, override, or change potential legal solutions or loopholes that would enable some contact and cooperation is the most telling evidence of his break with Conservative and Reform Jewry. When compared to his attitude towards the *mehallel Shabbat befarhesia* who belongs to an Orthodox synagogue, or towards other Orthodox-affiliated deviants, this lack of loyalty and concern is even more evident. As stated above, the important question in the sphere of membership is the following: When do marginalizing sanctions in the sphere of loyalty outweigh the significance of formal membership? At the very least, it is clear in which direction Feinstein is tipping the balance.

Prescriptive and Descriptive Marginalization

Moshe Feinstein's policy on this issue is dependent on the denomination of the deviant in question. When it comes to the Orthodox-affiliated *mehallel Shabbat befarhesia*, he maintains a strict descriptive policy. Consequently, he refuses to change their status, and he overrules or reinterprets prior precedent in order to maintain their status in accordance with their self-definition, i.e. as members of Orthodoxy. On the other hand, when it comes to Reform and Conservative Jewry, he adopts a prescriptive policy, which given the historical circumstances, renders him one of the most extreme implementers of prescriptive marginalization in the history of halakhah.

As stated above, at the time of the Hatam Sofer, prescriptive marginalization nevertheless had a quasi-descriptive foundation. At the beginning of the nineteenth century, the denominations were starting to separate from one another, and staking out their own space. When he saw Reform Jews, he saw individuals who were consciously choosing to be non-Orthodox. As a result, the Hatam Sofer may have been justified in perceiving Reform Jews first and foremost as individuals who had broken with him and his community. Consequently, his marginalization of them could still be quasi-descriptive in the sense that Reform was separating from Orthodoxy and marginalization by Orthodoxy merely reaffirmed this fact.

By the time of Moshe Feinstein, this was no longer the case. Reform, and subsequently Conservative, Jews had both existed and, in many ways, also coexisted with Orthodoxy within the collective structure of the Jewish people for over 100 years. In addition, Reform and Conservative Jews were no longer defined by their breaking with Orthodoxy and setting out on a new path. They had already arrived, and had lived their lives for decades as full members of the Jewish community. To marginalize them to the status of intolerable deviants, while ignoring their clear self-identity as Jews, regardless of what one thinks of the nature of their Judaism, is clearly prescriptive.

What makes their marginalization even more prescriptive and extreme is the fact that, by the mid-twentieth century Reform and Conservative Jews had already become the majority of the Jewish people in America. Their primary identity was no longer as the 'non-Orthodox'. They had established an alternative within the Jewish people and in fact constituted the Jewish mainstream, determining the shared cultural space of the Jewish people more than their Orthodox counterparts. Nowhere in the history of Jewish boundary policy has anyone called for the imposing of marginalization policies, and extreme ones at that, on a group that is both established within the Jewish community and in fact representative of the majority of the Jews. When the overwhelming proportion of Jews are classified as intolerable deviants, one's boundary policy no longer serves to define the people but rather to re-define it.

Through his prescriptive marginalization of Reform and Conservative Jews, Feinstein thus constructs a boundary policy not in order to create frameworks for living with difference, but rather to remove from the community all those whose beliefs and practices, or more accurately, whose formal affiliation, is different from his own. The purpose of his boundary policy is not to strengthen Jewish collective life, but to create walls around Orthodoxy, championing it as the new Jewish people. In the past there was some legal precedent for the prescriptive marginalization of small groups within the Jewish people, in particular if they were also enemy deviants. Nowhere is there any precedent for the type of extreme move called for by Moshe Feinstein.

Modernity redefined the scope of the challenges facing Jewish individual and collective identity, creating a reality of an unprecedented nature. Feinstein's response was to create a boundary policy of an equally unprecedented nature that in many ways gave up on Jewish collective life, at least as we have known it, and attempted to offer a new foundation and basis for the Jews as a people.

Notes

1 For an analysis of the Jewish Community in North America during this period, see: N. Glazer, *American Judaism* (Chicago, 1989); B. Martin, 'American Jewry Since 1945: An Historical Overview', in B. Martin (ed.), *Movements and Issues in American Judaism* (Westport, 1978), pp. 3–24; A. Hertzberg, *The Jews in America* (New York, 1990); 'The American Jew and His Religion', in J. Neusner (ed.), *Understanding American Judaism* (New York, 1975), pp. 5–24; C. Leibman, 'The Religion of American Jews', in J. Neusner (ed.), *Understanding American Judaism*, pp. 25–68; L. P. Gartner, 'Immigration and the Formation of the American Jew: 1940–1925', in M. Sklare (ed.), *American Jews – A Reader* (New York, 1983), pp. 5–22.

2 See M. Sklare, M. Vosk and M. Zborowski, 'Forms of Expression of Jewish Identification', in *Jewish Social Studies* 17 (1955), 205–9. On the basis of an analysis of the religious affiliation of Jews in 1952 with that of their grandparents in a large city on the East Coast of the United States, as an example of a general trend, Sklare *et al.* bring the following significant statistics. While 81% of the grandmothers' and grandfathers' generation were Orthodox, only 16% of their grandchildren's generation were Orthodox. Five per cent of the grandparents were Reform as opposed to 30% of the grandchildren, while 11% of the former were Conservative in comparison with 43% of the latter. Furthermore, while more than 60% of the Conservatives and Reforms declared their intention to remain as such, only 20% of Orthodox planned to remain Orthodox, and the majority planned to become Conservative.

3 For an historical analysis of Orthodoxy during this period, see Charles Leibman, 'Orthodoxy in American Jewish Life', in *American Jewish Year Book* 66 (New York, 1965), pp. 21–97.

4 *Ibid.*, p. 249.

5 See J. S. Glock, 'Twentieth-Century American Orthodoxy's Era of Non-Observance, 1900–1960', *The Torah U-Madda Journal* 9 (2000), 87–107.

6 For an analysis of the history of the development and ideology of the

Conservative Movement, see David Rudavsky, *Modern Jewish Religious Movements: A History of Emancipation and Adjustment* (New York, 1972), pp. 317–45. Also M. Davis, *The Emergence of Conservative Judaism* (Philadelphia, 1963); M. Waxman, 'Conservative Judaism – A Survey', in M. Waxman (ed.), *Tradition and Change* (New York, 1970); D. Elazar and R. M. Geffen, *The Conservative Movement in Judaism* (Albany, 2000); E. Dorff, *Conservative Judaism: Our Ancestors to Our Descendants* (New York, 1979); N. Gillman, *Conservative Judaism: the New Century* (West Orange, 1993).

7 For a historical survey of the Reform Movement and its ideology in America, see Michael Meyer, *Responses to Modernity* (New York, 1988); David Rudavsky, *Modern Jewish Religious Movements*, pp. 285–302.

8 M. Feinstein, *Igrot Moshe*, Oreh Haim 2.51.

9 See for example, *Igrot Moshe*, Yoreh Deah 4.58.3.

10 See *Igrot Moshe*, Oreh Haim 2.51.

11 See *Igrot Moshe*, Yoreh Deah 4.58.3

12 See for example, *Igrot Moshe*, Oreh Haim 2.51; Yoreh Deah 3.39: Even ha-Ezer 1.52, 1.82.

13 See for example, *Igrot Moshe*, Oreh Haim 1.33, 2.2, 4.39, 5.18; Yoreh Deah 1.235, 2.3, 2.140, 4.14, 5.10; Even ha-Ezer 1.40, 1.52, 1.152, 1.73, 1.121, 3.4, 3.28, 3.30, 4.23, 4.104, 4.112, 4.120, 4.121.

14 See for example, *Igrot Moshe* Oreh Haim 1.23, 1.33, 2.19, 3.22, 4.96, 5.20.35, 5.28.22, 5.29, 5.37.8; Yoreh Deah 1.1, 1.70, 2.3, 2.4, 2.5, 2.43, 2.47, 2.78, 4.37.17, 4.58.3, 4.61.6; Even ha-Ezer 1.42, 1.52, 1.121, 2.20, 3.49, 4.62; Hoshen Mishpat 2.50.

15 See for example, *Igrot Moshe*, Oreh Haim 2.50, 3.28, 4.39, 4.91.6; Yoreh Deah 1.139, 1.174, 2.3, 2.101, 2.107, 2.140, 4.14; and Even ha-Ezer 1.82, 1.135, 2.20, 3.30, 4.13.3, 4.26,4.80.

16 *Igrot Moshe*, Oreh Haim 1.23, 1.33, 2.19, 3.22, 4.96, 5.20.35, 5.28.22, 5.29, 5.37.8; Yoreh Deah 1.1, 1.70, 2.3, 2.4, 2.5, 2.43, 2.47, 2.78, 4.37.17, 4.58.3, 4.61.6; Even ha-Ezer 1.42, 1.52, 1.121, 2.20, 3.49, 4.62; Hoshen Mishpat 2.50.

17 *Igrot Moshe*, Oreh Haim 3.28, 4.91.6; Yoreh Deah 1.139, 1.174, 2.101,2.107; Even ha-Ezer 1.135, 4.26,4.80.

18 *Igrot Moshe*, Oreh Haim 2.50; Yoreh Deah 1.174; Even ha-Ezer 1.82, 1.135, 2.20, 4.13.3.

19 *Igrot Moshe*, Yoreh Deah 4.58.3.

20 See *Igrot Moshe*, Oreh Haim 1.33. The language of Feinstein's ruling is as follows.

'In my commentary, I commented regarding the rationale for distinguishing with regard to Shabbat being like idolatry, between the public and private (desecration of the Shabbat). Initially, this distinction (between public and private) does not make sense given the fact that private violations are as severe with regard to the Shabbat as are public violations. Furthermore, from the perspective of the heresy involved, private is even worse than public, as seen in Baba Kama page 79 regarding the distinction between the robber who hides his identity (*ganav*) and the robber who does not (*gazlan*). I explained that the cause for comparing the violator of the Shabbat to an idol worshipper is due to the fact that he (the Shabbat violator) looks like a *kofer* and this applies only if it is for this reason (i.e. that he is a *kofer*) that he is violating the Shabbat. But if it is due to the fact that he does not withstand the temptation of earning money or to fulfil his desires, he is not to be considered a *kofer*. Therefore, when he violates the Shabbat in private, he can claim that the reason for the violation is to fulfil his desires and even if he does not make this claim we are to grant him the presumption of being innocent and in good standing (*kasher*) and that the impetus was desire, and not him being a *kofer*. Similarly, we have seen that even one who eats forbidden foods out of desire (*teiavon*) has the presumption of innocence (*hezkat kashrut*) that he would not eat *lehakhis* for one suspected with regard to a light violation is not suspected regarding a more severe one. In public, however, his inner thoughts and intentions are a matter of the heart that is not known to the onlookers. They [upon seeing his behaviour] will interpret it as resulting from him being a *kofer*. Consequently, he has done an act of heresy (*kefirah*) even though in his heart he is a believer in God and is so doing out of desire. This is due to the fact that he did the act in front of onlookers, so it is necessary that it be judged in accordance with how the onlookers will assess his actions, i.e. as the actions of a *kofer*. However, here (in our times) since it is known that most violators of the Shabbat do so because of the desire for money and many go to synagogue to pray and then go to their place of work, it is possible that even public violations should be judged similarly to private violations. This is because the onlookers will not in any way assess the act as heresy, but rather, that the violation of the Shabbat is the result of desire. Consequently [today, the violator of the Shabbat in public] is in all matters, not like the idolater.'

See also, Yoreh Deah 2.5, 4.58.3; and Even ha-Ezer 2.20.

21 It is interesting to compare the position of Rabbi Feinstein regarding the Orthodox desecrator of the Sabbath, with the two halakhic precedents – that of R. Ya'akov Ettlinger (1798–1871), the famous rabbi of Altona and teacher of Azriel Hildesheimer and R. Samson Rafael Hirsch, and that of R. David Zvi Hoffman (1843–1921), head of the Rabbinical Seminary of Berlin. In *Responsa Binyan Zion ha-Hadashot* 23, regarding the wine of one who desecrates the Sabbath publicly, R. Ettlinger presents for the first time the claim that we later find in the writings of Rabbi Feinstein, which differentiates between a desecrator of the Sabbath considered a *kofer*, and one who is not considered a *kofer.*

'The stipulation of the exalted teacher, may his light shine, namely the prohibition against the imbibing of wine touched by a Jew who desecrated the Sabbath publicly because he is a *mumar lekol hatorah kullah*, is supported by the Mabit [R. Moshe Ben Yosef of Tirani], who wrote in *Responsa Nekudat HaKesef* (14.124) that the imbibing of wine touched by Karaites is prohibited since they desecrate the festivals and are like desecrators of the Sabbath. However, some disagree with him, and he therefore asked my opinion on the matter.

In my humble opinion, he is correct, since one who desecrates the Sabbath publicly is like a *mumar lekol hatorah kullah*, and his legal status is like that of a heathen ...

Until this point we have discussed the original intent of the law regarding treatment of one who desecrates the Sabbath publicly. However, regarding the transgressors of our days, I do not know what to rule in their case since in our manifold iniquities the infection has spread so widely to the point where in most cases they desecrate the Sabbath as if it is permissible. Perhaps we should regard them legally as if they deem it as permissible for themselves, such that would be considered only close to deliberate sinning (*meizid*), since there are those who recite the Sabbath prayers and sanctify the Sabbath over wine (*Kiddush*), and afterwards desecrate the Sabbath, performing tasks forbidden by the Torah and by the Sages. Since a desecrator of the Sabbath is considered a *mumar* only because when one denies the Sabbath, one denies creation and the Creator, yet these individuals recognize [the creation and Creator] through prayer and *Kiddush*. Moreover, the children whom they have raised have not known or heard the laws of the Sabbath, and are thus like the Sadducees, who were not considered *mumarim* even though they desecrated the Sabbath, since they did as their ancestors, and are like *tinok shenishbah* (a child taken into captivity) by idolaters, as is explained (*ibid.*, 385), and as the Mabit wrote (*ibid.*, 37): They can also be viewed as Sadducees who were not used [to observe the halakhah] among the Jews and did not know the basics of the religion, and do not take on a spiteful attitude against the wise men of the generation, and are not thought of as deliberate sinners, (see *ibid.*) ... Therefore, in my humble opinion, the stringent ruling that considers the wine of these transgressors as the wine of Gentiles should be blessed. Nevertheless, those who rule leniently have grounds (on which to base their ruling), unless it is clear that one who knows the laws of the Sabbath and defiantly desecrates it in the presence of a gathering of ten Jewish men, in which case he is certainly a complete *mumar* and it is forbidden to touch his wine. And this is my humble opinion – Ya'akov.'

R. Ettlinger is aware of the fact that the characteristics of the deviance of one who desecrates the Sabbath in public has changed. The acts of the desecrator who prays and makes *Kiddush* testify to the fact that he does not deny the Creator or creation. Therefore, Ettlinger raises the possibility of ruling leniently regarding such a person's wine. This, however, is contingent on it being 'clear that one who knows the laws of the Sabbath and defiantly desecrates it in the presence of a gathering of ten Jewish men' is a *mumar*. This additional condition renders R. Ettlinger's precedent unsatisfactory for R. Feinstein, who seeks to unequivocally clarify the position of the Orthodox Jew who desecrates the Sabbath publicly, despite his familiarity with the laws of the Sabbath. In quoting R. Ettlinger, R. Feinstein only refers to and rejects the former's claim regarding the possibility that one who desecrates the Sabbath publicly is not a deliberate sinner because 'in our manifold iniquities the infection that has spread so widely to the point where in most cases, they desecrate the Sabbath as if it is permissible.' See also *Responsa Igrot Moshe*, Even ha-Ezer, 2.20.4. In addition, the connection R. Ettlinger makes between one who desecrates the Sabbath publicly in his generation, and the law regarding *tinok shenishbah*, was not mentioned by R. Feinstein. This omission enabled him to avoid altering the desecrator's status, since such a connection would necessitate a change in the status of every desecrator of the Sabbath in public, and is not restricted to the Orthodox.

The Responsa that does use this argument regarding *tinok shenishbah* is that of R. David Zvi Hoffman, *Melamed le-ho-il,* Oreh Haim 28, where he deals with the question of whether one who desecrates the Sabbath in public can be counted in a *minyan.*

'Question: In our *minyan,* there are one or two men who desecrate the Sabbath publicly not only in their occupations, but also in general, and they do not even perform *Kiddush* and *havdalah,* but their inclusion in the *minyan* was approved.

Answer: ... regarding the above, although the law regarding one who desecrates the Sabbath in public is to not include him in a *minyan,* in our times, there is a tendency towards leniency, even in Hungary, and even more so in Ashkenaz. I recall that once there was a man whose store was open on Shabbat, who was in mourning, and he was one of the well-to-do of our community, Adath Israel, and he led the prayers in our synagogue. But the *gabbai* knew how to please him and placate him so that he would not lead prayers any more since the congregation complained about it, and afterwards, this man went to the Hevrat Shas synagogue, and although the *gabbai* there was a God-fearing man, he let him lead the prayers without hesitation, and when I asked the *gabbai* why he didn't prevent it, he told me that this has been the practice since days of old in this house of study, that they do not prevent those whose businesses are open on the Sabbath from leading the prayers, and because the rabbis there did not protest, they probably had a reason and substantiation, and they may have based themselves on what is also written in *Responsa Binyan Zion ha-Hadashot* 23, that desecrators of the Sabbath in our day are considered to a degree as *tinok shenishbah* amongst the heathens since in our manifold iniquities, most Jews in our land desecrate the Sabbath, and it is not their intention to deny the mainstays of our faith.

Indeed, our rabbi and teacher R. Zalman HaCohen of blessed memory in the name of the *gaon* author of *Sho-el u-Meishiv* [R. Shaul Nathanson], wrote that the Jews in America are not disqualified by their desecration of the Sabbath because they are like the *tinok shenishbah* amongst the heathens. Later, I found a similar stipulation in the writing of R. Akiva Eiger, Yoreh Deah 264 ... Be that as it may, one who is lenient regarding the inclusion of such persons in a *minyan* relies on someone, but if one can attend a different synagogue without bringing shame upon anyone, it is better that he should not rely on this *heiter,* and should pray with worthy people. An additional reason for leniency in our day is that they are not considered as those who desecrate the Sabbath publicly, since most people behave in this way. The reasoning would apply if most Jews were observant and few dared to violate this prohibition, since one would be a *kofer* against the entire Torah, and considered as carrying out an abomination in an uninhibited manner. But in our manifold iniquities, in the case of those who break the law, the misdeed becomes their saving grace. The individual believes that it is not such a great transgression, and does not need to be performed privately, and for him, publicly and privately are one and the same; indeed, the God-fearing are today referred to as the Sadducees and set apart, and the transgressors are the norm.'

By determining the status of the desecrator of the Sabbath in public, or as a *tinok shenishbah*, or as a violator of the Sabbath in private, R. Hoffman makes a categorical distinction between the law regarding one who violates the Sabbath publicly in the past and one who does so in his times. In this sense, the ruling of R. Feinstein follows from it, but with one significant difference. Both the law regarding *tinok shenishbah* and desecration committed publicly (*befarhesia*) – a function of rebellion and separation from the community, and conditioned on a reality in which most of the people observe the Sabbath – create a halakhic basis for converting the status of every public desecrator of the Sabbath into one of a tolerated deviant. However, R. Feinstein, as stated, is interested only in changing the status of Orthodox desecrators of the Sabbath. As far as the others are concerned, he applies the law: 'leave the evil one to his own devices and he will die.'

For a broader discussion on the positions of R. Ettlinger and R. Hoffman, see J. Bleich, 'Rabbinic Responses to Non-Observance in the Modern Era' in J. Schachter (ed.) *Jewish Tradition and the Non-Traditional Jew* (Northvale, 1992), pp. 72–6; A. Ferziger, *Exclusion and Hierarchy*, (Philadelphia 2005), pp. 90–109, 173–7; S. Morrell, 'The Halakhic Status of Nom-Halakhic Jews', *Judaism* 18, 3 (1969), 455–7. See as well, Avi Sagi, and Zvi Zohar, *Ma-agalei Zehut Yehudit be-Sifrut ha-Hilkhatit* (Tel Aviv, 2000), pp. 137–9.

22 *Igrot Moshe*, Oreh Haim 4.91.6.

23 *Igrot Moshe*, Oreh Haim 2.50, 3.21, 3.25, 4.91.6; Yoreh Deah 1.139, 1.149, 2.100, 2.107; Even ha-Ezer 2.26.5, 3.3, 3.23, 4.13.3, 4.21.6, 4.46, 4.80.

24 *Igrot Moshe*, Oreh Haim 2.50, 4.91.6; Yoreh Deah 1.160, 2.12, 2.100; Even ha-Ezer 1.77, 1.85, 1.135, 2.26.5, 3.3, 3.4, 3.23, 4.13.3, 4.77, 4.78.

25 *Igrot Moshe*, Even ha-Ezer 4.13.3.

26 Maimonides, Hilkhot Mamrim 3.3. See also Hilkhot Sheggaggot 2.6 where Maimonides gives the *tinok shenishbah*, the law of *shogeg*.

27 *Igrot Moshe*, Oreh Haim, 4.91 (6).

28 *Igrot Moshe*, Oreh Haim 1.99.

29 *Igrot Moshe*, Yoreh Deah 2.107. See also *ibid.*, 106.

30 *Igrot Moshe*, Yoreh Deah 2.107. In 106, Moshe Feinstein suggests switching Torah Studies in girls' schools to afternoon hours in order to expand the work hours of teachers teaching boys in the morning, thus freeing them from the financial need to take up teaching positions in Reform and Conservative schools functioning in the afternoon.

31 The *mumar ledavar ehad lehakhis* is not to be called to the Torah, given the fact that Feinstein, in defining him as a heretic, declares that he does not believe in God and the Torah. However, in cases where the *mumar* in question plays an important role in the community, and sanctions will harm the community, one can honour him with the opening and shutting of the ark, as the fulfillment of these acts does not necessitate proper faith. See *ibid.*, Oreh Haim 2.51, and 3.21. Their testimony is invalid, even without witnesses attesting to their deviance, (*Igrot Moshe*, Even ha-Ezer 1.52, and 1.82). Thus any wedding where they serve

as witnesses is invalidated and does not necessitate a *get* to annul it. *Igrot Moshe*, Even ha-Ezer 1.52. One sanction that does pertain to the sphere of loyalty involves permission to both charge a *mumar* and pay him interest. This is the result of the abolishment of the responsibility to sustain and assist (*le-hah-yoto*), a responsibility which applies exclusively to Israelites in good standing. See *Igrot Moshe*, Yoreh Deah 3.39.

32 *Igrot Moshe*, 2.43, and 2.47.

33 *Igrot Moshe*, Even ha-Ezer 1.52.3.

34 *Igrot Moshe*, Yoreh Deah 2.78.

35 *Ibid.*, 2.3. See as well, *ibid.*, 1.1, where even the *mehallel Shabbat leteiavon* is called a *kofer* and disqualified to serve as a *shohet*.

36 *Igrot Moshe*, Oreh Haim 3.22.

27 *Ibid.*, 5.20.35.

38 *Ibid.*, 1.23, 2.19.

39 See *Ibid.*, 5.28.22 and 5.29. Feinstein further argues that the building of an *eruv* can create a stumbling block for the righteous who may carry even when the *eruv* is not functional.

It is interesting to compare this ruling of Feinstein with slightly different circumstances facing the Hatam Sofer. He was asked about the need to build an *eruv* in order to prevent righteous Jews from sinning.

'Therefore it is self-evident to anyone of sound mind that it is impossible for the community of Israel to prevent throughout the Shabbat all the children of their household, nor their wives and those of weak intellect, from taking minor things or small cloths, or children carrying bread in their hands, from going outside the gates of their home. In addition, how great will be the extent of the anguish which will be caused to the adults who are careful, in particular with regards to prayer in synagogue on the Shabbat day regarding the bringing of prayer books to pray from and prayer shawls and the like. Therefore simple logic requires that it is worthy and required to erect in the courtyards an *eruv* which permits one to carry.' (*Responsa Hatam Sofer*, Orekh Haim 99).

40 *Igrot Moshe*, Oreh Haim 3.25 and 4.91.6.

41 *Igrot Moshe*, Yoreh Deah 2.101

42 *Igrot Moshe*, Oreh Haim 3.25.

43 *Igrot Moshe*, Yoreh Deah 1.139, and 2.106.

44 *Ibid.* 1.139.

45 *Ibid.* 2.107. See as well, *ibid.*, 106 where Feinstein recommends moving Torah studies in the girls' schools to the afternoon, thus opening up the educational positions there to the teachers who also teach the boys in the morning, consequently alleviating the financial need to take teaching positions in Reform and Conservative afternoon schools.

46 *Ibid.* 2.100. Feinstein does not specifically mention here Avodah Zarah page 17, but the rationale is the same. This Responsa was written in 1970. However, in *ibid.*, Yoreh Deah 1.149, written in 1959, he specifically allows Orthodox to join communal institutions together with Reform and Conservative Jews, limiting partnerships and co-operative ventures with idolaters alone, and not with

'wicked Israelites'. However, even there he argues that contributing to Federation is forbidden if monies are allocated to Reform and Conservative institutions. Feinstein argues that to do so is 'worse than contributing to non-Jewish idolaters to assist them in building a house of worship for themselves'. Orthodox contributions to Federation are only permitted under the following condition: If by the observers of Torah not contributing, nothing will be given to Torah institutions, it is still forbidden to contribute unless if by the contributions of the observers of Torah a greater sum of monies will be allocated to the Torah institutions than was contributed by the observers of Torah. For then, not only did they not assist the institutions of the *kofrim*, but they actually harmed them.

47 See *Igrot Moshe*, Oreh Haim 4.40.26 and Yoreh Deah 3.129.6

48 *Igrot Moshe*, Oreh Haim 4.91.6.

49 In Maimonides, Hilkhot Yisodei ha-Torah 6.8. the proper reading is *min*. Feinstein, however, often reads it as *apikorus*. Given the parallel meanings for the categories in Feinstein, the issue is rendered insignificant. See *Igrot Moshe* 4.39 where Feinstein refers to the scribe of the *Sefer Torah* sometimes as *apikorus*, sometimes as *min* and sometimes as *kofer*.

50 *Igrot Moshe*.

51 *Igrot Moshe*, Oreh Haim 2.50 and 4.39.

52 In addition he also reiterates the literal application of the Maimonidean ruling and applies it to a *Sefer Torah* or holy work written by a *min/apikorus* as well as to the writings of missionaries in which God's name is recorded. See *Igrot Moshe*, Oreh Haim 4.39; and Yoreh Deah 2.137, 2.172. Such documents, he rules, are not sacred scrolls and need not be treated as such.

53 *Igrot Moshe*, Oreh Haim 2.50.

54 *Ibid.* See as well, *ibid.*, 2.51, 3.21, and *Igrot Moshe*, Even ha-Ezer 2.80.

55 *Igrot Moshe*, Oreh Haim 3.22. See as well, *ibid.*, 3.12.

56 See, *ibid.*, 2.50.

57 See *Igrot Moshe*, Yoreh Deah 3.39.

58 *Igrot Moshe*, Even ha-Ezer 1.82.11. See as well, *ibid.*, 1.52.3, 1.85, 1.86, 1.135, 2.26.5, 3.23, 4.13.3, 4.24, and 4.41.

59 *Ibid.*, 4.13.3.

60 *Ibid.*, 3.23. See as well, *ibid.*, 1.76; 1.77, and 3.25

61 *Igrot Moshe*, Yoreh Deah 1.160.

62 *Igrot Moshe*, Likutei She-eilot ve-Teshuvot 89. See as well, *ibid.*, 86, where the Hatam Sofer states that the fate of Jews who incline towards Reform practice 'are not our responsibility'.

63 See BT Tractate Gittin 81a–81b; Maimonides, Hilkhot Gittin 10.17–19 and Hilkhot Ishut 7.23; *Tur*, Even ha-Ezer 149, and Beit Yoseph, on the Tur, *ibid.*

64 See *Igrot Moshe*, Even ha-Ezer 1.75, where Feinstein is also willing to remove the necessity for a *get* even in civil marriages, in the event that it is impossible to get a *get*, and the women is an *agunah*. He does so on the grounds that under these circumstances one can accept the argument that those who are willing to violate all of the laws of the Torah are not bothered if their sexual relations constitute an act of *zenut*. See as well *ibid.*, 1.74, 3.77, 3.25, 3.85. See as well *ibid*, 3.25, where

Feinstein also argues that a student in a Reform seminary, who is therefore a *kofer* in the Torah and violates all of Torah arrogantly, is also willing to have sexual relations which are characterized as *zenut*.

65 *Ibid.*, 3.25. See as well *ibid.*, 1.76, 1.77, and 3.85

66 *Ibid.*, 1.135.

67 *Ibid.*, 4.13.3.

68 On the issue of *yibum*, the only issue he is willing to consider is whether the husband was an apostate, and whether the original intent of the wife was to such a marriage (*de-adata de-hakhi lo kidshah nafshah*), thus possibly nullifying the marriage in the first place. The question of whether the *mumar* has the status of Israel and *ahikha* is not even raised. See for example *ibid.*, 1.152 and 1.162. Furthermore, on the issue of paying and charging interest, Feinstein assumes that the *mumar* is *ahikha*. He nevertheless permits the charging of interest because there is no obligation with regard to the *mumar* to maintain him (*le-hahyoto*), an issue in the sphere of loyalty and not basic membership. As to paying him interest in light of the rule of *lifnei iver lo tasim mikhshol*, i.e. not placing a stumbling block in front of the blind, Feinstein also permits it because he argues that the law of *lifnei iver* does not apply in this case. See *Igrot Moshe*, Yoreh Deah 3.39.

69 See *Igrot Moshe*, Orekh Haim 1.23; Yoreh Deah 3.39; Even ha-Ezer 4.7, 4.83.

70 See *Igrot Moshe*, Yoreh Deah 3.146.

CHAPTER SIX

Towards a Contemporary Theory of Boundaries

Diversity is the defining and central feature of contemporary Jewish life. It is so pervasive that one is hard-pressed to identify anything that all those who declare membership in the Jewish people hold in common today. The absence of commonality is frequently the source of tension and discord. Nonetheless, in the contemporary context it is important to remember that diversity is in fact one of the central forces enabling and sustaining Jewish continuity.

Diversity is not merely a by-product of the multiplicity of denominations that characterize modern Judaism. These multiple approaches are symptoms of a deeper revolution, a revolution in the nature of Jewish identity. For most of Jewish history, one's identity was self-evident. People did not choose their Jewish identity, it chose them. One was born a Jew and, for the most part, one by and large died a Jew. However, in the modern context, genetic origins cease to be the determinant factor in one's identity, especially with anti-Semitism on the wane. What characterizes modernity is choice, by which I mean not simply the freedom to choose, but the opportunity to choose. Modern men and women are offered participation and membership in multiple spheres of identity, and one is required to choose where one wants to belong.

Futhermore, this choice is often between multiple identities that are expected to coexist. In the past one's identity was not only inherited but was also singular and all-encompassing. Being a Jew defined most aspects of one's life, from one's belief system, to one's values and behaviour, to one's neighbourhood, friends and socio-economic status. Modern identity, on the other hand, is more often that not, complex and limited, with one identity coexisting simultaneously with multiple others, each inhabiting only a partial space within the life of an individual, each claiming only a part of a person's loyalty. We rarely have one dominant membership commitment, but rather many, with each playing a role and taking turns to lead in different contexts. Thus, one can be a Jew, an American, a Republican or Democrat, a lawyer, a woman, etc. In the modern world one travels between these identities, focusing on some and relegating others to insignificance depending on the needs each fulfills and the joy and meaning each provides.

In the context of choice, vis-à-vis both one's identity and, more significantly, the place and significance of this identity in comparison to others, it is critical that the framework be in place to motivate and inspire that choice. That framework is diversity. It is only when Judaism offers a diverse product with multiple access points that there is a chance that different individuals with varied sensibilities and needs will find within Judaism an identity to which they both want to belong and to which they will pledge loyalty. On the other hand, when these access points are limited or under the control of a certain ideology, most Jews will opt out, failing to choose or to give to their Jewish identity a place of prominence. Diversity is that which inspires and enables the critical decision to be Jewish, and must remain so, if Jews are to continue to make this choice.

In the midst of this reality of choices, the enterprise of building and maintaining Jewish collective identity is exceptionally complex. It requires boundary policies of special sensitivity and adeptness. Too limiting a policy will overly constrain the choices that Jews can make and compel masses of Jews to locate their identity elsewhere. In addition it will feed the forces of sectarianism and provide the framework for ideologues to re-construct Jewish collective identity in terms that exclusively reflect their own affiliation and ideology. If that happens, the Jewish people as one people will cease to exist. In their stead will be a plethora of minor and insignificant denominations and interest groups, all identifying their roots in a people with a great past but with no future. At the same time, as discussed in the Introduction, a boundary policy which is too expansive and porous will not provide the Jewish people with a meaningful collective identity, and will thus undermine any motivation for choosing a Jewish identity in the first place.

In this chapter, I seek to suggest a boundary policy for the contemporary Jewish community. In so doing, I am not attempting to overcome Jewish diversity but rather to celebrate it. At the same time it is true that by its very nature, a boundary policy must have notions of intolerable deviance, so not every self-expression of Jewishness will find a place in the Jewish collective space.

There are two critical prerequisites which must be in place prior to actually defining the boundary policy. The first, and in some ways most crucial is that there must exist a presumption of loyalty, by which I mean an *a priori* decision to work to ensure that one's boundary policies encompass as wide a spectrum of those who identity themselves as Jews as possible. *Af al pi shehata yisrael hu*, i.e. deviants are still Israelites, must be one's standard, not merely as a statement of irrevocable status within the sphere of basic membership, but as a commitment within the sphere of loyalty. The exemplar of such a commitment, although in too limited a fashion, is Moshe

Feinstein. The essential critique against him is that he limited his loyalty to Orthodoxy alone, whereas a constructive boundary policy must apply to all Jews. Nevertheless, he serves as a model of how one can both shape legal precedent and re-interpret deviance as tolerable when one has in place a presumption of loyalty.

To reiterate, the presumption of loyalty does not mean that everyone must by definition find themselves within the boundaries, for that will render them meaningless. Rather it means that every attempt must be made to ensure that as much as possible of the ideological, practical and denominational diversity that finds expression in Jewish life remain within one's boundaries of the tolerable. To fail to do so is to offer a boundary policy which, instead of serving to define Jewish collective identity, works to redefine it and ultimately damage it.

The second prerequisite is the decision to apply the category of intolerable deviance descriptively and not prescriptively. That which is classified as intolerable must be shaped by the living reality that is the Jewish people. One may reject certain expressions of Jewish life, but the minute that that expression is the policy or ideology of more than a small minority of Jews, that rejection must remain within the confines of tolerance or tolerable deviance. Prior to the modern period, with the exception of Maimonides, this condition was by and large religiously maintained. Even Maimonides ruled that all second generation deviants fall under the category of *tinok shenishbah*, i.e. are not held responsible for their actions, thereby effectively overruling his prescriptive tendencies as well. Maimonides was more interested in prescriptively defining the essence of Judaism than prescriptively marginalizing deviants.

A powerful model for a wide-reaching presumption of loyalty and for a commitment to descriptive marginalization is offered by the Orthodox rabbi and head of the Rabbinical Seminary of Berlin, David Zvi Hoffman (1843–1921). Hoffman was confronted with the question as to whether one can count in a *minyan* [the quorum of ten] a *mehallel Shabbat befarhesiah* who does so not merely for the sake of making a living. He rules as follows:

> The people from America are not disqualified [from being counted in a *minyan*] as a result of their violation of the Shabbat, since they are like babies who were taken captive (*tinok shenishbah*) ... Whatever the case may be, those who are lenient and count those types of people in a *minyan*, do have something on which to base their ruling. However, one who can go to another synagogue without embarrassing anyone should do so. It is self-evident that it is preferable not to base oneself on the above ruling, but rather, one should pray with upstanding Jews.

There is, however, another basis for leniency, for in our generation one is not called a *public* violator of the Shabbat for the majority of people do so. When the majority of Israel are innocent and it is a minority who dare violate this prohibition [regarding Shabbat], then one is a *kofer* in the Torah, a brazen performer of abominations and an individual who separates himself from the community of Israel. However, given our multitude of sins, the majority breaches the barrier [and violates the Shabbat in public]. Their deficiency is the source for their correction, for the individual thinks that it is not such a significant sin and it need not be hidden. As a result his or her *public* violation is as if it was done in private. Quite to the contrary, the pious in our generation are considered as if they were separated and distinguished [from the community], while the sinners function in a manner that is considered normal.[1]

In the above ruling, David Zvi Hoffman, as distinct from Moshe Feinstein, works to remove the *mehallel Shabbat befarhesia* in general, Orthodox and non-Orthodox alike, from the status of intolerability. He applies the ruling of *tinok shenishbah* across the board and utilizes it not merely for the removal of sanctions, but as a catalyst for allowing full membership in the sphere of ritual. No fear with regards to social contact and interaction is mentioned. While preferring participation in a synagogue whose members are not Shabbat desecrators, he rules that before leaving one must ensure that one's actions do not cause others to be embarrassed. This consideration reflects a concern and care which lies at the core of the presumption of loyalty which fellows members, even those who disagree, must grant each other. Finally, basing himself on the lived reality of the Jewish people, wherein the majority of Jews are now violators of Shabbat, he eliminates the classification of the *mehallel Shabbat befarhesia* as an intolerable deviant. So large a number of people violating a law precludes the possibility that the act be classified as intolerable deviance, for such a classification is conditional on the individual in question separating himself from the community. Instead, these deviants now see themselves as the standard bearers and choose to remain inside.

The only major exception to descriptive marginalization, as evident in rabbinic sources, is the prescriptive marginalization of enemy deviants. It is important to reiterate that while others may find different ideologies to be tempting and seductive, this does not mark their adherents as enemy deviants. This status is reserved exclusively for those who engage in an active campaign to attack and undermine the validity and strength of others' Jewish beliefs and practices. In contemporary Jewish life the majority of those who are guilty of such actions are those on the more traditional side who prescriptively marginalize. Liberal Judaism that fully identifies with Jewish collective life and a liberal reading of Torah does not function as enemy deviance and as such must be exempt from prescriptive marginalization.

The only group that may fail to satisfy this condition are Jews for Jesus. The majority of Jews view them as a group whose primary loyalty is to the Christian community and who are merely using the Jewish nomenclature in order to attack from within and undermine classic Jewish identity. As such, regardless of their self-professed affiliation, prescriptive marginalization may be warranted.

Once these two prerequisites are in place, it is safe to turn to the charting of the actual boundaries of Jewishness. I will divide the discussion in two, as was the case in the preceding chapters, between the definition of intolerability itself and the forms of marginalization that such a classification engenders. As seen from the previous analysis, throughout Jewish history there are only two consistently and universally adopted conditions for intolerability, which are the *meshumad lekol hatorah kullah,* i.e. one who completely rejects all of the Torah and who separates himself from the community, and the *min* as enemy deviant. While some Ammoraim expanded these conditions to include any *meshumad ledavar ehad lehakhis,* and Maimonides, for example, attempted to include heresy, these positions were not universally accepted. The Ammoraic expansion, while taking root in Jewish law, was nevertheless foreign to Tannaitic thinking, rejected by some Ammoraim and most importantly, often functionally ignored in later codifications and Responsa. In addition, while a legal case can be made for the intolerability of the *meshumad ledavar ehad lehakhis,* such a move would violate the two prerequisites outlined above. In the ideologically diverse Jewish world, everyone is a *meshumad ledavar ehad lehakhis* from someone else's perspective, creating too broad and too prescriptive an application of intolerable status. As to the Maimonidean position, it remained a minority one, rejected by the vast majority of halakhic authorities over the centuries. In its stead, the rabbinic model, in which pure heresy was not subjected to sanctions, dominated the halakhic landscape.

The *meshumad lekol hatorah kullah* and the *min* as enemy deviant create a clear and operable boundary for collective Jewish identity. An individual is classified as within the Jewish people's shared cultural space as long as he or she has some engagement and commitment to some part of Torah, identifies as a member of the Jewish people, and is not engaged in actively attacking and undermining the Jewish life and commitments of some member of the Jewish community. On the other hand, one for whom no component of the 3000–4000-year-old tradition of Jewish values and life is relevant is basically playing a different game and is outside the boundary of Jewishness.

Similarly, one for whom Jewishness is not connected to a people and who does not require any conversation and relationship with this people is in fact engaged in a different collective enterprise. In both cases marginalization is but a reflection and recognition of the status that the individual has adopted. Finally, one who sees themself as committed to some notion of Torah and to belonging to the Jewish people, but is engaged in actively attacking and undermining the Jewish life of some, may be prescriptively defined as intolerable by those being threatened. If one wants to remain within the parameters of Jewish collective identity, one needs to exhibit loyalty to the different members of that collective, a loyalty which entails ensuring that our collective space is a safe space, a space where individuals do not feel attacked or undermined. These are the boundaries of Jewishness.

Whom do these boundaries include and whom do they exclude? On an empirical level, every one of the major Jewish denominations and ideologies, be it Orthodox, Conservative, Reform, Reconstructionist, Renewal or Secular, all fall or can fall within the parameters of the Jewish collective space. That is not to say that everyone must assimilate the differences between them under the category of pluralism or even tolerance, but if one classifies one of the above as deviant, then it must be as tolerable deviant. The only two possible exceptions lie at the two opposite extremes, each of which is worthy of consideration.

There are segments of Orthodoxy, such as the ultra-Orthodox anti-Zionist Neturei Karta sect, for example, who despite their obvious commitment to Torah, adopt isolationist and anti-Israeli policies of such extreme measures as to in essence advocate a break with the Jewish people as we know it, with those of their own persuasion serving as the new people of Israel. While Neturei Karta is the radical example, much of *haredi* or ultra-Orthodoxy exhibit similar, though less extreme, tendencies and need to be on guard less they cross over the line. Furthermore, the policies of some segments of Orthodoxy, especially in Israel, to actively attack and undermine the religious rights of non-Orthodox Judaism would constitute an act of enemy deviance and could justify prescriptive marginalization on the part of the liberal wing of Judaism.

The other group that may, in some contexts, be labelled as intolerably deviant is the secular Israeli. In most cases a secular ideology, while not placing the worship of God or ritual at the centre of its Judaism, nevertheless remains firmly Jewish. With their commitment to the value language of the Jewish tradition coupled with a deep dedication to collective Jewish identity, secular Jews are clearly insiders. However, this connection may be undermined in certain extreme cases. Unless its value agenda is connected through study and engagement with Torah to the larger Jewish tradition, it can, as we see in Israel, engender individuals who do not view the Jewish tradition as in any way a part of their lives, and who may opt for an Israeli, as distinct from a Jewish, identity. In such cases, intolerable deviant status will only be the descriptive response to the status that they have adopted for themselves.

One increasingly prevalent area where the above-demarcated boundaries are of extreme significance is in the classification of individuals who intermarry with a spouse from a different faith community. For much of Jewish history, intermarriage both signified and was perceived as entailing the decision to become in essence a *meshumad lekol hatorah kullah*. We saw this, for example, with the daughter of Bilgah in Tannaic times. However, as intermarriage rates outside of Israel approach and even surpass fifty per cent, the mere numbers and relative percentage of individuals engaging in the act by definition preclude it from being allocated an intolerable classification. One can read the above-quoted words of David Zvi Hoffman as if they were written for precisely this reality. 'Quite to the contrary, the pious in our generation are considered as if they were separated and distinguished [from the community] while the sinners function in a manner that is considered normal'.

In addition, on the basis of the above analysis, the significant factor in determining the status of intermarriage cannot be the act itself, but rather the connection to Torah and the Jewish people which it implies. In this, the intermarried must be regarded similarly to the *mehallel Shabbat befarhesia*. The latter served as the paradigm of intolerability for approximately the last 2000 years; yet, as seen above, the status of these individuals was changed to that of tolerable deviant in light of the fact that the desecration of the Shabbat ceased to imply either a complete rejection of Torah or a separation from the Jewish people. One of the more interesting features of contemporary intermarriage is that this is often similarly the case. Ever-increasing numbers of intermarried couples are maintaining their Jewish communal identity, belonging to Jewish synagogues and institutions and giving their children Jewish educations. The critical factors for intolerability in the case of intermarriage are the decision of the Jewish partner as to his or her personal and familial identity. Obviously, when the Jewish spouse adopts the non-Jewish partner's identity, be it Christian, Muslim, or even secular humanist, the fact remains that the act of intermarriage thus signifies a transition moment out of one's Jewish identity and, as such, is to be descriptively classified as intolerable. However, when the intermarriage act is in fact only (in the Hatam Sofer's sense of 'only') an expression of one's choice as to one's partner and not of one's personal religious and collective identity, the classification of intolerability is not warranted. While one can claim that such a distinction is impossible, the fact remains that precisely such a claim was made in the past with regard to the *mehallel Shabbat befarhesia*. Modernity and the choices it has engendered have created complex realities which we must take into account in our boundary policies.

It is possible, however, to make the case that the intolerability of intermarriage be contingent on a more subtle distinction beyond the one offered. Instead of simply assessing the intent of the Jewish partner, one might take into account also the couple's joint intent for their family. Obviously, if the non-Jewish spouse adopts a Jewish identity, even without a formal conversion process, on an ideological level the marriage ceases to be an *inter* marriage. However, even if such an affiliation does not occur, the couple may decide that the formal religion of the family and the identity of the children will be exclusively Jewish. Here, too, the intermarriage may be classified as tolerable. It is precisely when such a decision is present at the outset that the Jewish partner is making the necessary reaffirmation as to the place of Judaism and Jewish collective identity in his or her life, a status which was brought into question by the act of intermarriage itself. On the other hand, to claim to want to remain an insider but to not want such a status for one's children is viewed as internally contradictory, and as indicative of a subtle transformation in one's chosen identity outside Judaism and the Jewish people. To claim that as a parent one has decided not to take a stand and to 'let the children decide for themselves' would involve intermarriage of an intolerable form.

When it comes to intermarriage there are two possible statuses: tolerable and intolerable. We must learn to distinguish between the two and direct our responses accordingly. Once it is understood that intermarriage is not inherently intolerable, it will strengthen our resolve to ensure that when it does occur, we do everything within our power to direct it towards a tolerable course. Such resolve involves the redoubling of our efforts at 'in-reach' towards intermarried couples and their non-Jewish spouses, and the broadening of our membership and welcoming policies in our synagogues, schools, camps and community centres. Above all, it is crucial that we remember that intermarriage, while not necessarily tolerable diversity, need not be intolerable. It no longer has to signify the end of one's Jewish identity and commitments, and it requires that we as a community respond accordingly.

One area of much contention and debate is whether rabbis should be involved in any way in the intermarriage ceremony. Given the fact that it no longer necessarily constitutes an act of intolerable deviance, coupled with our collective responsibility to work to ensure that the intermarried maintain their ties to parts of Jewish law and the community, do rabbis have a responsibility to officiate at intermarriages of the tolerable deviant nature, in order to affect this outcome and to further keep the Jewish channels of communication open? The answer to this question is not simple, nor, I believe, self-evident; and those rabbis who do choose to officiate are clearly not themselves intolerable deviants. At issue is whether in our boundary policies we are able to not merely maintain the distinction between tolerable and intolerable deviance, but between tolerable deviance and tolerable diversity. There are forms of behaviour, as we have seen throughout this book, which encompass a wide spectrum of our society and which do not entail any act of self-separation and identity transformation. This does not, however, mean that this behaviour is to be viewed as positive and embraced as one of the expressions of our shared collective identity. Intermarriage poses a grave threat to the continuity and vitality of the Jewish identity of the future generations of our community, as we have yet to succeed in creating educational and communal mechanisms which ensure that all intermarriages be of the tolerable form. When that happens, the status of intermarriage may move from deviance to tolerable diversity, as was the case in the Bible. Until that time, however, we need to not only reach out to the intermarried but also to educate and advocate as to its dangers and challenges.

However, the critical challenge faced by the distinction between tolerable deviance and tolerable diversity is to maintain it not only intellectually but socially. In some cases, especially when the deviance is so predominant, the community ceases to ascribe to it any deviant stigma, and the attempt to maintain the distinction is not only ineffective but irrelevant. As the Rabbis in the Talmud have taught, just as it is a *mitzvah* to say that which will be heard, so it is a *mitzvah* not to say that which will not be heard.[2] The responsibility of rabbis is to be heard and to use their voices to positively influence and shape the depth and commitment of people's Jewish lives. In this capacity it is of critical significance for them to maintain the boundary between tolerable deviance and tolerable diversity, yet at the same time to acknowledge those cases where the distinction has been rendered mute. Such an acknowledgement is not merely important to ensure that religious leaders remain relevant and are not fighting yesterday's battles, but to ensure that they direct their efforts at that which can be achieved and where their limited resources can positively effect the future identity of the Jewish people. Whether intermarriage has crossed this line or not is a question of judgment. What is clear is that if current trends continue, it will not remain a question for long. At that point, rabbis of the different denominations will not be able to live vicariously off the decisions of some Reform rabbis, publicly criticizing them while privately recognizing that in the case of a tolerable intermarriage, the rabbi's participation has merit. We will need to recognize that the boundary has changed and incorporate policies that enable us to respond accordingly. Whether this involves officiating in a *kiddushin* or creating a new form of marriage ceremony will need to be determined. What is clear is that silence will not serve our end.

The second dimension of a contemporary boundary policy pertains to the process of marginalization. The significance of this dimension is relatively minor when there is a consensus as to the definition of the intolerable. In such a case, the vast majority of Jews perceive each other predominantly through the categories of pluralism, tolerable diversity or tolerable deviance and, as such, are immune to the effects of marginalization. In the modern context of extreme diversity and debate, where, as we have seen, a mutual commitment of loyalty is often missing, where there may be a willingness to marginalize prescriptively, and there is no consensus as to the definition of the intolerable, a controlled policy of marginalization can serve as a last-resort safety net for Jewish collective survival. Thus, even if we reject the above-outlined boundary policy and instead classify each other as intolerable deviants, but agree to limit the implications of intolerability, we can still establish a functional system of coexistence. As is evident from the above rabbinic and mediaeval analysis, the preponderance of halakhic precedent supports and in fact requires just such a policy. This policy, I believe, must be founded on two central principles.

The first is to carefully maintain the distinctions between the different spheres of marginalization fastidiously maintained by the rabbis. By this I mean, in particular, the distinction between sanctions which affect the sphere of ritual and those which impact on the sphere of loyalty. As seen above, with the exception of the enemy deviant *min* and the subsequent forms of marginalization which result from the rule of 'keep yourself far from her', the vast majority of sanctions directed towards the *meshumad lekol hatorah kullah* are in the sphere of ritual. The one major exception is the law of *moridin ve-lo ma-alin*, which in the modern political context has no practical manifestation in the sphere of loyalty. Even Moshe Feinstein, who uses the law extensively, does so only with regards to the validity of the intolerable deviant's testimony, an issue which predominantly bears on the sphere of ritual.

Where the Hatam Sofer and Moshe Feinstein went wrong, I believe, and deviated from halakhic precedent, is in the application of sanctions intended to be directed exclusively against the *min* as enemy deviant and in using them on deviants who are either more accurately classified as *meshumadim* or *mumarim*, or who are not enemy deviants. Were Moshe Feinstein, for example, to limit the marginalization of Reform and Conservative Jews to the sphere of ritual, the fact that he classified the majority of Jews as intolerable would have been tolerable in itself. Given our ideological differences, it is eminently plausible to argue that we should not pray together. The joke about two Jews on an abandoned island creating three synagogues, one to which each goes, one that each individually will not attend, and one that they both together reject, may in fact be the prescribed response to the ideological debates engendered by modernity. We can agree not to pray together, and even not to allow each other a place or role in our respective synagogues, but we nevertheless can live with and care for each other when it comes to all other affairs. A community which doesn't pray together can still stay together. Sectarianism can be avoided even when fellow members marginalize each other in the sphere of ritual so long as they maintain each other's status in the sphere of loyalty. It is only with regard to the latter, wherein social contact is forbidden, non-ritual institutional cooperation is banned and mutual concern and assistance is outlawed, that the community ceases to be a singular collective entity. When such polices are applied to a majority of members, the social fabric is destroyed. As a result, the first order of the contemporary marginalization policy is to recognize that while one may classify others and even many others as intolerable deviants, if they are not enemy deviants, the sanctions must be limited to the sphere of ritual. The bifurcated state of world Jewry is not served by innovative use of sanctions in the sphere of loyalty but rather by returning it to its traditional, limited role.

Secondly, just as the distinction between the spheres of ritual and loyalty must be maintained, so too must great care be taken to avoid marginalization within the sphere of basic membership. By this I do not merely mean the formal adoption of the rule of *af al pi she-hata yisrael hu* with its subsequent recognition of all intolerable deviant marriages. I mean, rather, that it is necessary to ensure that even when sanctions are directed within the sphere of loyalty, great care be taken not to create so extreme a marginalization as to effectively and practically construct a *de facto* outsider status. In fact, it is precisely because it is so universally assumed that one cannot lose one's status within the sphere of basic membership that we often allow ourselves to direct virulent attacks and marginalization policies against each other, finding support and self-congratulation in the claim that 'I am not saying that they are not Jews'. It is important to remember that a functional outsider is socially indistinguishable from a theoretical one, with both creating an irreparable social rift. If indeed *af al pi she-hata yisrael hu*, this must determine, as stated above, a commitment of loyalty towards each other on an ongoing basis, and not in merely accepting the relatively trivial legal validity of each other's marriages.

Finally, the last feature of the contemporary boundary policy is a commitment to use the various halakhic vehicles that enable mutual accommodation, such as Maimonides' notion of the *tinok shenishbah* outlined above. Here too, Moshe Feinstein serves as example both for what needs to and can be done, as well as that which must be avoided. His utilization of categories such as *nasseh lahem ke-heter* or *shogegim* with regard to Orthodox deviants is a model of how to maximize halakhic precedent to ensure the maintenance of ongoing contact. On the other hand, his efforts to minimize and get around the implications of the status of *tinok shenishbah* when it comes to Conservative or Reform Jews serve as an opposite illustration of a policy which must be avoided.

The notion of *tinok shenishbah* does not entail respect for the difference in question; quite to the contrary, it rejects its value and only tolerates the individual by classifying him as not responsible for his decision. In the contemporary context, however, this is not a weakness but a strength. Any attempt to create Jewish social cohesion by demanding that we assimilate our differences through the prism of pluralism is destined to fail, for it does not give sufficient credence to the depth of the ideological debate among the various Jewish denominations and ideologies. We see each other as deviants, and the relevant question is whether we can tolerate each other or not. In this context a category such as *tinok shenishbah* is exactly what is prescribed. It allows individuals to be honest to their value judgments and commitments but still gives them the halakhic foundation for setting aside their marginalization policies. In the reality which is the contemporary Jewish community, while more pluralism may also be required, anything that engenders some measure of coexistence, even if it is a tense one, is of significant value nonetheless.

In summary, the modern boundary policy proposed in this book is built on a set of key features. Its implementation must be preceded by an *a priori* presumption of loyalty to the various and diverse members of one's society, as well as a decision to institute this policy in a descriptive (as distinct from prescriptive) manner. The actual boundary must be constructed by a notion of the intolerable which is limited exclusively to one who rejects all of Torah and completely separates himself from the community, the operative terms being 'all' and 'completely'. In the absence of this, the only other intolerable deviant is one who is an enemy deviant, actively working to undermine the religious life of other Jews. Marginalization of intolerable deviants, with the exception of enemy deviants, must be limited to the sphere of ritual. Care must be given to ensure that if one does sanction within the sphere of loyalty, it is not done to such a degree as to affect the sphere of basic membership and thus create functional outsiders. Finally, there must be a commitment wherever possible to utilize those halakhic vehicles which can create possibilities for mutual co-existence.

While the above guidelines are intended to serve as a comprehensive policy, they are at the same time modular in the sense that even if there is no agreement as to the proposed definition of the intolerable, an agreement on marginalization policies will suffice. Furthermore, even if there is no consensus on the latter, a commitment to utilize notions such as *tinok shenishbah* wherever possible will also serve enable the continuity of Jewish collective life.

As stated above, diversity is not something to fear but rather a reality which must be embraced. Its preponderance in the Jewish communal context requires that instead of building our collective identity on that which we share, we build it through the erection of boundaries and the instituting of marginalization policies which demarcate the lines that those who are Jews do not cross. The complexity of our reality must be matched by the complexity of our boundary policies. Jewish collective life demands and indeed is dependent on the development of ever-increasing levels of sophistication on this issue, so that we neither attempt to function without a boundary policy, nor to erect one in the wrong place, nor marginalize incorrectly so as to further divide and undermine our collective enterprise.

Jewish collective life will not survive without a shared boundary policy. At the same time, however, I do not believe that it alone will suffice, especially if the agreement is limited to constrict or even suspend marginalization. In addition to its boundaries, a community's shared collective space requires also some things that the various members share in common. As a people with a history which is over 3000 years old, we did not merely survive as a result of shared boundaries, but also by virtue of some shared beliefs and practices. In the Bible, it was primarily ethnicity that was shared. With the onset of the common era, commonality was increasingly expressed in certain agreed principles of faith and halakhic behavior. Such agreement has been lost in the modern era and it is my belief that without a concentrated effort to re-identify some features that all who declare themselves to be Jews actively share, Jewish collective life will remain in peril. While anti-Semitism and crises may at times serve as a stop-gap measure, creating a semblance of shared purpose, it is neither worthy of our people nor increasingly, I hope, sufficiently active, to existentially effect people's identity choices.

In our sectarian reality, it is difficult to imagine both what such a commonality will be or even how to go about thinking about it. The complexity of the issue warrants a work of it own. It is a worthy goal, however, to remember Maimonides' Responsa regarding the Karaites. Despite his clear rejection of their ideology and approach to Jewish life, things which on their own warrant intolerable deviant status, Maimonides maintained their status in the sphere of loyalty. He does not do so by classifying them as *tinok shenishbah*, as was the case in his halakhic codification. Rather, in the Karaites' case, he identifies their belief in the oneness of God as an essential principle, which for Maimonides is sufficiently powerful to serve as a counterweight to their deviance. In doing so, Maimonides takes two courageous steps. The first entails a choice to assess the deviant member from a broader perspective. It is not that Karaite ideology ceases to be intolerable, but that Maimonides is able to put this intolerability in the perspective of a complete picture in which the heresy and delinquency are positioned together with those aspects of Karaite ideology which he respects. One can choose to see what is deviant or to focus on what is shared. Maimonides here chooses to focus on the latter. The second step is Maimonides' recognition that the fact that the Karaites are intolerable deviants does not mean that everything they do is intolerable. The ability to recognize complexity and to refrain from portraying the other in simple and simplistic categories is the essence of the Maimonidean move. Because one is a heretic it does not follow that everything by definition that comes out of one's mouth will be heresy.

A measure of Maimonides' courage would serve us well today. Were we able to step back from the issues that divide us and concentrate on those areas of value that certainly exist in the other, were we able to see our denominational counterparts in the broader context that is their Jewish life and cease to focus merely on that which we reject, we could begin the process of identifying our common foundations. While there is much that we renounce in the other, there may be much that we can also appreciate. We must, however, make the decision to look. It is possible that this decision must be the first expression of our mutual presumption of loyalty – not a loyalty to try not to exclude, nor a loyalty to refrain from radical marginalization, but a loyalty which allows ourselves to dare to find features in the other which we respect.

Notes

1 *Melamed Le-ho-il* Part 1.29.
2 BT Tractate Yevamot 65b.

Bibliography

Primary Sources

Avot D'Rabbi Natan (New York: Schecter, 1967).

Babylonian Talmud Mahadurat Nahardeah (Jerusalem: H Wagshal, 1991).

Ben Asher, Y., *Arba Turim Hashalem* (Jerusalem: Machon Yerushalayim, 1990–1994).

Feinstein, M., *Responsa Igrot Moshe.* (New York: Rabbi M. Feinstein, 1974).

Karo, Joseph, *Shulchan Aruch.* Mahadurah Mada'it (Jerusalem: Mifal Shulchan Aruch Hashalem, 1944).

Karo, Joseph, *Shulchan Aruch* (Jerusalem: Shulchan Aruch Hagadol).

Maimonides, M., *Mishneh Torah* (Jerusalem: Machon Mishnat HaRambam, 1985).

——, *Hakdama L' Perush HaMishna* (Jerusalem: Mossad HaRav Kook, 1961).

——, *Introduction to the Commentary on the Mishnah* (ed. M. D. Rabinowitz) (Jerusalem: Mossad Harav Kook).

——, *T'shuvot HaRambam* (ed. Y. Blau) (Jerusalem: Reuven Mass, 1989).

——, *The Guide to the Perplexed* (trans. S. Pines) (Chicago: University of Chicago Press, 1963).

Mechilta D'Rabbi Ishmael (Jerusalem: Horowitz–Rabin 1930).

Midrash Bereishit Rabbah, (ed. C. Albeck) (Jerusalem: Shalem Books, 1996).

Midrash Tanhuma (Vilna: Shlomo Buber, 1885)

Rashi, *Teshuvot Rashi* (Bnei Brak: Yahadut, 1980).

Schreiber (Sofer), Moses, *Teshuvot Hatam Sofer* (Jerusalem: Machon Hatam Sofer, 1982).

Seder Eliyahu Zutta, (ed. M. Ish Shalom) (Jerusalem: Wahrmann, 1969)

Sifrei Devarim, (ed. L. Finkelstein) (New York: Jewish Theological Seminary, 1969).

Tosefta (ed. M. S Zuckermandel with 'Supplement to the Tosefta' by S. Liebermann) (Jerusalem: Wahrmann, 1970).

Tosefta (ed. S. Lieberman) (New York: Jewish Theological Seminary, 1988).

V'Eleh Divre Ha-Berit (Altona: Germany, 1819).

Secondary Sources

Alon, G., *Toldot ha-Yehudim be-Eretz Yisrael be-Tekufat ha-Mishnah ve-Hatalmud* (2 vols) (Tel Aviv: Kibbutz HaMeuchad, 1977). (Hebrew)

Angel, M. (1988), 'A Study of the Halakhic approaches of Two Modern Poskim', *Tradition* 23, 3 41–52.

Becker, H. S., *Outsiders – Studies in the Sociology of Deviance*. (New York: The Free Press, 1963).

Berger, P., *The Heretical Imperative* (New York: Doubleday, 1980).

Berger, P. L. and Luckman, T., *The Social Construction of Reality* (New York: Anchor Press, 1967).

Berlin, I., 'Two Concepts of Liberty' in *Four Essays on Liberty* (Oxford: Oxford University Press, 1969).

Bildstein, G. (1976), 'Who is not a Jew', *Israel Law Review*, 11,3, 369–90.

——, (1988) 'ha-Gisha la-Karaim be-Mishnat ha-Rambam', *Tehumin* 8 502–3.

Black, D. J. and Reiss, A. J. (1970), 'Police Control of Juveniles', *American Sociological Review*, 35,1,63–77.

Bleich, J., 'Rabbinic Responses to Nonobservance in the Modern Era' in J. Schachter, (ed.), *Jewish Tradition and the Non-Traditional Jew* (Northvale: Jason Aronson, 1992), pp. 37–115.

Boyarin, D., *Dying for God*, (Stanford: Stanford University Press, 1999).

Brubaker, R., *Citizenship and Nationhood in France and Germany* (Cambridge: Harvard University Press, 1992).

Buchler, A., *Studies in Jewish History* (London: Oxford University Press, 1956).

——, *Studies in the Period of the Mishnah and the Talmud* (Jerusalem: Mossad HaRav Kook, 1967).

Chinitz, J., *In My Opinion* (Tel Aviv: Peninim, 2000).

Cohen, S., *The Beginnings of Jewishness* (Berkeley: University of California Press, 1999).

Cranston, M., 'John Locke and the Case for Toleration' in S. Mendus and D. Edwards (eds), *On Toleration* (Oxford: Clarendon, 1987).

Davis, M., *The Emergence of Conservative Judaism* (Philadelphia: Jewish Publication Society, 1963).

Dentler, R. A. and Erikson, K. T., 'The Function of Deviance in Groups', in R. A. Farrell and V. L. Swigert (eds), *Social Deviance* (Philadelphia: Lippincott, 1975).

Dorff, E., *Conservative Judaism: Our Ancestors to Our Descendants* (New York: United Synagogue of Conservative Judaism, 1979).

Douglas, J. D., 'The Experience of the Absurd and the Problem of Social

Order' in R. A. Scott and J. D. Douglas (eds), *Theoretical Perspective on Deviance* (New York: Basic Books, 1972), pp. 189–214.

Douglas, M., *Purity and Danger* (London: Routledge, 1984).

Elazar, D. and Geffen, R. M., *The Conservative Movement in Judaism* (Albany: State University of New York Press, 2000).

Elbogen, Y. M., *Hatfillah be-Yisrael be-hitpat-hutah ha-Historit* (Tel Aviv: Devir, 1972).

Ellenson, D., *Tradition in Transition: Orthodoxy, Halakha and the Boundaries of Modern Jewish Identity* (Lanham: University Press of America, 1989).

——, 'Germany Jewish Orthodoxy: Tradition in the Context of Culture' in J. Wartheimer (ed.), *The Uses of Tradition* (New York: Jewish Theological Seminary of America, 1992), pp. 7–11.

——, 'For the Heretics Have Arisen: Maharam Schick and the 1876 Controversy over Orthodox Secession from the General Jewish Community in Germany' in D. Ellenson (ed.), *Between Tradition and Culture: The Dialectics of Modern Religion and Identity* (Atlanta: Scholars Press, 1994), pp. 41–58.

——, 'Traditional Reactions to Modern Jewish Reform: The Paradigm of German Orthodoxy' in Ellenson, D. (ed.), *After Emancipation: Jewish Religious Responses to Modernity* (Cincinnati: Hebrew Union College Press, 2004).

Erikson, K. T., 'Notes on the Sociology of Deviance' in H. S. Beker, *The Other Side – Perspectives on Deviance* (New York: The Free Press of Glencoe (MacMillan)1964). pp. 9–21.

——, *The Wayward Puritans* (New York: John Wiley & Sons, 1966).

Ferziger, A., 'Hierarchical Judaism in Formation: the Development of Central European Orthodoxy's Approach to Non-Observant Jews (1700–1918)' (Doctoral Thesis, Bar Ilan University, 2001).

——, *Exclusion and Hierarchy: Orthodoxy, Nonobservance and the Emergence of Modern Jewish Identity* (Philadelphia: University of Pennsylvania Press, 2005).

Finkelman, S., *Reb Moshe* (New York: ArtScroll Mesorah, 1986).

Finkelstein, L., *Mabo le-Massektot Abot ve-Abot d'Rabbi Natan* (New York: JTS, 1950).

——, 'The Development of the Amidah' in *Pharasism in the Making* (Hoboken: Ktav , 1972).

——, *Sifra* on Leviticus (New York: JTS, 1989).

Fischel, H., in *Rabbinic Literature and Graeco-Roman Philosophy* (Leiden: Brill, 1973).

Fletcher, G., *Loyalty* (New York: Oxford University Press, 1993).

Flusser, D. (1992), 'Miktzat Ma-asei ha-Torah u-Birkat ha-Minim', *Tarbitz* 61, 333–46.

Gartner, L. P., 'Immigration and the Formation of the American Jew: 1940–1955' in M. Sklare (ed.), *American Jews – A Reader* (New York: Behrman House, 1984), pp. 5–22.

Geiger, Y. (1973), 'Letoldot ha-Munakh Apikorus', *Tarbitz* 42, 499–500.

Gilman, N., *Conservative Judaism: the New Century* (West Orange: Behrman House, 1993).

Glazer, N., *American Judaism* (Chicago: University of Chicago Press, 1989).

Glock, J. S. (2000), 'Twentieth-Century American Orthodoxy's Era of Non-Observance, 1900–1960', *The Torah U-Madda Journal*, 9, 87–107.

Goode, E., *Deviant Behavior*, (Englewood Cliffs: Prentice Hall, 1990).

Greenwald, Y. Y., *Sefer Mekorot ha-Torah ve-ha-Emunah be-Hungariah* (Jerusalem: Hod, 1972).

Gusfield, J. R. (1967), 'Moral Passage – The Symbolic Process in Public Designation of Deviance', *Social Problems* 15, 175–188.

Guttman, A., *The Struggle over Reform in Rabbinic Literature*, New York: The World Union for Progressive Judaism, 1977.

Halbertal, M. and Margalit, A., *Idolatry* (Cambridge MA: Harvard University Press, 1992).

Hengel, M., *Judaism and Hellenism* (Philadelphia: Fortress Press, 1974).

Herford, R. T., 'The Problem of the 'Minim' Further Considered' in S. Baron and A. Marx (eds), *Jewish Studies in Memory of George A Kohut* (New York: The Alexander Kohut Memorial Foundation, 1935).

——*Christianity in the Talmud and the Midrash* (Eugene, OR: Wipf and Stock, 2003).

Hertzberg, A., 'The American Jew and his Religion' in J. Neusner (ed.) *Understanding American Judaism* (New York: Ktav, 1975), pp. 5–24.

——*The Jews in America* (New York: Simon and Schuster, 1989).

Heyd, D., *Toleration, an Illusive Virtue* (Princeton: Princeton University Press, 1996).

Horton, J., and Nicolson, P., *Toleration: Philosophy and Practice* (Aldershot: Avebury, 1992).

Hyman, A., 'Maimonides' ''Thirteen Principles'' ' in Altmann, A. (ed.), *Jewish Medieval and Renaissance Studies* (Cambridge: Harvard University Press, 1967), pp. 119–44.

Ir-Shai, O. (1984–1986), 'Meshumad ke-Yoresh be-Teshuvot ha-Gaonim', *Shenaton ha-Mishpat ha-Ivri* 11–12, 435–61.

Katz Jacob, *Out of the Ghetto* (Cambridge: Harvard University Press, 1973).

——, *Jewish Emancipation and Self-Emancipation*, (Philadelphia: Jewish Publication Society, 1986).

——, 'Orthodoxy in Historical Perspectives', in P. Medding (ed.), *Studies in Contemporary Jewry II*, (Bloomington, IN: Indiana University Press, 1986), pp. 3–17.

——, *Halakhah and Kabbalah* (Jerusalem: Magnes Press, 1986).

——, *A House Divided: Orthodoxy and Schism in Nineteenth Century Central European Jewry* (Hanover: Brandeis University Press, 1988).

——, *ha-Halakhah be-Meitzar* (Jerusalem: Magnes, 1992).

——, *Tradition and Crisis* (New York: New York University Press, 1993).

Kimelman, R., 'Birkat Ha-Minim and the Lack of Evidence for an Anti-Christian Jewish Prayer in Late Antiquity', in E. P. Sanders, A. I. Baumgarten, and A. Mendelson (eds), *Jewish and Christian Self-Definition, Vol. Two: Aspects of Judaism in the Graeco-Roman Period*, (Philadelphia: SCM Press, 1981), pp. 226–44.

Kellner, M., *Dogma in Medieval Jewish Thought: From Maimonides to Abravanel* (Oxford:Oxford University Press, 1986).

——, *Must a Jew Believe Anything* (London: Littman Library, 1999).

Kirshenbaum, A. (1996), 'Rabbi Moshe Feinstein's Responsa: A Major Halakhic Event,', *Judaism* 15,3, 364–73.

Klineberg, O. (1967), 'The Multi-National Society: Some Research Problems', *Social Sciences Information*, 6, 81–99.

Lazerwitz, B., 'Denominations and Synagogue Membership: 1971 and 1990', in D. Gordis and G. Dorit (eds), *American Jewry, Portrait and Prognosis* (West Orange: Behrman House, 1997), pp. 199–220.

Lemert, E., *Social Pathology: A Systematic Approach to the Theory of Sociopathic Behavior* (New York: McGraw-Hill Book Company, 1951).

Liebermann, E. (ed), *Nogah ha-Tzedek* (Dessau: C Schlieder 1818).

——, *Or Nogah* (Dessau: C Schlieder 1818).

——, *Eleh Divrei ha-Brit* (Altona, 1819).

Lieberman, S., (1944–1945),'Roman Legal Institutions in Early Rabbinics and in the Acta Martyrum' *JQR*, 35, 20–21.

——*Tosephta ki-Fshuta* (New York: Jewish Theological Seminary, 1955–1988).

——*Greek and Hellenism in Jewish Palestine* (Jerusalem: Bialik, 1962).

——, 'How Much Greek in Jewish Palestine' in A. Altmann (ed.), *Biblical and Other Studies* (Cambridge: Harvard University Press, 1963).

——, 'Some Aspects of After Life in Rabbinic Literature', in S. Leiberman (ed.), *Harry Austryn Wolfson Jubilee Volume, English Section Volume II* (Jerusalem: AAJR, 1965).

——, 'Notes on Chapter 1 of *Koheleth Rabbah*' in E. E. Urbach, R. J. Zwi Weblowsky, and C. Wirszubski (eds), *Studies in Mysticism and Religion presented to G. G. Scholem*, (Jerusalem: Magnes, 1968).

Liebman, C., 'Orthodoxy in American Jewish Life' in *American Jewish Yearbook 66* (Philadelphia: Jewish publication Society, 1965), pp. 38–9.

——, 'The Religion of American Jews' in J. Neusner (ed.), *Understanding American Judaism* (New York: Ktav, 1975), pp. 25–68.

Martin, B., 'American Jewry Since 1945: An Historical Overview' in B. Martin (ed.), *Movements and Issues in American Judaism* (Westport: Greenwood Press, 1978), pp. 3–24.

Mendes-Flohr, P. and Reinharz, J., *The Jew in the Modern World* (New York: Oxford University Press, 1980).

Mendus S. (ed.), *Justifying Toleration* (Cambridge: Harvard University Press, 1988).

Meyer, M., *The Origins of the Modern Jew* (Detroit: Wayne State University Press, 1967).

——(1975), 'Where Does the Modern Period of Jewish History Begin', *Judaism* 24, 3 329–38.

——, *Response to Modernity* (New York: Oxford University Press, 1988).

——, *Jewish Identity in the Modern World* (Seattle: University of Washington Press, 1990).

Milikovsky, H. (1986), 'Gehenom ve-Poshei Yisrael al pi Seder Olam', *Tarbitz* 55, 3 332–3.

Miller, Stuart. S. (1993), 'The *Minim* of Sepphoris Reconsidered', *Harvard Theological Review* 86 4 377–8.

Morrell, S. (1969), 'The Halakhic Status of Non-Halakhic Jews', *Judaism* 18 3 455–7.

Petuchowski, J. J., 'The *Mumar*. A Study in Rabbinic Psychology' in *Hebrew Union College Annual XXX* (1959) (New York: Hebrew Union College Press, 1968), pp 179–90.

——, *Prayerbook Reform in Europe* (New York: WUPJ , 1968).

Philipson, D., *The Reform Movement in Judaism* (New York, The MacMillan Company: 1907).

Plaut, W. G., *The Rise of Reform Judaism – A Sourcebook of its European Origins* (New York: World Union for Progressive Judaism, 1963).

Rabbinovics, R., *Sefer Dikdukei Sofrim* (Jerusalem: Ma'yan ha-hokhmah, 1960).

Rackman, E. (1964), 'Halakhic Progress: Rabbi Moshe Feinstein's Igrot Moshe on Even ha-Ezer', *Judaism* 13 3 365–73.

Rand, A., *Toldot Anshei Shem* (New York: Hevrat Toldot Anshei Shem, 1950). (Hebrew)

Raphael, D. D., 'The Intolerable' in S. Mendus (ed.), *Justifying Toleration* (Cambridge: Harvard University Press, 1988).

Robinson, I. (1986), 'Because of Our Many Sins: The Contemporary World as Reflected in the Responsa of Moses Feinstein', *Judaism* 35 1 35–46.

Rokeah, D. (1970), 'Ben Sitra Ben Pantira Hu', *Tarbitz* 39 9–92. (Hebrew)

Rosner, F. (ed.), *Medicine and Jewish Law* Vol. II (Northdale: Jason Aronson, 1993).

Rudavsky, D., *Modern Jewish Religious Movements: A History of Emancipation and Adjustment* (New York: Behrman House, 1972).

Sagi A., (1995) 'ha-Dat ha-Yehudit: Sovlanut ve-Efsharut ha-Pluralism', *Iyyun* 44 175–200. (Hebrew).

Sagi, A. and Zohar, Z., *Giyur ve-Zehut Yehudit* (Jerusalem: Bialik, 1994). (Hebrew)

——, *Ma-agalei Zehut Yehudit be-Sifrut ha-Hilkhatit* (Tel Aviv: Kibbutz HaMeuchad, 2000). (Hebrew)

Samet, M., 'Halahkah ve-Reformah' (Doctoral Thesis, Hebrew University, 1967).

——, 'Kavim Nosafim le-Biographiah Shel ha-Hatam Sofer' in M. Breuer (ed.), *Torah im Derekh Eretz* (Ramat Gan: Bar Ilan University Press, 1987), pp. 65–74.

——, (1988), 'The Beginning of Orthodoxy', *Modern Judaism* 2 249–69.

Schiffman, L. H., *Who was a Jew?* (Hoboken: Ktav, 1985).

——, *Ha-Shinuim be-Sidrei Beit ha-Knesset: Emdat ha-Rabbanim Keneged ha-Mihadshim ha-Reformim*, *Asufot* 5 (Jerusalem, 1991): 345–404.

Schremer, A. (1990), 'The Manuscripts of Tractate Moed Katan', *Sidra* 6 121–150.

Schur, E., *Labeling Deviant Behavior* (New York: Harper and Row, 1971).

Scholem, G. G., *Major Trends in Jewish Mysticism* (New York: Schoken, 1971).

Scott, R. A., 'Framework for Analyzing Deviance as a Property of Social Order', in R. A. Scott and J. D. Douglas (eds), *Theoretical Perspectives on Deviance* (New York: Basic Books, 1972).

Segal, A. F., *Two Powers in Heaven* (Leiden, Brill, 1997).

Shemesh, A. (2001), 'King Manasseh and the *Halakhah* of the Sadducees', *Journal of Jewish Studies* LII, 1, 27–39.

Shohet, A., *Im Hillufei Tekufot* (Jerusalem: Bialik, 1960).

Silber, M., 'Shorshei ha-Pilug be-Yahadut Hungariah' (Doctoral Thesis, Hebrew University, 1985).

——, 'The Emergence of Ultra-Orthodoxy: the Invention of a Tradition' in J. Wartheimer (ed.), *The Uses of Tradition* (New York: JTS, 1992).

Simon, M., *Commentary on the Talmud, Soncino Talmud* (London: Soncino Press, 1990).

Sklare, M., Vosk, M., and Zobrowski, M. (1955), 'Forms of Expression of Jewish Identification', *Jewish Social Studies* 17 205–9.

Sussman, Y. (1989–1990), 'Heker Toldot Ha-Halakha U-Megliot Midbar Yehudah', *Tarbitz* 59, 11–76

Trepp, L., 'The Controversy between Samson Raphael Hirsch and Seligman Bar Bamberger and its Significance' in S. F. Chyet and D.

H. Ellenson (eds), *Bits of Honey* (Atlanta: Rowman & Littlefield Pub, 1993), pp. 289–310.

Twersky, I., *Rabad of Posquieres* (Cambridge MA: Harvard University Press, 1962).

Urbach, E. E., *The Sages* (Jerusalem: Magnes, 1982).

——, *The Halakhah: Its Sources and Ddevelopment* (Ramat Gan: Yad La-Talmud, 1984).

Walzer, M., *Spheres of Justice* (New York: Basic Books, 1983).

——, *On Toleration* (New Haven, Yale University Press, 1997).

Wartheimer, J. (ed.), *The Uses of Tradition* (New York: JTS, 1992).

Waxman, M., 'Conservative Judaism – A Survey' in M. Waxman (ed.), *Tradition and Change* (New York: Burning Bush Press, 1970).

Weiss H. D., *Mekorot Umesorot* (Jerusalem: American Rabbinical Bet Midrash,1982).

Williams, B., 'Toleration: an Impossible Virtue', in D. Heyd, *Toleration, an Illusive Virtue* (Princeton: Princeton University Press, 1996), pp. 18–27.

Wolfe, A. 'Democracy versus Sociology: Boundaries and Their Political Consequences', in M. Lamont and M. Fournier (eds), *Cultivating Differences* (Chicago: University of Chicago Press, 1992), pp. 309–325.

Zerubavel E., *The Fine Line* (New York: Free Press, 1991).

Index